THE UNBORN CHILD

& the pain held in" p188

THE UNBORN CHILD

Beginning a Whole Life
and Overcoming Problems of Early Origin

Roy Ridgway

updated and extended by
Simon H. House

Forewords by
Barbara Findeisen
Michael A. Crawford

KARNAC

LONDON   NEW YORK

Extracts reprinted with permission: p. 19, from Aldous Huxley, "The Fifth Philosopher's Song", in: *Brave New World* (ch. 3) (London: Penguin, 1920); pp. 174–175, from Mildred Bressler-Finer, "Dreams of Pregnant Women", *Birth Psychology Bulletin* (1981).

First published in 2006 by
H. Karnac (Books) Ltd.
6 Pembroke Buildings, London NW10 6RE

First published by Wildwood House, Great Britain, 1987, under the title,
The Unborn Child: How to Recognize and Overcome Prenatal Trauma

British Library Cataloguing in Publication Data

A C.I.P. for this book is available from the British Library

ISBN-13: 978-1-85575-420-1
ISBN-10: 1-85575-420-7

Edited, designed, and produced by Communication Crafts

Printed in Great Britain by the MPG Books Group, Bodmin and King's Lynn

www.karnacbooks.com

to Frances, Ben, John, Susie,
to our families
and coming generations

CONTENTS

PART D Psychological healing and protection

Figures and tables

Figures

Tables

ABOUT THE AUTHORS

SIMON H. HOUSE   Always intrigued by tracing life to its origins, Simon House was inspiringly supervised at Cambridge by Dr John Kendrew of the Crick-Watson team, just when they cracked the DNA code. As a result of recalling some early-life experiences when he was marketing health products, he came on "primal integration therapy", as did Frederick Leboyer while he and Michel Odent were minimizing the trauma of birth to sustain the mother–baby bond. The ministry of healing helped Simon when a parish priest to see how much a sense of well-being depends on prenatal and birth "imprints". He began networking and writing on bringing children into the world healthy and well-loved. He came upon *The Unborn Child* and its author, Roy Ridgway, and then Professor Michael Crawford, who alerted him to the importance of preconception nutrition and with whom he still works. He worked closely with Roy until he died. Roy's devoted widow, Dorothea, asked him to update his book.

ROY RIDGWAY [1916–2000]   Roy Ridgway's background was literary and philosophical, moving through prison as a conscientious objector and the wartime Friends' Ambulance, into medical journalism and psychotherapy. He minded passionately about the things he felt really matter. He disregarded costs and threw himself in for the sake of his patient, reader, or audience, or for life in the large. To enlighten people, he launched new medical journals, wrote books, co-initiated a global medical campaign to prevent nuclear war, directed a psychotherapy centre, and then turned his mind to the *next* generation's health, founding a charity. As an octogenarian, he was still visiting Russia and Ukraine to improve children's health, an effect reaching cities throughout the former Soviet Union. He deserved the thrill of his share in the 1985 Nobel Peace Prize and his 2001 Albert Schweitzer Gold Medal.

FOREWORD

Barbara Findeisen

In the first edition of *The Unborn Child*, Roy Ridgway went beyond his training as a medical journalist to include realms of the heart as well as the intellect. He spoke of a deeper truth, a place we all know, though we may have forgotten. He covered subjects ranging from biology to emotional trauma, from embryology to psychology, and from the historical perspective to current treatment of birth trauma. He wrote then, in 1987, that he hoped there would be further research that would shed more light on the neglected field of pre- and perinatal psychology.

Since then, there has been a great deal of further research. Certainly there has been a flood of medical information concerning the technology of fertilization, inter-uterine intervention, and birth itself. Less well publicized is the research done towards the advancement and understanding of the emotional and psychological issues around birth and pregnancy. In his latest edition of *The Unborn Child*, Roy Ridgway expands his original work to include latest information and research on the earliest stages of our development as thinking, feeling, physical, social, and spiritual Beings. This knowledge is vital if we are to understand and prevent the escalating increase of violence

---

Barbara Findeisen is President of the Association of Prenatal and Perinatal Psychology and Health of North America (APPPAH).

in our societies, most especially among younger and younger individuals.

Children are killing children at an alarming rate. Child abuse is epidemic. Children are harming themselves, committing suicide, at increasingly younger ages. In an effort to stem the tide of this tragedy, we would be wise to step back and re-evaluate many of our beliefs, attitudes, behaviours, and institutions. We need to revisit the roots of our humanity as members of the human family and take a good look at what we are doing. Nowhere is this more important than concerning the births of our children, which includes the first nine months from conception through birth. It is then that basic imprints are made of fear or love, of mistrust or trust, upon which later behaviour and personality are formed.

There is scientific data that now proves the presence of consciousness in the womb. The fetus is thinking, sensing, feeling, and learning about life in that watery world. Perhaps the intellect and technology are out of balance with the wisdom of our hearts.

Anyone who has even a slight interest in the field of consciousness, pregnancy, or birth would be well advised to read Roy Ridgway's book. It is always one of the first books I recommend for data and research. It is well documented and presented in a clear and exciting manner. The reader will be given an overview of the field of pre- and perinatal psychology from many different aspects: historical, developmental, psychological, and philosophical. It is fascinating to read how the theories of pre- and perinatal pioneers have grown over the years.

The reader is exposed to the writings of remarkable people such as Dr Frank Lake, Otto Rank, R. D. Laing, Donald W. Winnicott, Phyllis Greenacre, and Francis Mott. Though many of these pioneers are no longer living, their works and knowledge are with us, continuing to inspire and teach us. Roy Ridgway includes information on professionals currently working in classrooms, therapy rooms, conferences, and research facilities, carrying forward and expanding knowledge of pre- and perinatal psychology. Articles, books, and websites on the subject are appearing more frequently. Stories of actual cases, peoples' experiences, dreams, drawings, and poetry affirm again and again the validity of the psychological life of the unborn child, which is corroborated in scientific studies.

Roy Ridgway's vast scope entices us to explore the subject further. The author's training as a journalist creates a very readable and well-researched volume. Beyond that, one gets a sense of the author himself. When I first met Roy Ridgway, I was immediately taken by his warmth, his open-hearted way of speaking and relating. I had already read the first edition of *The Unborn Child*, and I expected his grasp of pre- and perinatal psychology and the keenness of his intellect. He writes eloquently of the need of children to be loved, of the damage caused when love is absent. He explores fundamental facts that all human relationships originate in parental attitudes and behaviour, which begins before conception.

From the first stirrings of life in the womb, we are reacting to environmental conditions. The ways we learn to respond in that watery world will be reflected in later life. When there is damage early in life, it will be manifested in many different symptoms in childhood and adulthood, and into the next generation. Denial of love in childhood is a predictor of later violence. In his second edition, Roy Ridgway includes the latest research of the importance of bonding and the dire consequences that follow its absence. Certainly no one can ignore the psychological condition of many, many of our children. It is time for all of us at every level of society, institutions, individuals, and the medical world to become aware of the vital importance of this information. Scientific research corroborates the importance of changing some of our methods of carrying, birthing, and parenting our children. Properly, scientists are beginning to see love as a verifiable—respectable—area for research. It is a vital necessity if we are to stem the tide of violence and emotional spiritual pain among us. This is the way we can touch the future, for the children are the future.

Roy Ridgway's concern and dedication to people of all ages is felt throughout *The Unborn Child*. The hearts of all who read it will be touched, and the consciousness of all who read it will be expanded. We will all benefit, but most importantly the next generation will be blessed.

2006

FOREWORD

Michael A. Crawford

Roy Ridgway was clearly a man passionate to see people happier and healthier in a world protected from the worst ravages. He had witnessed a world war, and its damage to family lives, physical and mental, that lasted last long after the trauma of battle, the bomb-ravaged loss of home and belongings, or the loss of a father, mother, brother, or sister. Roy's research with pioneer psychotherapists and obstetricians identified the source of much chronic depression and violence. In Freud and Winnicott, Leboyer and Odent, and Frank Lake—cell biologist as well as psychiatrist—he recognized the salient factors that were being widely overlooked. What then struck Roy Ridgway and Simon House alike was the powerful evidence emerging over several decades from my own fields of brain chemistry and human nutrition. Before a woman is aware she is pregnant, her child's development and health is more affected by her nutritional status on the one hand, or the exposure to toxins on the other, than at any subsequent time. The brain again becomes particularly vulnerable during its very rapid cell division and growth, before birth and its continued maturation in the months when the infant is fed and emotionally nourished at the breast of the mother. It is hardly a surprise that the brain is a

Michael A. Crawford, PhD, CBiol, FIBiol, FRCPath, is Director of the Institute of Brain Chemistry and Human Nutrition, London Metropolitan University.

major target of disorder associated with low birthweight or preterm delivery.

From the 1930s nutrition was becoming more objective, with the chemical identification of the vitamins and essential fatty acids. The widening interest in the epidemiology of disease by pioneers like Sir Robert McCarrison was identifying the link between bad diets and much disease defining the converse links between nutrition and health that was to serve the country so well during the Second World War under the direction of Sir Jack Drummond. In the aftermath of the war, the heady days of nutrition research were considered over, the answers were known. Despite the evident success of Drummond's nutrition and health policy, that strategy of feeding the nation was abandoned. The new way was the thirst for production and profit. The rates of heart disease, breast, colon, and prostate cancers rose, and although new pioneers of nutrition and health such as Cleave and Burkitt spoke out, the march for productivity raced on unabated, ending in Salmonella and Bovine Spongiform Encephalitis (BSE).

But it was not only the animals that were affected. By 1972, when cardiovascular disease had become the major burden of ill health, it was simple for us to predict (Crawford & Crawford, 1972) that the brain would be the next to suffer from the modern, lipid malnutrition. The evidence base for the prediction was, first, that lipids are the major structural material of the brain; second, that the lipids of the brain required specific essential fatty acids that were being eroded in the food chain by the enthusiasm for production; and, third, that its prenatal development and growth is dependent on efficient blood supply. With the arteries under attack, it was logical the brain would be next. Today, disorders of the brain have overtaken heart disease. Across the 25 member states of the European Union, brain disorder now costs 386 billion euros at 2004 prices. It accounts for 25% of the total burden of ill health, with heart disease relegated to second place at 17% (Andin-Sobocki et al., 2005).

Of course not all brain disorder is nutritional. Psychology, until the 1980s, had relied on anecdotal material and qualitative analysis. Now the biochemistry of hormones, Candace Pert's work, and Curt Sandman's, notably, and Jaak Panksepp's neuroscience, could quantify and bring objectivity to emotional states. The brain could be observed not only as a telephone exchange but as a wine-cellar of hormones, ready to be dispensed through the bloodstream to act on receptors throughout the body–brain regions included.

The mechanisms of gene expression, too, were becoming clear: Bruce Lipton was among those explaining the lifelong biochemical effects on the individual of emotions and nutrients—or their deficits. Biochemicals, switching genes on or off, prepare a person for life beyond the womb, beyond childhood. All this came to a head when, in 2001, the Human Genome Project revealed, rather than the predicted 150,000 genes, merely one-fifth that number of genes in the human genome. Moreover, powerful evidence emerged of major genes conserved for millions of years. Our genome is only 1.5% different from that of a chimpanzee. As Professor Ted Tuddenham said at a recent McCarrison Society conference, the modern epidemic of thrombotic and vascular disorders cannot be due to changes in genetic material but, rather, to environment and diet acting on "ancient genes" to manipulate their expression.

What Simon House has done is to work in both camps. In this single book he has brought together in a readable manner the recent findings of nutrition and psychology, biochemistry and emotion. Prenatal and perinatal care vitally needs to progress as an integral wavefront. That the nutrition and health of the mother has been neglected is evidenced by the increase in low birthweight from 6.6% in 1973 to 7.6% in 2002 (H.M. Government, 2004). UNICEF (2004) puts the United Kingdom at 8%. "The window of opportunity" that seals the intelligence, behaviour, and health of those about to be born is lost for many of the 55,000 babies born at low birthweights in the United Kingdom. This book presents the case for a paradigm shift towards the nutrition and emotional health of the mother and her unborn child. In my opinion there can be no more effective and economical way to benefit people's health, happiness, and peacefulness. The book is not just about the United Kingdom. The issue is global. Roy Ridgway in his life certainly saw the worldwide implications, and his efforts to help Russia stand as a great tribute to his perseverance, compassion, and effectiveness. Ridgway and House, with their own perception from experience, review a global range of expertise. Fully referenced, this is an authoritative book in the quest for global health and peace.

2006

PRELUDE TO THE 2006 EDITION

Simon H. House

In 1992 I was working on a book about bringing children into the world healthy and happy, based largely in the experience of psychotherapy and life as a parish priest. Happily, while browsing in a bookshop in Winchester, I came across a second-hand copy of Ridgway's *The Unborn Child*. It was out of print, they told me, and brought in by the author, who lived along the road. This well-researched book was a ready-made part of my book-to-be. Within three conversations, Roy Ridgway said, "I can help you with your book, and I'd like you to be a trustee of my new Charity." We worked closely for eight years, until his death. Our minds were at one on what we wanted to achieve.

Roy had been a high-flying medical journalist, launching his own successful journals, and with several books to his name. He was an initiator of a Nobel Peace Prize-winning venture by International Physicians for the Prevention of Nuclear War (IPPNW). He had also begun setting up medical exchanges with Russia, which led to his first co-founding the Charity HealthProm, and then founding and directing another, which his widow and successor Dorothea has wisely renamed Child Health International. Our prime aim in the new charity became the Health of Future Generations, based on the evidence we had accumulated. Soon we had potential projects in Russia and Ukraine, but they seemed too forward-looking yet to win funds from the West. Nonetheless, Child Health International led to the updating of cystic fibrosis treatment across the "Former Soviet Union". Not only did those affected begin to live beyond childhood, but their quality of life was transformed.

After *The Unborn Child's* first edition, Roy, for long a believer in nutrition, became associated with Professor Michael Crawford (Director of the Institute of Brain Chemistry and Human Nutrition). Sharing the concept of health from the beginning of life, Roy and I grasped at once the huge importance Michael attributed to nutrition from before conception. I proceeded to assemble the evidence in a 50-page review, "Generating Healthy People" (S. House, 2000), with great help from Michael and his associates, Arthur and Margaret Wynn. Roy, always looking at things as a whole, would be keen to include the nutritional aspect, which I have made Part C of this new edition. It is largely the work of these associates that is behind the remarkable breakthrough by the bold television chef Jamie Oliver, in raising public awareness about school meals.

Also since the first edition, Frank Lake's well-founded yet controversial conclusions have been corroborated by biochemistry and genetics. Lake's extensive findings showed the lasting effect of a mother's emotional state on her child, especially in the first three months in the womb. Candace Pert's work on biochemistry of the emotions (Pert, 1998) and Curt Sandman's on the build-up during pregnancy of a shock-repressing hormone (Glynn, Sandman, & Wadhwa, 2000) provide further rationale. Even before the result of the Genome Project, Bruce Lipton was clarifying how environment affects genetic expression, especially in early development (Lipton, 1998). This concept was not widely acknowledged until, in 2001, the Genome Project revealed the number of a human being's genes to be only some 30,000—about one-fifth the number predicted. Developmental flexibility is explained by environmental effects on genetic switches rather than a higher number of genes. No surprise to Darwin, whose *first* principle of evolution, much overlooked, was "conditions of existence"—"The law of Unity of Type and of the Conditions of Existence embraced by the theory of Natural Selection" (Darwin, 1859). Environmental conditions, we would say. No surprise to Crawford (Crawford & Marsh, 1995) or Ridgway either. The mother's environment affects her own nutritional and emotional/hormonal state, which, in turn, affects her child, since she *is* the environment of her child-to-be. Her state, even from before conception, powerfully affects her child in the intricate processes of his development.

Roy and I would talk for hours, philosophically and about practicalities of our work. Drawing us together were his medical experience and writing and my physiology and pharmaceutical marketing; his experience directing a psychotherapy centre and my experiences of early-memory recall; his interviews with Frank Lake and others, my experience with Lake's primal integration therapy. Yet his leaning was more literary, mine more scientific; his emphasis more on "changing our manner of thinking", mine more on "changing our way of feeling"; but the difference was merely in emphasis. Protection from early life trauma leaves people's feelings more intact. The spread of such protection, through understanding and cultural change, increases the number of people whose capacity to feel is less impaired. A world with deeper feeling will be more averse to violence, to war, and to reckless development. The powerful and the self-seeking will have more heart for the needs of all. Change of heart leads to change of mind, of the way we think and the way we work.

In this edition, I have shifted the emphasis from overcoming early trauma towards prevention of early damage, in keeping with our shared aim, the health of future generations. Roy would have been more than happy with this. I have also restructured it more as a handbook so that, when there is so much to read in so little time, readers can readily find their way about it.

We have reached a stage in evolution of such rapid change to our environment that we can no longer rely on natural evolution for "quality control" of our own reproduction. We have ourselves to evolve means of quality control to keep up with rapid change. Recent research has been prolific. The current gap is our slowness to act on its findings. This is not the way in progressive industries. For computers, or mobile phones, poor quality control would be regarded as folly. For humans perhaps it will become regarded as criminal folly.

Roy and I discovered how hard many find it to realize that we can recall early memories, though with skill this is not difficult and can be so healing. Many found it hard to recognize the importance of nutrition from before conception, though generations of farmers have recognized the truth of this for their animals. For many this will be a hard book to take. To others it will seem like common sense. Every few years understanding deepens of how the creation of human beings happens, and how we can introduce new generations in a healthier and happier state, more stable and peaceable.

* * *

I wish to endorse Roy's acknowledgements and thanks in his original Prelude, reprinted verbatim immediately below, and include my thanks to Dorris Halsey of Reece Halsey North for kind permission to print a verse from Aldous Huxley's *Brave New World*.

My warmest thanks to Roy himself, of course, for a great friendship and all those good times together, and for introductions to new networks. To Dorothea, his devoted widow, particularly for inviting me to update the book, and their son Michael for his interest and encouragement. For exciting ideas and events and great company and for many papers I want to thank profoundly Michael Crawford, coupled with David Marsh, and Arthur and Margaret Wynn; Lutz Janus for his warm welcomes to platforms in Heidelberg and elsewhere. I am immensely grateful for everyone's resources, and for amazing patience in editing various aspects; Joe Hibbeln, Bruce Lipton, Jaak Panksepp, and Nim Barnes for their generous sharing of experience and knowledge; my siblings, Julia Chappell and Adrian House, for publishing and editorial wisdom; my wife, Frances, for her special perception, and our children, Ben, John, and Susie, for all I learn from them and for constantly keeping me computer-capable; for the enjoyment of working with all at Karnac—Oliver Rathbone, Kate Smith, Catherine Foley, and Elizabeth English—and Klara King of Communication Crafts, for her amazing skill in unearthing anomalies and her wise editing.

PRELUDE TO THE 1987 EDITION

Roy Ridgway

"Every man is some months older than he bethinks him, for we live, move, have being, and are subject to the actions of the elements and the malice of diseases, in that other world, the truest microcosm, the womb of our mother."

Thomas Browne, Religio Medici, 1642

"Yes—the history of man for the nine months preceding birth would probably be far more interesting and contain events of greater moment than all the three score and ten that follow it."

Samuel Taylor Coleridge, 1802,
in the margin of his copy of Browne's book

I should like to record here my gratitude to John Heron, assistant director of the British Postgraduate Medical Federation. No doubt he will be surprised to find his name coming first in these acknowledgements, but he it was who first aroused my interest in prenatal psychology when he ran a weekend workshop at the Sparsholt Centre, sometime in the mid-1970s, I forget precisely when. The workshop was concerned with advanced co-counselling, but it included a practical demonstration of "re-birthing".

As director of the Sparsholt Centre, I learnt a great deal from people who called themselves facilitators but were in fact leaders, and others who visited us to practise various forms of psychotherapy. They were exciting days, never to be forgotten. They opened my eyes to vast areas of human experience that scientists tend to ignore because they defy classification. They also taught me the meaning of what Krishnamurti calls "inexhaustible innocence". One becomes attached to knowledge, which sometimes accumulates, layer on layer, to form a brick wall dividing you from the world, in the same way as one becomes attached to material possessions, which give the illusion of security. Knowledge—the response of memory—can hold you back. Not to know, on the other hand, can open up a whole new exciting world where many things are possible.

Among those who shared in our adventure at the Sparsholt Centre were Michael Green, Chris Fraser, Oded Manor, Mike Pegg, John Crook, Helen Davies, James Kilty, Graham Whale, and Neil Grant. They and many others have, through their influence, their validation of whatever one feels, their unconditional positive regard for the other person, helped to make this book possible.

Later, when I was editing BMA News Review, I came across a British Postgraduate Medical Federation programme, which included a workshop run by the psychiatrist Dr Frank Lake, mainly for GPs, with the title "Fetal Memory—Fact or Fiction?" It intrigued me and rekindled my interest in prenatal psychology.

I met Dr Lake at Lingdale, his home and the centre for the Clinical Theology Association, in Nottingham, where he ran many of his workshops. This meeting was, for me, the beginning of a fascinating journey that led to the writing of this book. I and many others are still travelling along the same road. Who knows where it will lead? In recent years we have learnt a great deal about how the child develops in the womb, not only physically but psychically. Could the next step be to follow this journey back to before conception? Or even to previous lives, perhaps? It may sound farfetched, but it was not so long ago that much that we now know about life before birth was regarded as superstition. The folklore and superstition of today often become the science of tomorrow.

When I met Dr Lake in Nottingham, he did not scoff at the possibility of taking his research back to before conception (healing the ills of the collective unconscious?). He had a sensitive, receptive, and lively mind, and I should like to acknowledge here all the help he gave me at that original meeting and in subsequent correspondence. Sadly, he died just after I got started on this book.

I should also like to express my gratitude to the Rev. Martin H. Yeomans, who took over from Dr Lake as acting director of the Clinical Theology Association, and to Mrs Sylvia Lake for permission to use material on the small group and the paranoid family from *Studies in Constricted Confusion*, published privately by Dr Lake.

I must also thank Vivian Milroy for permission to use material from *Self and Society*, the journal of the British Association for Humanistic Psychology; and Leslie Feher for permission to use material from the *Birth Psychology Bulletin*, the official journal of the Association of Birth Psychology, New York.

I am grateful to Stanislav Grof, of the Esalen Institute, Big Sur, California, for permission to use material from his book, *Realms of the Human Unconscious*; and to Dr Erich Blechschmidt for permission to use material from *The Beginnings of Human Life*.

Among others who have helped me in various ways are: Dr S. Schindler, chairman of the International Society for the Study of Pre-natal Psychology; Dr Martin Bax for the fascinating material that emerged from his radio programme on the prenatal origin of language; Dr John Launer, for introducing me to the metaphysical poet Henry Vaughan and for reading the proofs to check for medical accuracy; Dr William Emerson, for permission to quote from *Infant and Child Birth Refacilitation*; Dr David L. Kay, for permission to quote from a paper published in the *Journal of Analytical Psychology*; Dr Jean Goodwin, Director, Postgraduate Education, The University of New Mexico School of Medicine, and Dr James Jaramillo, for permission to quote from their paper on "Post-Partum Psychosis in an Artist", presented at the Sixth World Congress of Social Psychiatry, 1976; Angela Fawley for providing me with much interesting information; my wife, Dorothea, for helping in many practical ways, including translating from the German; and also Mrs M. Wagner and Charles Lewis for their help with translations from the German; my sons and daughter, Michael, Tony, and Jane, who have pushed and prodded me into completing this book, which I found so daunting at first; also a special word of thanks to Fred Yarrow, for his helping hand and his friendship for the family at a very difficult and stressful time during the writing of this book; and my ever-patient editor, Matthew Reisz, for his guidance and help in giving the book a shape.

Introduction:
inner nature and outside world

"We had to go for a medical and Michele stood shuddering in her knickers when the doctor came near her. He said: 'My goodness, she is nervous, isn't she?' I said, 'Well, I was pregnant with her in a cellar during the war; I should think that counts for something.'"

Motherland (Ann McFerran, 1988)

Care to last a lifetime

Violence towards children is endemic. In 13 years following publication of this book's first edition, over 2 million children were killed in wars and civil conflicts, and between 4 million and 5 million have been disabled (UNICEF, 1998). Nearer home, in Britain, the NSPCC reports an appalling record of cruelty and neglect. An advertisement headed "Cruel Britannia", placed by the Children's Society in the British press, points out that we march for animal rights, respond generously to humanitarian tragedies across the globe, and campaign for a better environment. Yet we have the worst record in Western Europe for caring for our children.

Another press report points out that Britain shares with Romania (UNICEF–WHO, 2004) one of the worst records in Europe for babies seriously underweight, with increased risks of death within a month, mental handicap, blindness, deafness, cerebral palsy, epilepsy, and autism.

In the first edition of this book I wrote about child suicide in the United States. According to Dr Perihan Rosenthal (Rosenthal & Rosenthal, 1984), a director of child ambulatory services at the University of Massachusetts Hospital, doctors dismissed child suicides as accidents, but he said he found children as young as 2 who deliberately attempted to take their own lives.

A little boy was asked by Rosenthal why he had injured himself. "Daddy and Mummy don't love me any more", he replied, as if he was trying to punish himself because his parents had left him and he felt that their rejection was his fault. Sadly, the problem of child suicide is still with us. In the Children's Society advertisement referred to above, Josie (aged 12), who had tried to commit suicide, said, "I wish I'd never been born." What a terrible thing to say in the springtime of life!

We talk about educating our children in numeracy and literacy while many of them are more in need of help with their emotional problems—even more essential to their wellbeing, and also to their skills. The Mental Health Foundation's report on mental health of children (1999) states that "at any one time 20% of children and adolescents experience psychological problems" (http://www.mentalhealth.org.uk/html/content/young offenders.pdf).

This world-wide epidemic of child cruelty leads many to mental and physical ill-health, and often to a lifetime of misery, lawlessness, and exclusion from society. How can it be prevented? There is, of course, no easy fix, but one important factor in human development and behaviour that is not yet taught in our schools is that all human relations have their origin in parental attitudes from before conception.

And this brings me to the reason why I have been persuaded to bring out a second edition of this book: its main message has so far been widely ignored.

The book presents a concept of care that spans a lifetime, the whole lifecycle, from before conception onwards. It describes new ways to protect new lives. It tells how people are finding new ways of healing. The book has powerfully influenced a small but worldwide community of dedicated people, including experts in prenatal and perinatal psychology, but they have not yet received the recognition they deserve. They are researching into the beginnings of life, but society is scarcely aware of the problems and their causes, or of the newfound possibilities of healing.

Bonding

Environmental conditions significantly determine health from before life begins in the womb. Genes play an important part in establishing who we are and how we behave, but there is mounting scientific evidence that, in the age-old dispute between nurture and nature, nurture usually wins.

The American developmental neuropsychologist James Prescott has demonstrated this in his studies of the long-term consequences of lack of bonding, which formed part of a broad programme of systematic research on the origins of violence carried out over 25 years at the US National Institute of Child Health and Human Development (Prescott, 1996). They showed that neural circuits were damaged through rejection or abandonment of a child by parents or through inadequate bonding. The degree of bonding depends on the amount of attention given to the physical and emotional needs of a developing child at each stage of development—preconception, pregnancy, infancy, childhood, and adolescence. Economic and social pressures also affect these natural developmental processes.

Prescott found abundant evidence to show that bonding rests on three emotions: trust, affection, and love, each in a system of the brain (Prescott, 1996). Trust rests on the vestibular-cerebellar sensory system. Affection rests on the somesthetic, touch-sensory system. Intimacy rests on the olfactory, smell-sensory system. The love-bond consists of these three combined. Feelings of pleasure arise, says Prescott, and bonding, when these three systems are fully integrated in development. Lack of this integration is the principal neuropsychological condition for expression of violence.

Prescott carried out cross-cultural studies on 49 primitive cultures distributed throughout the world. Among these, he found 29 violent cultures and 20 peaceful ones. His findings showed that the degree of physical and psychological bonding in the maternal–infant relationship was a reliable predictor of the degree of peaceful or violent

behaviour in those cultures. He concluded that violence was cultur-
ally determined—a fact that can also be demonstrated in the learned
behaviour of chimpanzees.

Main cause of violence particularly sexual

"The failure to integrate the physical pleasure of bonding into
the higher brain centres associated with consciousness", says James
Prescott, "is the main neuropsychological condition for the expression of violence, particularly sexual violence."

He was talking about different degrees of pleasure, from pleasure
experienced as purely physical or sexual to a love in which the physical and spiritual are integrated. Love is described in different ways
by different people. To the neuropsychologist, it has something to do
with neural circuits in the brain. To the lover it is the physical pleasure of intimacy, a feeling of closeness. All relationships begin with
physical pleasures of touch, smell, and a sense of trust. But it is not
just a matter of determinacy—as if we cannot help ourselves being
who and what we are. It is more a matter of the choices we make, our
intentionality. To be human is to be responsible for one's own feelings and thoughts, being attentive to the feelings and needs of others,
acknowledging what Heidegger called our state of "being with others in the world" (Heidegger, 1953). In other words, being a human
being means being in relationship with others and with nature; and,
I would add, an awareness of a spiritual or creative intelligence at
work in the universe, with an attitude, "Not my will, but the will of
a creative intelligence be done". Looked at from the point of view of
the psycho-neurologist, these basic physical pleasures should in all
healthy nurturing and development go on to become integrated into
the higher brain centres as transcendental states of human spirituality. However, as a result of incomplete bonding, pleasure is experienced by some only at the genital-spinal reflex level or limbic level
of brain function. We then become slaves of our animal instincts—of
those parts of the brain that have been described as reptilian and
mammalian.

Love can, of course, include the sexual appetite; but when it becomes integrated into the higher consciousness, there is regulation
and restraint or, in neurological terms, there is "regulation and in-

hibition of those neural circuits that mediate depression and violent behaviour" (Prescott, 1996).

The transcendental state of human spirituality is described by the Jewish mystic Martin Buber as the "I–Thou relationship"—a feeling of oneness between two people—that is experienced at the beginning of life before a child feels separated from its mother (Buber, 1958). Later, as this state becomes integrated into the higher consciousness, it is experienced as trust, affection, and physical closeness, and we do not think in terms of an object to love (which is the I–It relationship, expressed in the purely sexual relationship—i.e. sex without love); there is just a loving relationship where there is mutual respect and tenderness.

Blake wrote of love moving "silently, invisibly" (*Love's Secret*). This is a poetic way of saying it happens without words or definitions or protestations. It is a force that is there at the beginning, in the nurturing of a child, and it can become a "guiding light" throughout life. "Never seek to tell thy love", Blake wrote, "love that never told can be." Love often becomes distorted by words, degenerating into possessiveness or dependency, except in the powerful lines of a Blake or Shakespeare or Shelley or Elizabeth Barrett Browning. But love needs no words; it exists in its purest sense pre-verbally. It is the state of being described in the East as our unborn Buddha nature, or *kensho*, when the self vanishes, leaving a state of absorption in the activity of the moment: being present to the Other.

Love is experienced as a common bond with humanity. It includes relationships with nature and animals as well as human beings, which Wordsworth, with his universal sense of religion, saw as a powerful force at the very centre of life.

As we enter the new millennium, I believe the best way for science to ensure a more peaceful world is not by playing about with genes, as some believe, but by getting to grips with the psychological, social, cultural and religious problems of human love; and the place to begin is before conception, with the understanding of what it means and what it requires to create another life.

"The understanding of the nature of human love", James Prescott says, "is a proper subject for scientific study and such studies are essential if human violence is to be understood and prevented."

Love spans a whole lifetime and begins when a couple take on the responsibilities of parenthood. As scientists such as Prescott have demonstrated, bonding during pregnancy and at birth lays the foundation for much that follows in life. But science is just one way of knowing. Other ways of knowing are through art and religion.

Condemned to please

What science is teaching us today is that we can never be certain of anything. And we know from the lives of many people that even if there is love at first, even if the bonding goes well, it does not necessarily lead to loving relationships later in life. The denial of love increases the likelihood of violence. Truly caring love reduces its likelihood. The main trouble as the child begins to gain a sense of independence is that socio-economic pressures interfere with the healthy development of relationships within the family, and love is perceived as synonymous with social approval. The good—"love-able"—boy or girl is one whose behaviour is socially acceptable. This, as Sartre said in his autobiography (Sartre, 1964), means that the child is "condemned to please". Love, which most people experience at the start as both spiritually and physically nurturing, becomes confused with dependency and possessiveness, and this is probably the origin of much that goes wrong in interpersonal relations in the home, the community, and even on the world stage of international relationships.

If I may bring a personal note into this thesis, I am aware, when looking back at my own childhood and boyhood, that the real problem (in the 1920s and 1930s) lay outside the family home. Being loved—that is, winning approval—in the outside world was mainly a matter of obeying rules of social behaviour, but in the home you could break the rules and still feel loved. But although you enjoyed loving or caring relationships in the home, the world outside could be very cruel and have a damaging effect on your character, sometimes, as I remember, splitting the male breadwinner in two—into a tender home-loving father and thick-skinned businessman, the latter perceived as supportive to the former. Cruel, indifferent behaviour is justified as a means to an end. Not only is this true on the small stage of business and family relations, it happens on the big stage of international relations. But means and ends are one process, and, as Eliot wrote in *East Coker*, "in my beginning is my end". Means determine ends. The wrong means cannot produce the right results any more than wrong motives.

Yet most of us separate outside from inside. We live in two different worlds. Even some of the most ruthless dictators experienced the unconditional love of a mother, which they continued to respond to in loving ways. For instance, Stalin's mother, a peasant woman in the last few years of her life when Stalin was at the height of his power, talked of her "loving, considerate son". Stalin visited her regularly in her two-roomed flat in Tiflis, Georgia. There was a very close bond between them.

When Stalin was a child, life was hard for his mother, Katherine Djugashvili, in the family's little dark house with its leaking roof and empty larder. The family was very poor and suffered ill-health and malnutrition. Then later, when Stalin—the man of steel—became one of the most ruthless dictators of all time, the memory of a loving mother remained with him, but it could not prevent him from committing acts of terrible savagery. Indeed, the memory of his mother's suffering may have contributed to his ruthlessness in creating what he regarded as a fairer society, where the State looked after its people. It was mainly the economic and social circumstances of Stalin's childhood that had moulded his personality, which saw danger everywhere, making him turn on people who had done him no real harm. In his case, violence was linked both to a cruel father and to the poverty and injustice he had experienced early in life: currently referred to as "structural violence". The bonding was not strong enough to counter this.

Alice Miller blames Stalin's persecution mania on the brutality of his father, who had mercilessly beaten him when he was a child. There are many instances in the past, and even in recent times, of fathers who ruled their families with rods of iron. It was also once common practice for the State to inflict brutal physical punishment on citizens who broke the law. Those who perpetrated these crimes were part of a social system that not only condoned but encouraged such behaviour. In blaming them, we are blaming the victims of an unjust system; the fault lying in the thinking that creates such systems. Fragmented thinking fails to see the whole of life from beginning to end as one continuous process. Holistic thinking, seen from the outside as development or progression or deterioration, is felt inside as harmony, following a universal design that we call intelligence.

Life was hard for many of us in Britain before and after the Great War of 1914–18, especially when I was a boy during the depression years on Merseyside, where there was a lot of misery brought about by poverty and malnutrition. I remember the despair outside the family home, but I also remember all the love within the home in spite of a bad-tempered father, who worked in Liverpool in a job he hated. This was the pattern in many homes on Merseyside—loving mother, hard-working, battle-weary, bad-tempered father.

It was a time when many families were bereaved after four years of trench warfare. There were men suffering from post-traumatic stress disorder (PTSD), which they called shell shock in those days; and every family had lost someone or knew of someone who had been killed in the trenches of the Great War. No one came out of that war without some form of psychological damage. To paraphrase Yeats, too much exposure to suffering can make a stone of the heart. I have experienced the numbness myself in wartime. I worked for a while as a medical orderly in the resuscitation tent of a field hospital where the worst casualties were brought—men with their legs crushed by mines or their brains hanging out, or with bits of shrapnel lodged in the spine or lungs or stomach. I put up with it as part of the reality of war; there was nothing else I could do. I had to go about my work concentrating on the routine of care without becoming too much involved.

In the language of today's neuropsychology, we would say that too much suffering damages the limbic system, which does most of the brain's learning and remembering. Cutting off was an automatic reflex, the only possible response if one was to remain sane. But when the dust of battle settled, there were terrible feelings of guilt and inadequacy; and many cracked up. What saved me, I believe, from coming to much harm in spite of these ghastly experiences was healthy nurturing right at the start of my life—the memory of a loving mother and an environment that was not too unkind to me.

Memory of just being

For me, fortunately love remained as solid as a rock in a turbulent sea, a memory and a comfort, and indeed a lifeline in times of distress or failure. It encouraged me to go on trying to be the person

I knew I was and wanted to be. And also, if I went into that feeling more deeply, what I discovered was not a self-image but a memory of "being"—just being alive, awake, true to my nature—my unborn Buddha nature. The reality of that memory negated a lot that had been imposed on me by way of culture since early childhood. It took me back to a time before conditioned thought processes constructed fears out of physical distress.

What does it mean to endure? To keep going because one believes in something? Endurance was not only a lesson taught by the Victorians, but in my case it took me back to a very early "visceral" memory in which love (endurance of pain for the love of a child) overcame the trauma of a difficult birth—the kind that can leave a horror imprint on the memory, becoming a template for later behaviour. However, in spite of the pain of birth, my primal or "visceral" memory, which is a part of me, is essentially one of love and protection.

The importance of parental attitudes and close contact between mother and child were topics discussed at the Eighth Congress of the American Association for Prenatal and Perinatal Psychology and Health (APPPAH) held in San Francisco in December, 1997, which had as its theme "Birth, Love and Relationships".

I attended the conference because I was planning this new, updated edition of my book, originally published under the title of *The Unborn Child: How to Recognize and Overcome Prenatal Trauma* (1987), which, at the time it was published, did not attract much attention in the United Kingdom (though it goes on selling in Japan). At that time people thought it absurd that the nine months in the womb could have any great significance in the development of personality. It was therefore very interesting for me to hear of the mounting scientific evidence demonstrating that those nine months and the conditions in and around birth are indisputably of tremendous importance in creating a style for what follows, both physically and psychologically: physically, for instance, in the way even before conception poor nutrition—deficiencies of vitamin, minerals, or fatty acids—or pesticides in food, or smoking or drinking, can lead to birth defects (Crawford, 1993; Crawford et al., 2003) or can result in heart disease or other illnesses later in life (Barker, 1998), and psychologically because of the damage that can be done during pregnancy and birth to the neurobiological systems that are the foundations for psychological states. But beyond all this is a sense of something "far more deeply interfused" (Wordsworth, *Tintern Abbey*).

Teaching the heart to think

The main message of the San Francisco conference was, I believe, best expressed by Joseph Chilton Pearce, when he said: "Our great task today is to teach the heart to think."

It is a message that is implicit in Daniel Goleman's popular book, *Emotional Intelligence*, in which it is argued that our emotions play a far greater part in our thinking and decision-making than we are prepared to admit (Goleman, 1996).

Goleman writes about horrors of war that are frozen in the memory, leading to the hypervigilance and other symptoms of post-PTSD. This, to some extent, had happened to me, though I did not know it at the time. I had a bad time in the post-war years, but fortunately I was not scarred for life, as many are. Just as there are vitamins that will offset the risk factors of a poor lifestyle, in my case close family bonds prevented serious psychological damage that can occur when victims of war have no good early memories of being loved, no solid foundation of love and trust. This, I believe, is why some people can stand the stresses and strains of life more than others.

The San Francisco conference dealt with this physical and psychological damage, which goes back to the first trimester of pregnancy, when the embryo's developing neural system is so vulnerable. This, I learned at the conference, includes the development of the heart cells, 65% of which, according to Joseph Chilton Pearce, are neural cells. The brain, Pearce said, developed from a mass of undifferentiated heart cells before they had formed into the four cardiac chambers. Pearce talked a lot about research that was going on in the new science of neurocardiology and explained how the heart and brain worked closely together. The heart, he said, was more than a pump: it was connected to all the organs of the body and was linked to the cognitive and learning processes.

There were many surprising things said at the conference. For instance, Harvard biologist Bruce Lipton challenged the primacy of the gene concept and turned this round to talk about the primacy of the environment or the primacy of nurture—not nature (Lipton, 1998). "Genes cannot control themselves", he said, "and therefore they cannot control the system. It is a false assumption to say that our character is determined by our genes." Other scientists are in agreement. The Human Genome Project has been attacked as "an extreme example of reductionism". "Subscribers to the philosophy of genetic determinism", said Professor Michael Baum, "need a strong dose of humility" (Baum, 2002).

The mathematician Illya Prigogine, in his study of the thermodynamics of nonequilibrium systems, has shown that many things attributed to biological pre-wiring are actually the consequence of social interactions in nonequilibrium conditions (Prigogine & Stengers, 1984). Out of chaos comes order; out of all the forces that impinge on the developing human life comes a reaction that is an attempt to establish or restore order. Sometimes the effort is too much and neural circuits are damaged.

In the end, what we are up against is not so much the social or psychological environment but our manner of thinking, which shapes that environment and perpetuates social injustices and concepts that create divisions between people, religions, classes, and so on. The divisions are in the mind, which accepts and rejects and has chosen an ethic that says, "Work to make money, to be successful, to go to the moon" and so on. It is our whole way of thinking that must be transformed.

Debris of emotional anxiety

The humanistic psychologist John Heron talks of the debris of emotional anxiety that exists in society itself. Individual hurts, he says, which stem from early anxieties of a personal kind, can be understood and discharged, but there is an anxiety that cannot be discharged in this way because it is fixated in society in the collective traumas of the past. It is experienced as a sense of helplessness, as in the Kosovo War. And many personal traumas, because they stem from this source—the undermining of the will and the anxiety created by a sense of being helpless victims—can therefore be described as innate. These feelings belong more to the collective unconscious, and therefore they can only be dealt with collectively in group work. Awareness is all-important in facing problems of interpersonal relationships, and this means an awareness of how we have been conditioned to think in the way we do.

In his talk at the International Co-counselling Teachers Meeting on "Co-counselling and the Paradigm Shift" (1995), John Heron stressed the need to recover spiritual identity and the expanded awareness that goes with it. Krishnamurti (1981) calls this awareness a discovery of "the seed of life that is hidden below the surface." Love, he says, is the "drawing forth of that seed from its hiding place."

Healing relationships

Speakers at the San Francisco conference—psychologists, gynaecologists, midwives, physicians, anthropologists, clergymen, biologists—talked of the power of love and of the need for love in preconception planning and in the development and birth of a baby. They talked of childbirth as a spiritual as well as a biological event.

Thomas Verny, the founder of APPPAH, said: "Through healing birth, we are healing this earth, and God knows this earth needs a lot of healing." Vice-President Barbara Findeisen talked of all the research that is going on now that affirms the reality of the soul, and about how prenatal and perinatal experiences supported or destroyed the connection with the soul.

James Chilton Pearce described the long-term consequences of supportive and non-supportive parents on the personality of the child as he/she grows up through adolescence to adulthood, and how early experiences (environment impinging on development) can have a lifetime effect on a person's behaviour. Pearce gave an example of long-term research carried out over 30 years at Harvard University (Pearce, 1997). Of the minority (160) of students who had described feelings of being loved and cared for in childhood, 25% had serious illnesses when questioned 30 years later. Of the majority of students, who had described feelings of being unwanted and badly treated, 80% later suffered from serious illnesses such as cancer, heart disease, and arthritis.

Healing a part of our consciousness

We need to heal that part of our consciousness identified with race, country, or religion, which we call history, through a change in our way of thinking—the sort of change that David Bohm describes as "the movement of thought becoming aware of itself". The body is aware of itself, of its movements, and we call this "proprioception". Thinking proprioceptively is more difficult, but possible. It is called "choiceless awareness" by Krishnamurti (1992) and "self-remembering" by George Ivanovich Gurdjieff (1950).

David Bohm (1992) points out that every time you do or think something, it leaves a bit of change in the nervous system; in this way it builds up a pattern, particularly in the early years, which then becomes fixed. A group of people looking at this process together will become aware of what is happening and, as a result, raise the consciousness of the group. But you cannot be aware of your thinking if you view it merely in abstract terms as a process or mechanism: this is the scientific way of thinking, and it is inappropriate when dealing with human relationships. When we are not thinking scientifically in symbols of measurement, we always think in some cultural or social context: our thoughts prepare us for action; or they are a rehearsal of some part we are going to play in a social or family setting, and they are usually related to our early conditioning in a particular culture.

I am sure that a transformation in our thinking will come, if we are aware that the way people relate to one another is mostly competitive—everyone striving to find a situation in which he/she excels. The psychologist Alfred Adler describes so eloquently in his *Individual Psychology* (1930) what he calls "the will to power". If we could replace the "will to power" with "the will to be", it could make all the difference. I do not believe that the satisfaction of exercising power over others is essential to our nature. Memories become distorted and stored as personal myths or fantasies or paranoid interpretations of what we see or experience—as they did with Stalin. It is obvious how these memories have such a hold on us, a safety wall we build around ourselves, propping up the ego.

Where and how do we search for the truth? Obviously seeing clearly means seeing the truth—that is to say, seeing in a way that is unclouded by personal prejudice or ambition. The more we look through the eyes of the ego or through the eyes of so-called experts, the more fixations we have, the less we see. By waking up, by becoming aware of our conditioning, we can gain a strong sense of where we are and who we are, thus changing our way of being in the world. It is up to those whose thinking was not irreversibly damaged in early development, who are close to their childhood and recognize the child in themselves, remaining innocent throughout life, to demonstrate that it is possible to live a different kind of life, where love and not violence holds sway. There is a growing number of these self-aware, self-remembering people today, thank goodness! The future of the world—no less—rests with them and every one of us, if we look and listen.

Roy Ridgway, 2000

PART A

CONCEPTION
AND LIFE IN THE WOMB

CHAPTER ONE

Beginning and adapting

"The universe resounds with the joyful cry I am."

Alexander Scriabin, *Poem of Ecstasy*

a.   *Development week by week*

The New Zealand gynaecologist, Professor A. M. Liley, pointed out that although in the temporal sense we spend a very short time in the womb, about 1% of our life, in terms of the division of cells, our physical development—apart from stature—is almost complete by the time we are born (Liley, 1977).

We begin life as a single cell; 45 generations of the doubling up of cells by growth division are needed to reach the thirty million million cells of an adult. Of the 45 divisions, 41 take place before birth. Yet even before this single cell there is "life before life". The sperm's life can be traced back months to its genesis in the testes, which were already formed in the father when in the grandmother's womb. The beginnings of the ovum itself existed in the mother when she was still in the grandmother's womb, where it is known to have been

---

For the sake of grammatical simplicity, the fetus/infant/baby is referred to as masculine throughout.

susceptible to the grandmother's environment. Nor should we lose sight of the genetic trace unbroken down the generations:

> From the point of view of the sort of person we are going to be, 90 percent of the excitement is over by the time we are born. It is for this reason that we regard the care of the pregnant woman, and this stage of life, as so important, because rapidly growing cells are so vulnerable to inimical influences, and if anything does go wrong, this can cast its shadow so far into the future. [Liley, 1977]

Not that the remaining "10%" is unimportant—far from it.

The various stages of development will be mentioned from time to time in this book, so I am going to start here with some biological facts essential to the understanding of what follows.

First, conception: a new life emerges through the encounter of a male sperm with a female ovum. There is only one sperm that fertilizes the ovum out of the many thousands that reach as far as the Fallopian tube, and there is usually one ovum that is fertilized out of the many hundreds that develop during the menstrual cycle.

The ovaries of the new-born female contain approximately 80,000 ova, which, of course, is a great deal more than she will need in her reproductive life. During each menstrual cycle 250 ova begin to develop, but usually only one is properly ripened and shed in the middle of the cycle. A developing ovum lies inside a small cyst called a Graafian follicle, which gradually enlarges and migrates towards the surface of the ovary, finger-top size. The follicle then ruptures and releases fluid, which carries the ovum into the fimbriated (bordered with hairs) end of the Fallopian tube. The muscular wall of the Fallopian tube contracts and relaxes rhythmically, so that the fluid is drawn into it and then guided down the tube by the hair-like structures called cilia.

The ovum is very tiny, a mere pinpoint; it is pale yellow, because it contains some yolk, and is round like a ball. The sperm is much smaller than the ovum: 2,500 sperm would be required to cover a full stop.

Fertilization takes place after hundreds of millions of sperm fight their way through a treacherous obstacle course at a speed of one inch in 20 minutes. Only 2,000 manage to reach the vicinity of the ovum, and then only one sperm penetrates it, an event described by Aldous Huxley in the famous lines:

A million million spermatozoa,
All of them alive:
Out of their cataclysm but one poor Noah
Dare hope to survive.

[Aldous Huxley, "Fifth Philosopher's Song", 1920]

It is not known precisely how a sperm penetrates the ovum; but it is believed that it hits the membrane—the zona pellucida—very hard and at great speed and bores its way into the cell, apparently with the cooperation of the ovum itself. When this occurs, the ovum rejects all other sperm, although many more try to attach themselves to the zona pellucida. The whole operation, which looks so chaotic, usually ends precisely as planned.

The fertilized egg subdivides into two, and each of the two cells splits again, for seven days. Four days after conception these cells— up to about 32—form a hollow ball called the blastocyst, which is wafted by means of the cilia (microscopic hairs) slowly down the Fallopian tube towards the uterus. The cells around the outer surface of the blastocyst continue to multiply, and by the seventh day have formed finger-like projections called the chorionic villi.

The blastocyst sinks into the lining of the uterus, and a hormone is released to prevent the lining being shed in menstruation. The villi digest their way through the uterine lining. At first the uterus reacts to the invasion of the blastocyst as if it were an invading intruder. The lining tissues swell to engulf the embryo, and at the same time thousands of white blood cells are marshalled to get rid of any debris. It is really a bloody battle. That tiny blastocyst, fighting for its life, has no more than a 50–50 chance of surviving.

Suddenly, for those who win the battle, all resistance ceases; the invading army is then treated like a friend, and the uterine tissues seem to make a place for it. The haemorrhaging tissues provide the embryo with its first outside source of nutrition: a starch called glycogen, which is broken down into glucose. The embryo immediately gorges itself on this.

By the end of the fourth week after conception there is a rudimentary brain and a spinal column as well as a spinal cord, and the first rudimentary heart and circulation are beginning to function. In the second month a threshold is crossed: the embryo becomes a fetus and, small though he is, it begins to look human. Usually by the time the embryo is five weeks old, the limbs are formed, with separate fingers and toes; the liver shows up as a dark shadow, and the heart begins to look human.

During the third month the baby begins to be very active and responsive to stimuli, although it is still small enough to fit into a goose egg and weighs only about one ounce. He can kick his legs, curl his toes, bend his wrist, squint, frown, and he can swallow—in fact, he swallows considerable quantities of amniotic fluid.

We now see our tiny human being behaving in ways that look human. So perhaps at this point it might be a good idea to define what we mean by behaviour. In the *Pre-Natal Origin of Behaviour*, Davenport Hooker (1952b) defines behaviour as "a fundamental characteristic of all animals, whether adult or developing, unicellular or multicellular". He goes on to describe how he sees behaviour as the sum total of the adjustments made by the organism to the internal and external environment. Bodily activity can be seen as the overt expression of the drive to maintain a dynamic balance of all the parts of the organism.

At the end of the twelfth week the baby reaches "an important age landmark, as the quality of response is altered. It is no longer marionette-like or mechanical . . . the movements are now graceful and fluid, as they are in the newborn . . . the fetus is active and reflexes are becoming more vigorous." But although all this is going on, the mother does not feel the movements, because the uterus, like all internal organs, is insensitive to touch, and the movements are not strong enough to be transmitted to the abdominal wall.

But the picture we see at the end of the twelfth week is recognizably of a baby with bodily features and facial expressions resembling the parents. The behaviour of the fetus is to some extent determined by hereditary qualities, such as the structure of the muscles, which varies from baby to baby; but the environment also plays an important part.

In *The Prenatal Origin of Behavior* Davenport Hooker says:

> In the normally developing organism, behaviour is an expression of inherited structure. . . . It is well known that maternal diet or certain diseases suffered by the mother may prematurely alter structure. Where these early changes in structure seriously affect the neuro-muscular mechanism, alterations in behaviour may be expected. [Hooker, 1952b]

In the fourth month the baby reaches half his height at birth. The baby then needs a good deal of sustenance, and it is during the fourth month that the placenta, which provides the fetus with food, oxygen, and water, is properly formed. Waste products are also carried away through the placenta: they are absorbed into the maternal circulation, and some of these, such as carbon dioxide, are exhaled by the mother from her lungs, while urea is eliminated by her kidneys.

In the fifth month the fetus grows to be one foot long and weighs a pound. He grows hair on his eyebrows and on his head; his heartbeat becomes louder, and he sleeps and wakes much as a newborn does. In the sixth month he can open and close his eyes, look up, down, and sideways. Most important of all, if he is born prematurely during the sixth month, he is capable of maintaining regular breathing and could survive in an incubator; but usually the lungs and digestive system are too immature to take over their full functions.

During the next three months the fetus continues to put on weight. Late in the seventh month the fetus becomes "viable"—that is, able to maintain breathing and with lungs and digestive system well developed. If he is born prematurely, he will have a better chance of survival than at six months, but he will still have to be placed in an incubator because he lacks the heat-insulating layer of fat under the skin and his defences against disease are weak. In the incubator, temperature and humidity will be kept under control and infection rigorously excluded.

The baby is born when he is so large that the uterus is stretched to its limits. This usually occurs within 11 days of the appointed 266 in the womb.

b.   *The personality of the fetus*

It is only in recent decades that the fetus *in situ* has been accessible to study. Now modern scanners can see things in such detail that it is possible to examine the heart and its four chambers when it is only 1 cm in diameter and the fetus is 18 weeks old. It is even possible to detect heart abnormalities and treat them in the womb. At a very early stage of development an incurable condition can be picked up—and the mother can then have the choice of terminating a pregnancy if that is her wish.

Modern technology's capacity to monitor the development of the fetus has corrected some false ideas, for instance about what the fetus feels—or does not feel. The fetus is not, as many people in the past thought, an inert passenger in the pregnant woman; and he does not have a mind like a clean, washed slate, a *tabula rasa*, which was the eighteenth-century belief of Jean-Jacques Rousseau and his pupils.

Freud (1922) described intrauterine life as a condition not unlike sleep, with an "absence of stimulation and avoidance of objects". And that great neurophysiologist, Sir Charles Sherrington (1951), spoke of "the miracle of the human ear developing in silent water for hearing in vibrant air", which we know now is quite untrue. Many people still picture the womb as a quiet place with little stimulation for the fetus, a peaceful place where everyone would like to return because they will find the peace of Nirvana. The womb is a metaphor for a safe, silent place—safe, perhaps, but it is certainly not silent. It is in fact a noisy place, and the fetus, far from being inert and soporific, is very active, responding to all kinds of stimuli that reach it from inside and outside.

According to Professor Liley, the fetus is not a passive, witless inhabitant of the womb but the dominant partner in the pregnancy (Liley, 1977): it is the fetus who guarantees the endocrine success of pregnancy and induces all manner of changes in maternal physiology to make her a suitable host. It is the fetus who, single-handedly, solves the homograft problem—no mean feat when you reflect that, biologically, it is quite possible for a woman to bear more than her own body weight of babies, all immunological foreigners, during her reproductive career. It is the fetus who determines the duration of pregnancy. It is the fetus who decides which way he will lie in pregnancy and which way he will present in labour. Even in labour the fetus is not entirely passive—neither the toothpaste in the tube nor the cork in the champagne bottle, as supposed by the old hydraulic theories of the mechanics of labour.

The gynaecologist Frank Hytten has also pointed out how ruthlessly selfish and active the fetus is in creating his own environment:

> The fetus is an egoist, and by no means an endearing and helpless little dependent as his mother may fondly think. As soon as he has plugged himself into the uterus wall he sets out to make certain that his needs are served, regardless of any inconvenience he may cause. He does this by completely altering the mother's physiology, usually by fiddling with her control mechanisms. [Hytten, quoted by MacFarlane, 1977]

In the first half of pregnancy the fetus moves about with ease in the buoyant amniotic fluid. When he rests, he chooses the most comfortable position, sometimes with his chin resting on his chest and sometimes with his head tilted back. In the first half of pregnancy the uterine cavity is relatively large and globular, so movement is not difficult, but in the second half it becomes ovoid, and the growing fetus feels cramped and uncomfortable. Usually he flexes his knees, and this is best achieved in the normal head-down position, but if he decides to extend his knees, which sometimes happens, he will fit in best in the reverse position, which results in the so-called breech birth—that is, feet first.

Sound

In the first half of the nineteenth century it was thought that the fetus was deaf and dumb, but in fact the inner ear is completely developed soon after mid-pregnancy, and at birth a child's hearing is very good.

The fetus responds to a wide range of sounds, some of them at frequencies so high or low that they cannot be heard by the human ear, which suggests that sensory pathways other than the ear are implicated.

Mothers have long known that whenever there was a loud noise of any kind, such as a car back-firing or a door suddenly slamming, it will startle the fetus. Ashley Montagu tells the story of a typist who was forced to give up her job during the eighth month of pregnancy because every time the typewriter carriage was returned to begin a new line, the clang caused the fetus to jump. With 30 lines to a page, the typist just couldn't take all that jumping (Montagu, 1978).

In the 1930s L. W. Sontag carried out the first experimental work on the effect of sounds and vibrations on the unborn child (Sontag, 1941). A vibrator, which produced 120 vibrations a second, was applied to the tummies of eight pregnant women during the last three months of pregnancy. Sontag found a marked increase in the movements of the fetus every time the vibrator was turned on. This, of course, would be no surprise today—mothers might be amused that such an experiment was thought necessary—but what is of interest is a follow-up experiment, which established that fetal activity was not caused by an hormonal change in the mother's body, which some thought could have been activated by the mother's alertness after hearing a startling sound. This would cause the uterus to contract slightly, and there would then be an increase in pressure in the fluid surrounding the fetus.

The question was resolved by transmitting high-frequency sounds by means of a vibrator attached to the mother's abdomen while at the same time providing the mother with headphones continuously playing different sounds, so she would not be able to hear or feel the high-frequency sounds. Within five seconds of the sounds being turned on, the fetus was kicking. There is evidence that some sounds heard by the mother will stimulate the fetus, but never within five seconds. A similar experiment with low-frequency sounds, which the human ear cannot pick up, established that the fetus was being stimulated in some other way, through another part of the body.

Liley found that from at least 25 weeks the fetus would jump in rhythm with the tympanist's contribution to an orchestral performance. It may not, therefore, be so absurd as it may sound to some that a Liverpool doctor said that when his wife was pregnant, he used to play the bagpipes a lot, and that the fetus could be felt jumping or—as the doctor put it—"dancing" to the sound of the music. Then, when the boy was 3 or 4 years old, he wanted to play the bagpipes. This may, of course, have been the result of the father's influence after birth, but the "dancing" was probably a genuine response to the rhythm of the bagpipes.

The Canadian Dr Thomas Verny recalls in his book, *The Secret Life of the Unborn Child* (1982b), how he heard Boris Brott, conductor of the Hamilton (Ontario) Philharmonic Symphony, describe in a radio interview how he became interested in music. He said that as a young man he was mystified by the unusual ability he had to play certain pieces sight unseen:

> I'd be conducting a score for the first time, and suddenly the cello line would jump out at me; I'd know the flow of the piece before I found the page on the score. One day I mentioned this to my mother, who is a professional cellist. I thought she'd be intrigued because it was always the cello line that was so distinct in my mind. She was; but when she heard what the pieces were, the mystery quickly solved itself. All the scores I knew by sight were ones she had played while she was pregnant with me.

It is not only external sounds that bombard the fetus; there are also the mother's body sounds, the loudest of which are stomach rumblings, which peak at 85 to 90 decibels. There are, however, the richer, all-pervading sounds that synchronize with the mother's heartbeat, such as the sound of blood in the arteries supplying the uterus and placenta.

Liley asks whether the long exposure to the sound of the mother's heartbeat explains why a baby is comforted when held close to a mother's breast. "Does this experience explain why the tick of a grandfather clock in a quiet study or library can be a reassurance rather than a distraction, why people asked to set a metronome to a rate which 'satisfies' them will usually choose a rate in the 50–90 beat per minute range?"

Elias Canetti points out that all the drum rhythms in the world belong to one or other of two basic patterns: either the rapid tattoo of animal hooves or the measured beat of a human heart.

> The animal hoof pattern is easy to understand, from the ritual and sympathetic magic of hunting cultures. Yet, interestingly, the heart beat rhythm is more widespread in the world—even in groups like the Plain Indians who hunted the great herds of bison. Is this rhythm deeply imprinted on human consciousness from fetal life? [Canetti, quoted by Liley, 1972]

Vision

Muscles within the orbit are present very early in pregnancy, and the eyes of the fetus move during sleep and when he changes position. Liley has noted that when a flash is used to photograph a pregnant abdomen, the fetus is startled. But although there is activation of visual pathways when light is present, the fetus lacks sufficient light to practise cone vision, so that after birth it takes a baby some five to eight months before he can recognize images with any confidence.

Dreaming

The fetus, particularly during the last three months of pregnancy, has the same sleep patterns as the mother. This was demonstrated in research carried out by the Swiss paediatrician, Stirnimann (1940, 1951), who compared the sleep patterns of neonates (newly-born babies) of housewives with those of mothers with quite a different sleep cycle, who worked at night in bakeries. In each case the fetus had the same sleep pattern as the mother.

Sleep restores the body and mind—recharges the batteries—usually during the hours of darkness. Nobody knows quite how this happens or why exactly we dream during sleep, though it is commonly believed that dreams clear the mind of behavioural problems that have been bothering us during the day and interfering with our natural patterns of behaviour: they attempt to put the person back on course, or, as a biologist put it, they replay the DNA code.

There is evidence that we learn to dream in the womb. Electro-encephalograph (EEC) examinations have shown that during sleep the fetus has phases of rapid eye movement (REM), which in adults usually means they are dreaming. Professor Sepp Schindler, once President of the International Society for Prenatal and Perinatal Psychology and Medicine, is one of those who believe that the fetus is indeed in a dream-like state during these phases. His explanation for neurological activity during sleep—"active sleep"—is that increasing restriction of movement experienced by the fetus as he grows during the last three months of pregnancy is replaced by increasing activity in the head. It is a kind of "wish-fulfilment" dream or a rehearsal of movements learned in the womb that will be needed after birth—in other words, it is a form of "action replay": the replaying of a photographic sequence of what has become an inhibited activity, a reminder of what the fetus can accomplish (Schindler & Zimprich, 1983).

This is all speculation, of course, but Schindler believes that something of this sort happens because, after birth, when the child is able to move freely again, REM phases are considerably reduced. The theory fits in with Freud's idea of dreams as "the royal road to the unconscious", freeing the individual from emotional blocks and allowing him to fantasize forbidden activities. Could the emotional block, or the way we deal with it in our dreams, have its origin—as Francis Mott believed—in some anxiety over an inhibited physical activity, going back as far as the womb?

American sleep researchers believe that the REM phases are training for intellectual activity: they are the beginning of thought processes. It is a fascinating area of study, which may eventually help us in the understanding of the sleep patterns and dreams of the adult.

Touch and response

The fetus is responsive to pressure and touch. As early as nine weeks after conception, the fingers have developed well enough to wrap the palm of the hand around objects. At 12 weeks the fetus is able to close his fingers and thumb. He touches parts of his body with his hands and feet; though early in pregnancy when he accidentally touches any object he moves away from it, later he moves towards it.

He at first turns away from his hand when it touches his mouth, though the mouth opens. Later he opens his mouth and puts a finger or thumb into it. This is the rooting reflex, which persists after birth: then it is usually the mother's nipple that touches the baby.

During labour, tickling the baby's scalp produces movement; stroking the arm produces a grasping movement, and tickling the soles of the feet during a breech birth produces upturned toes. He responds with violent movements to a needle puncture or an intra-muscular injection of a cold solution. Should anyone doubt that these are signs of pain, Professor Liley says:

> Although we would accept that these stimuli are painful for the newborn baby, we are not entitled, I understand, to assert that the fetus feels pain. In this context, I think Bertrand Russell's remark in his *Human Knowledge, Its Scope and Limitations* rather apt. He relates how "a fisherman once told me that fish have neither sense nor sensation but how he knew this he could not tell me!" It would seem prudent to consider at least the possibility that birth is a painful experience for a baby. [Liley, 1977]

Liley points out that radiological observations during contractions show the fetal hands and legs flailing about in what seems like a paroxysm of rage, and this, he says, must be because of the pain of the process. Liley suggests that the compression of the head during the contractions must be extremely painful.

Frederick Leboyer (1975) is in no doubt at all about the pain suffered by the child at birth. You don't need proof, he says: you can see the agony on the face of the newborn. You can see "the tragic expression, the tight-shut eyes, the howling mouth, the burrowing, desperate head, the outstretched hands beseeching. . . . You can't say a newborn doesn't speak. It's we who do not listen."

Karelitz (in Livingston, 1972) in New York has shown that, judging by the strength of the stimuli required to arouse a newborn child, his first sleep is more profound than any subsequent sleep. The child seems exhausted, which is hardly surprising after the prolonged stimulation and pain of labour.

Drinking and swallowing

The fetus drinks amniotic fluid at the rate of 15 to 40 ml per hour in the third trimester—that is, the last three months of gestation. There are more taste buds in his oral cavity than in the mouth of a child or adult.

He likes sweet things and dislikes bitter tastes; so he must learn something about pleasure and pain in the womb. Liley says that fetal drinking rates crash after an injection of Lipidol "R", which is a foul-tasting iodinated poppy-seed oil that any adult or child would spit out in disgust. The fetus, in fact, shows his dislike of a bitter taste by the sort of grimacing you might see on anyone's face who had just swallowed a spoonful of foul-tasting medicine. The fetus also shows his appreciation of a sweet taste. Saccharin increases fetal consumption of amniotic fluid: he gulps it down with great relish.

The fetus may have difficulty in swallowing. "Traditionally", said Liley, "it has been assumed that hunger is a brand-new sensation after birth, that *in utero* an obliging mother and faithful placenta have supplied baby's every need. However, the sight of babies with gross intrauterine malnutrition makes it rather hard to believe that every fetus lives in a metabolic Nirvana." (Liley believed that what is traditionally regarded as placental insufficiency is hypothalamic in origin, a glandular problem.) Fetal hiccups are fairly common and are sometimes induced by irrigating the amniotic cavity with cold solutions. Such a sound may alarm the mother, especially if there is a history of epilepsy in the family, and she needs to be reassured that it is quite harmless.

c.   Learning in the womb

We associate learning with repetition and the stick and carrot or reward and punishment—that is, habituation and conditioning. You get to know something if it is repeated often enough, or you like it enough, or you are afraid of being punished if you don't remember it.

The fetus certainly knows about pleasure and pain, which is the basis of a great deal of learning, particularly of the kind imposed on a reluctant student. Whether the sucking of a finger or thumb gives the fetus any pleasure is difficult to tell, but he certainly enjoys sweetened amniotic fluid and does not like it when it has a bitter taste.

Liley observed both habituation and conditioning in the fetus. The fetus will respond to a signal—say, a sound—on first hearing it, but after constant repetition the response becomes weaker and weaker, until eventually there is no response at all. He has become accustomed to the sound, knows it well, and becomes comfortable with it. This is habituation; and among the sounds the fetus must get used to are the mother's stomach rumblings, combined with all the other sounds in the uterus, including the flow of uterine blood. This is a continuous loud noise, varying in pitch but peaking, as I have said, at 80 to 90 decibels. It is not a sudden and unexpected sharp noise, which alarms the fetus. Could the loud background noise of the uterus account for the teenager's love of loud music at a disco? Does the disco, in fact, reproduce some of the conditions of the womb? A teenager was once reported as saying, "I feel safe at the disco." Safe back in the womb?

Conditioning is something quite different from habituation—more subtle; it is manipulative. A case of conditioning, dating back to 1948, is described by Ashley Montagu in *Life Before Birth* (1961). With the assistance of 16 pregnant women in the last two months of pregnancy and using sounds and vibrations, Dr D. K. Spelt (1984) demonstrated how the fetus could be conditioned.

First of all, he used an automatic clapper to produce a loud noise, and he set it off close to the pregnant woman's abdomen. In each case the fetus reacted by kicking wildly. Spelt then produced vibrations without any sound by removing the clapper from an ordinary doorbell and applying this home-made vibrator to the woman's stomach; this produced a gentle vibrating pressure. There was no reaction from the fetus. The vibrator and clapper were then set off at the same time. This was done between 15 and 20 times; and each time, of course, the fetus responded. Then the vibrator was set off without the clapper. There was a reaction. Spelt found he could do this 11 times, and then the response died away.

Can there be anything but very simple and basic conditioning of this kind? Can the fetus, for instance, be taught to love or hate or to react with hostility and aggression to certain stimuli? There is, in fact, evidence that maternal emotions can be communicated to the fetus and may have a lasting effect, influencing the personality of the child and later the adult. According to Liley, monitored fetal hearts do show abrupt changes, with sudden arterial pressures when the mother is emotionally disturbed. It has been argued, he points out, that since the fetus experiences only the consequence and not the cause of the emotion itself, the experience would mean nothing to him. This view, however, has been challenged, because of evidence that pharmacological responses to fear and anxiety also induce the sensation of fear and anxiety.

The fetus, as we have seen, also seems to learn something about sleep patterns. He learns that if his mother works at night in a bakery, she will sleep during the day, and he adjusts to this pattern. No problem. The problem comes when the mother suddenly changes her job and starts working during the day; this disturbs the fetus, who keeps the mother awake at night. He cannot adjust immediately to a sudden change of behaviour.

Most mothers have had some experience of what they regard as a child's perversity, doing the opposite of what is expected. Liley points out that the newborn baby is often restless at night and suggests that this is because the fetus has been subjected to the restlessness of the mother in bed during the later stages of pregnancy, when she may have suffered a great deal of discomfort, tossing and turning and possibly making frequent trips to the lavatory.

The fetus may become so accustomed to the mother's restlessness at night that the lack of restlessness at the expected time after birth, paradoxically, disturbs the child. This is the orienting reaction called "dishabituation". It is similar to the way a person living next to a motorway becomes accustomed to the noise of traffic and in the end does not notice it, but if he moves to a quiet area in the country, he is disturbed by the deafening silence. The silence, strangely enough, produces the same reaction as the initial reaction to noise. So we get the situation after birth of the infant sleeping when the mother is awake and active, and waking up and becoming very active when the mother is sleeping and the house is quiet.

It has been argued that sensation in fetal life cannot have lasting effects because the nerve fibres are not myelinated—that is, covered with a fatty sheath (myelin), signifying their readiness to function. However, there is recent evidence that the absence of myelin does not prevent the conduction of nerve impulses, though it slows it down. There must also be some kind of memory; otherwise the child would not be able to respond to his mother's voice, as he certainly does soon after birth. Detailed studies by W. F. Condon and others (see ch. 2[b]) have shown that the newborn baby sees and hears and moves in rhythm to his mother's voice in the first minutes of his life.

Arthur Janov, in *The Feeling Child* (1977), also mentions the sound of the heartbeat. The fact that this is always reassuring to the child (when played on a tape recorder) indicates, says Janov, that there must be some kind of systemic memory in the womb—what some people would call a "gut" memory.

Anxiety and behaviour

Janov (1977) tells the story of a mother who reported that, when she was eight months pregnant, she went to a park, which had a rifle range. Each time a shot was fired, said the woman, she felt her baby jump in the abdomen. When the baby was 8 months old, she returned to the same park; when a shot was fired, the baby had a startled reaction, more extreme than might be expected, according to the mother.

A sudden loud noise can have almost the same effect as a body blow, resulting in the tightening of the stomach muscles, screwing up of the face, and clenching of the fists. These are the physical signs of fear; and to get rid of these unpleasant sensations, we either fight the thing we are afraid of or we run away from it. If we are unable to do either, we are "petrified with fear". The fear remains, and it can remain as a stress condition long after the event.

Janov (1977) draws attention to research carried out by S. Rosen, a New York ontogenist, who wrote: "When a sudden noise strikes the ear, the heart beats rapidly, the blood vessels constrict, the pupils dilate and the stomach, oesophagus and intestines are seized by spasms. . . . You may forget the noise . . . but your body never will."

As Janov (1977) says, Rosen is discussing a stress or anxiety reaction. "An infant who is unable to focus on the source of noise", Janov goes on, "or to do anything about it will undergo this stress reaction. Whether the human organism is inside or outside the uterus makes little difference in terms of its physiological response to noise stress."

There are, of course, noises inside the uterus that don't disturb the fetus. They, however, are of a different quality, and the fetus undoubtedly recognizes them. The sudden noise in the park alarmed the mother, and she communicated her anxiety to the fetus. Since he also, presumably, heard the noise while in the womb, he later associated the sound with strong feelings of anxiety.

In one of the earliest papers on the subject, "War and the Maternal Fetal Relationship" (1944), Dr Lester W. Sontag described how he believed that pregnant women who were anxious about their soldier husbands disturbed the fetus and could possibly influence the behaviour of the child and adult. He noticed, he said, how babies born to these mothers frequently showed signs of disturbance.

This was little more than a hunch at the time, and Sontag's research findings were far from conclusive. He did, however, continue with his studies, and in 1966 he read a paper (Sontag, 1966) to the New York Academy of Science in which he described the results of ten years of research. He concluded—fairly cautiously—that severe maternal emotions during the last trimester (three months) "caused an immediate and profound increase in fetal activity".

He told the story, for example, of a young pregnant woman who had taken refuge in the Fels Institute in New York after her husband had tried to murder her. She had been having weekly sessions with Sontag, who had kept a record of fetal activity and fetal heart rate. When the young woman arrived at the hospital terribly distressed, Sontag examined her and found fetal activity enormously increased. We would be surprised today if the fetus had remained unruffled by the murder attempt and the mother's distress, but before Sontag's research it had not been established that there was any relationship between maternal anxiety and fetal activity. In a period of ten years Sontag and his team collected eight such dramatic incidents, all showing great increases in fetal activity in response to grief, fear, and anxiety.

"The children of such mothers didn't show any congenital defect", said Sontag. "They were, however, irritable, hyperactive, tended to have frequent stools, and three had marked feeding problems." He believed, he said, that there were prenatal predictors of the behaviour of the infant and the personality at a later age,

There have been various other studies of a similar kind showing the consequences of maternal anxiety during pregnancy: difficulties and complications in childbirth and a variety of disturbances in infants (Ferreira, 1960; Verny, 1982b, pp. 34–35, 64, quoting 1975 study by M. Lukesch).

Disadvantage and disability

One of the most interesting studies was one carried out by D. H. Stott (1978) in deprived areas in Glasgow and Lanarkshire, where there were histories of mental abnormalities in some families and not in others who lived in the same conditions. Sir Keith Joseph, when he was Minister of Health, challenged social scientists to find a solution to what he called the "cycle of deprivation".

No genetic method of transmitting social, biological, and mental impairments from one generation to the next had been demonstrated, nor could it be shown that postnatal influences played a part. There remained only one area of explanation, said Stott—events in the womb.

Stott had previously carried out research that showed that a variety of handicaps in the child—notably ill health, mental subnormality, and behaviour disturbances—could be traced back to maternal anxiety during pregnancy. But since this research was retrospective, it was not regarded as conclusive.

Stott therefore welcomed a follow-up study of prenatal influences on the behaviour of the child. Selecting every 200th baby born in Glasgow and every 100th baby born in Lanarkshire in a 12-month period, he collected all the information possible concerning the health, happiness, experiences, and circumstances of the mothers during their pregnancies and related this to the children's development during their first four years of life; 153 children were followed through to the end.

All the things that can go wrong with a child in its first four years—illness, neurological dysfunction, abnormalities of growth, malformations, and behaviour disturbance—were used to create a "morbidity score". This acted as a yardstick of ill effects, if any, of each prenatal factor:

What emerged with surprising significance was that the great majority of the mothers who had suffered from interpersonal tensions during their pregnancies had exceedingly unhealthy children . . . when the pregnant woman was subjected to continuous or recurrent serious interpersonal tensions, to which she could find no solution, the child ran twice the usual risk of handicap in health, development or behaviour. It could not be explained by birth complications, prematurity or postnatal influences. [Stott & Latchford, 1976]

What was difficult to ascertain was how far poverty had contributed to the results. Obviously, poverty can be a source of stress. For example, half of the mothers in the sample were under a great deal of stress because of the overcrowded conditions in which they lived, sharing a bathroom and lavatory with other tenants; in general, a woman of low social class would have little chance of a tension-free pregnancy. Stott admitted that poverty produced "a crude correlation with child handicap". This, however, did not mean that poverty itself caused these handicaps. Rather, since there is a greater likelihood of interpersonal tensions among the unprivileged, there seemed to be an important but "indirect" connection between poverty and child handicap.

He later carried out a study of pregnancy stress in Canada, employing a team of interviewers who obtained histories of the mothers' pregnancy and the postnatal development, up to the age of 5 years, of 1,300 children. He was able to compare the possible harmful effects of a wide range of factors. Among the surprising results of this survey was the fact that a child was at greater risk among the better housed. This seemed baffling at first, but then it was suggested that a middle-class family anxious to keep up with the Jones's and beset by financial problems could possibly be more disturbed than an ordinary working-class family (although this ad hoc explanation will not convince everyone). This result did show that poor accommodation was not the main factor in causing child handicap, though in the case of the Glasgow children it was obviously a contributory factor.

The Canadian survey also showed that quite a number of maternal illnesses were harmful to the child, as was heavy, tiring work and smoking during pregnancy. In the case of working-class women, distress at moving to a new locality far away from their mothers resulted in an 82% rise in the risk of child handicap. This was about the same as that for going into hospital for a digestive disorder, pneumonia, or pleurisy.

The remainder of the findings confirmed the results of the Scottish study to a remarkable degree:

Once again, it was stressful interpersonal relationships, which had by far the most damaging effects on the children. Marital discord during the pregnancy was associated with a 94 per cent above-normal rate of handicap in the child. This rose to 124 per cent among the better housed. The details of the marital discord show that it was more than just occasional quarrels: serious stress was involved, sometimes resulting in temporary separation. One factor was the husband's keeping his wife short of money while he spent heavily, which produced a great deal of stress and frustration. It was associated with 137 per cent greater risk of child handicap. [Stott, 1978]

One important conclusion was not in doubt: marital discord—often manifested in rows over money both in poor homes in Glasgow and in better-class homes in Canada—was very damaging. We can speculate further that such discord is so important because it makes it less easy for the mother to have positive, loving feelings towards her unborn child. In the last resort, such feelings, influenced by many things, including very centrally the attitudes of her partner or husband—if she has one—may be, as we shall see, the decisive factor.

Stott does not rule out genetically determined differences in vulnerability, which, he says, could explain why it is that not all children, even though they are brought up in extremely unfavourable conditions, are unhealthy, feeble-minded, maladjusted, or delinquent.

He also mentions overcrowding (important in Glasgow, no doubt, but not in the Canadian case?), which creates a lot of tension and may lead to violence. In animals there are genetic mechanisms to prevent overpopulation. They are triggered off by environmental factors, which act as barometers of population level. In humans, says Stott, the triggering-off agent is probably interpersonal tension. "The handicaps produced in the young", he says, "are caused by interactions between the mother's and the child's genetic constitution and specific types of environment."

Many of the children Stott examined were neurally damaged, and it was they who were the most vulnerable to postnatal stresses. The timid and dependent would probably take refuge in feeble-mindedness and the hyperactive would be restless and impulsive and could possibly turn to violence, to mugging, vandalism, and so forth.

On a wider scale, in Germany during Hitler's reign and the early post-war years, malformations of the central nervous system increased greatly, many attributable to the terrible malnutrition that persisted. It is hard to separate the effects of stress and malnutrition since they tend to subsist together under poor conditions. These will affect not merely one generation but the next one as well (Stein, Susser, Saenger, & Marolla, 1975). Only in the last few years have we recognized the remarkable association between depression and violence—including homicide and suicide—and a low consumption of fish.

The relationship of mental health to diet is the subject of Part C. The importance of attending to diet globally is underlined when we contemplate suicide attacks on New York's Twin Towers or bombs on London Transport, and the pandemic of violence, including nuclear threats. Everyday economic problems and unemployment may be causing some pregnant women as much anxiety as do more obviously personal problems. These, of course, have adverse effects on a mother's feelings for her unborn child, especially if she bottles up her feelings of anxiety rather than acknowledging and expressing them. Such feelings can be leaving their effect on children before they are born. But there are new hopes on the horizon, such as finding that a mother responds to the expressions of her unborn child viewed with ultrasound scanners.

Under a front-page headline blown-up scan of an unborn baby it was reported that

> scientists at the University of Portsmouth hope images like these will hold the key to stopping women smoking during pregnancy. In Portsmouth nearly one in four women smokes during pregnancy—23 per cent, compared to the national average of 18 per cent. In a trial, around 400 women who smoke will be given the cutting-edge scans in a study to see if the pictures help them kick the habit. Problems caused by mums-to-be smoking include premature and small babies, asthma in children and an increased risk of cot death. Will this early sight of their babies-to-be help mums to kick the habit? Fiona Fletcher of Buckland . . . said: "I felt like he was saying 'please Mum, don't smoke or you will hurt me'. The pictures are just unbelievable. It's really emotional. I'm not going to smoke any more. I really don't want to harm him."
> [Caws, 2005]

CHAPTER TWO

Characteristics—
intrinsic and being imprinted

"I am a little world made cunningly."

John Donne, *Holy Sonnet V*

a. *Abilities acquired before birth*

In the nine months a child is growing in the womb, he acquires a number of skills, which he puts to good use within a few hours of birth. Within minutes he can communicate with his mother. He can recognize her voice. Later, a short time after birth, he can imitate some of her gestures; he can smile; he can reach out to objects (Bower, 1984). He has other skills, other abilities, which he has learnt in the womb. His entire world, the way he perceives it, the way he adjusts to it, is determined by what happens in the womb.

If everything has gone according to plan and there has been no damage to the fetus, then the bonding process that began in the womb will go on developing after birth, when mother and child are pulled together by signals—by touch, scent, and sound—which produce behaviour designed to protect the child and reward the mother (Klaus & Kennell, 1976).

As in the womb, the child plays the dominant role in the partnership: it is his desires that must be gratified, otherwise he will torment the mother with his screams and tantrums. His mother learns to understand the messages the baby sends with his crying. It can mean different things and produce different reactions in the mother. His hunger cry, for instance, will produce a physiological change in the mother, which will induce her to feed the child.

The child can work out what is going on around him and make choices, signalling approval or disapproval. He is not the helpless creature he was once supposed to be, with a brain that is empty and needs to be trained to think, look, perceive, discriminate between people and between objects, sounds, tastes, distances. He can do all these things soon after he is born without any further training—it has all happened in the womb.

Professor Tom Bower of Edinburgh University, a persistent and critical baby watcher, contributed a great deal to our knowledge of how the newborn baby sees his world, what he thinks and feels. He showed us that the baby is born with certain intellectual skills. No one had thought this possible, and the baby had usually been placed in an environment that offered him no stimulation.

In the 1960s, said Tom Bower, "the standard baby's environment was often like a sensory deprivation. The infant lay in a white crib with a white liner, in a white room with a high ceiling and nothing else to look at. They were religiously kept lying down. Now they are sat up much more—it engages their posture, which engages their alerting system".

Tom Bower showed us that one of the things a newborn baby can do is to imitate. According to classical developmental psychology he would not be able to do this until he was one year old. For instance, he can stick out his tongue in imitation of his mother. "In no way is this a reflex", said Tom Bower. "He's miming what he sees in a very complicated way. It's the acquisition of a new skill."

This may be the first social gesture; and it is remarkable that the baby knows that the mother's tongue is similar to his own, which he has never seen. He can only feel his tongue; so the sight of his mother's tongue must be accompanied by a feeling of what it is like to stick out the tongue.

Within a short time after birth a baby can reach out with his hands and play with an object—correctly judging its distance: he used to be supposed not to be able to do this until he was 5 months old. He can also smile—something he was supposed not to do until he was between 6 and 8 weeks old. Of course, you will have to be very observant to notice some of the baby's expressions and gestures: they can only be detected by close analysis of videotape and film and are not immediately obvious to the eye.

Perhaps the most surprising thing Tom Bower discovered was that the baby can see the world according to abstract notions. For instance, a baby knows that objects can go behind one another. You can demonstrate this by moving one object behind another—say, an electric car behind a row of bricks—and watching the baby's eyes as this is going on. "It's a problem for the child", said Bower. "What has happened to the object? Has it vanished? Is it still there? The baby has to work it out."

The baby will tell you what he thinks is going on with his eye movements. In the film of this experiment you see the baby watch the object go behind a screen: his focus of attention then switches to the other side of the screen, where the object should emerge. He has worked out that if the object is moving when it goes behind the screen, it will probably go on moving until it reappears at the other side.

All this shows how highly organized the baby is at the moment of birth. There are many other things he can do in response to appropriate stimuli. He can try to crawl if he is put face downwards on a firm surface; he can put his hands up to stop a large heavy ball when he sees it rolling towards him; he can detect whether a sound is coming from the right or left; and so on.

A problem that has intrigued both linguists and child psychologists is the problem of just when and how a child starts to communicate with words. How does he learn to speak?

In the 1960s Noam Chomsky startled the academic world by saying that people who studied linguistics did not really know what they were doing. Language, he said, was not so much a matter of Latin verbs and French pronouns but, rather, understanding something much more fundamental: the rules that all languages had in common (Chomsky, 1966).

How did human beings, as distinct from other species, acquire their speech? That was the problem linguistics should be trying to solve. Chomsky himself believed that all human beings had an innate grammar-learning mechanism, which was as much a part of our biological make-up as any other human characteristic. "Our grammar depends", he said, "upon a genetic endowment that's on a par with ones that specify the structure of our visual or circulatory systems, or determine that we have arms instead of wings" (Chomsky, 1968).

Since Chomsky first propounded his controversial theory, there has been a tremendous interest in the way children acquire language, and it is becoming obvious that language is not just a cultural creation, as some people think. Certain important aspects—in fact, the very basis of language, the way it is structured—may well have their origin in the way certain parts of the brain develop in the womb. Is a child born with the ability to speak grammatically?

When child psychologists began to study the speech of children at the age of 2, they were puzzled by the way they began to construct sentences without being taught. It had always been believed that a child acquired language through imitation, but obviously he was not imitating anyone when he said things like "goed" instead of "went", or "doed" for "did": he was obviously working things out for himself. He must have noticed, without being told, that the past tense of such words as "walk" and "play" was formed by adding "-ed". Perhaps Chomsky was right in supposing that a child had an innate aptitude for the grammatical construction of sentences?

b.   The grammar organ in the brain

Chomsky's theory of a grammar "organ" in the brain found support among neuro-psychologists, notably Karl Pribram, who said that there was evidence for a brain "organ" responsible for the processing of natural languages and that any damage to this organ before or after birth can impair speech (Pribram, 1971).

Pribram explained that language and language-like processes result from interactions between the functions of different brain systems. Usually in the brain's left hemisphere, the posterior intrinsic cortex is involved in the coding operations that we recognize as "natural languages". If this cortex is injured, the result may be aphasia—the failure to recognize the character of some or all of the sounds in the spoken language.

There are different types of aphasia, including one in which the meaning of words is lost, in spite of the fact that they can still be strung together in grammatical sentences. In extreme cases, according to Pribram, patients can express sounds with inflections and apparent sentence structure, but the phrases are meaningless, the utterances pure jargon.

In another aphasia, produced by lesions in the frontal intrinsic cortex (which can occur during delivery), patients can understand the meanings of words, but the flow of speech is severely restricted. Missing from their speech are pivotal words, vital to the understanding of a sentence, inflections, the prosodics of speech and parsing that makes for sentence structure. The patient therefore speaks in a sort of telegraphic language, which is rather like the speech of a child who uses single, unlinked words.

All this lent support to what Chomsky (1983) had said about pre-programmed subsystems:

> In the last three or four years there's been a major conceptual change in the underlying theory. We now assume that universal grammar consists of a collection of pre-programmed subsystems that include, for example, one responsible for meaning, another responsible for stringing together phrases in a sentence, a third one that deals, among other things, with relationships between nouns and pronouns. And there are a number of others. [Chomsky, 1983]

Early development of speech

After studying the efforts of 2-year-olds to construct sentences, child psychologists began to study earlier forms of speech, starting with the cries and howls at birth. Most people had believed that these had something to do with getting air into the lungs; they did not consider that perhaps the child was in pain. "Ah, the little darling, isn't he beautiful! There, there! It'll soon be over. . . ."—words like that spoken by the traditional midwife brought some humour to the situation, and the mother found the cries reassuring; they immediately gave her a sense of contact with the child. But today she is not so sure: the cries tell her that at least he is breathing. But is he in pain? Shouldn't she hold him? Perhaps his cries are directed at her.

That is the beginning of communication. Later a mother is able to distinguish what the different cries mean. There is one cry that tells her he is hungry: this has the effect of increasing the blood flow to her breasts. Another cry says he is wet and uncomfortable and wants his nappies changed; yet another that says he is not getting enough cuddling. And so on.

What surprised psychologists was how soon after birth a baby recognizes his mother's voice. It is obvious to any mother that this is so, but the psychologists had to make sure by carrying out a number of tests. In the tests the mother spoke in her normal voice, which the child recognized. Then she changed the pitch or spoke in a monotone, which the child failed to recognize. The child did not respond to anyone else's voice in the same way as the mother's. It was also discovered that the child does not like a monotone but likes patterned sound; it also likes a high-pitched voice, which is probably why parents speak to their small children in a squeaky way.

The child psychologists came to the conclusion that the baby had got to know his mother's voice in the womb. The background noises in the womb—the mother's stomach rumbling, the sound of the blood flow, and so on—helped the child to focus his attention on the mother's voice, and, in fact, that was one of the first regulatory processes the child developed: already at birth he has learnt to ignore quite a lot of noise.

Some interesting research was carried out in 1984 by a team under Dr Anthony DeCasper at the University of North Carolina on what a newborn baby could remember of words spoken to the fetus during the last six and a half weeks of pregnancy. Could a fetus, for instance, hear and retain the words of a story read to him so that he could recognize them—the sounds, not the meanings of the words—after birth? This is what the team set out to discover (DeCasper & Spence, 1986).

Sixteen pregnant women were asked to read a children's story called *The Cat in the Hat* to their fetuses twice a day for six and a half weeks, so that by the end they would have heard the story for a total of about five hours. The problem was how the doctors would be able to prove that the fetuses recognized the story. Was there a test that would be scientifically infallible? The groundwork had been done in some previous research to show that the newborn baby recognized his mother's voice. In this study an ingenious opinion-sampling technique was worked out by Drs DeCasper and William P. Fifer (DeCasper & Fifer, 1980). There was one thing, they said, babies were keen on: sucking nipples. So nipples were used as a medium of communication.

A rubber nipple was wired up to a tape recorder, and the baby controlled what he heard by altering his sucking patterns. If he did not like the sound of a voice, he simply stopped sucking. The baby got the hang of it in about a day; and it was found that he sucked enthusiastically when he heard his mother's voice but was indifferent to the sound of his father's or anyone else's voice.

In the story-reading test two tapes were made available to the babies—one of *The Cat in the Hat* and another of a completely unfamiliar story, *The King, the Mice and the Cheese*. And, of course, they chose *The Cat in the Hat* every time. The other story left them cold. This was further proof that individual sounds or words are registered in the womb and auditory preferences after birth are influenced by what is heard prenatally.

Child psychologists are being led back to the womb. The more they study the infant, the more obvious it becomes that his behaviour cannot be fully understood without knowing what goes on in the womb. They can no longer draw a line at birth and pretend that that is where everything begins. The question now is: where do you draw the line? How far back can you go?

Another development in the understanding of how speech begins is the discovery that it has something to do with the relationship between movement and sound. In *The Magical Child* Joseph Chilton Pearce (1979) mentions one of a number of studies showing this. Sylvia Brody and S. Axelrod (1970), who were doing some research on the effect of maternal anxiety on ego formation, discovered that there were no random movements in the fetus: every movement, they said, had meaning. One of the discoveries of recent years is that particular movements can be linked to particular sounds.

In a 1974 study, two Boston University doctors, William F. Condon and Louis Sander, in an analysis of high-speed sound films of many newborn babies, found that their movements coordinated with speech (quoted in Pearce, 1979). Computer studies later showed that each infant had a complete and individual repertoire of body movements that synchronized with speech. A left elbow might be moved slightly when a "k" sound was used, or an "ah" sound might produce a movement in the right foot.

These movements proved consistent. After cataloguing and computerizing a child's repertoire of movement coordinates, Condon and Sander made up an artificial sound tape of random speech parts and fed this to the computer to match the tape to the infant's personal repertoire (quoted in Pearce, 1979). The computer then predicted the precise movements the infant would make to each of the sounds as they played. They then played the tapes to the child, making their high-speed films as they did so. When they checked the results frame by frame, they found that each sound produced the matching physical movements as computerized and catalogued.

This, as reported by Pearce (1997), is truly remarkable. The matching of movements to words must have started in the womb. Musical sounds, we know, are matched by the rhythmic movements of the fetus; probably other sounds that reach the fetus also produce characteristic movements. Later in childhood these movements are accompanied by hoots of delight, gurgles, cries, screams, sighs; eventually, out of these sounds words are formed.

Whatever aspect of behaviour you look at in the child or the adult—at language, mathematics, feelings of anger or love, music, art—you can trace it back to some physical activity in the womb.

Touch, meaning, and movement

Many of our movements and gestures were initiated in the early embryonic stages of development. The tiny arms that begin to form at the beginning of the second month of pregnancy already have a grasping movement, described by the embryologist Erich Blechschmidt (1977) as "growth-induced grasping". And this grasping movement, which is a growth activity, is seen in the newborn baby as he reaches out for objects. Reaching, stretching, grasping, which we must do as we develop in the womb in order to grow, are also activities associated, at least metaphorically, with intellectual growth: stretching the mind and so on.

There is a general embryological law that states that the earlier a function develops, the more fundamental it is likely to be. The sense of touch—the mother of the senses—is the earliest to develop in the human embryo. Before the embryo is eight weeks old and less than an inch long, it responds to touch. If you stroke the upper lip or the wings of the nose, the neck and trunk will bend away from the source of stimulation. This happens at a stage in embryonic development before the eyes and ears have been formed.

In the womb, physical development takes place as a reaction to some force or forces impinging on the organism. Its growth depends on stimulation. And this is true of the child. There would be no grasping, no reaching out, without stimulation. The child must be held, touched, cuddled, stroked, kissed. A child could survive without eyesight or hearing, but not without touch.

In his poem *Song of Myself*, Walt Whitman (1891) talks about touch "quivering me to a new identity". This is precisely what happens to the child: he gradually develops a sense of identity through touch. The child does not have a highly developed sense of purpose—or what psychologists call "intentionality"—to enable him to reach out to the environment. He would not do this if left alone. The child in the white crib mentioned by Bower just lay there without protest, and it was thought that he was not capable of imaginative play or any intellectual activity. Intellectual growth depends largely on stimulation from outside, and such stimulation begins to impinge on the fetus in the womb.

c.   The embryo/fetus develops: basic principles

At this point it might be as well to discuss some basic principles in embryonic development. Humanistic psychology, particularly the psychology of one of its founders, Abraham Maslow (1968)—who described it as "the science of Being"—is based on the assumption that man's deepest need is to be fully human, to realize his full human potential, which means becoming the person he truly is. From the start he has an essential inner nature, in part unique and in part species-wide.

This fits the facts of modern embryology. For instance, the embryologist Erich Blechschmidt (1977) maintained that development in the womb is about preserving what is there at the start. In embryonic development the external changes to the organism are the best way of preserving the inside. That seems the most staggering fact about human existence, a fact that is not always appreciated. Each one of us has a unique inner nature that is there from conception to death—smothered perhaps as we grow older, but struggling all the time to assert itself.

Ashley Montagu, in *Life Before Birth*, puts it like this:

> The basic fact is simple: life begins, not at birth, but at conception. This means that a developing child is alive not only in the sense that he is composed of living tissues, but also in the sense that from the moment of conception things *happen to him*. Furthermore, when things happen to him, even though he may be only two weeks old (in the womb), and he looks more like a creature from another world than a potential human being, and his birth date is eight and a half months in the future, *he reacts*. In spite of his newness and his appearance, he is a living, striving organism from the very beginning. [Montagu, 1961]

Blechschmidt saw that human development was no mere endogenous process initiated from within; it was brought about by external changes. "Growth", said Blechschmidt, "is stimulated by forces impinging on metabolism from outside." This does not, of course, mean that genes are merely passive and play no part in growth. They have a decisive influence. Without the genes there would be no central point of impact, but without the external forces the genes would be ineffective.

Every stage of development is an adaptation to external changes in accordance with genetically coded instructions. Blechschmidt described growth as the operation of two complementary forces: those of heredity and adaptation. "Without the cellular membrane there would be no food intake and, consequently, no growth: without the nucleus there would be no heredity influence in propagation. Without the nucleus, no retroactive process against external stimulated growth would be possible."

From the point of view of the growing organism, the operation of these forces—one coming from inside and the other from outside—sounds like the yang and yin of Taoism: the "firm" and assertive (yang) establishing a direction according to the genetic code; and the "yielding" or accepting (yin) allowing the penetration by a benign force that provides nourishment for growth.

Some of our cherished beliefs of the past (scientific myths) have been overturned by modern embryology. It has, for example, been established that there is no "centre of organization". There have been other common misconceptions. For instance, embryonic development is not an evolutionary process in the sense of proceeding from the simple to the complex. At every stage there is a complex set of circumstances that leads to the next stage. The mistake is seeing small as simple and big as complex.

The so-called basic law of biogenetics, formulated by Ernst Haeckel in 1866 (1899), postulated that human ontogenesis (or development in the womb) recapitulated phylogenesis (or the evolution of the species) in abbreviated form. Blechschmidt saw this as one of the most serious errors of biology. The embryo is developing not by an evolutionary process but simply by what it is now, in interaction with its environment now. Some evolutionary stages are clearly evident in human embryonic development and are relevant, for instance, in relation to the brain (as we see in ch. 8[b]). But this does not mean that the embryo or fetus is repeating an evolutionary process of its own, just that development follows in a similar order.

There is no straight-line development towards some target; there is no evidence at all that the way we develop is goal-directed. That is thinking backwards, beginning at the end with the adult and calling him the goal. But, said Blechschmidt, that sort of thinking is unscientific and subjective. There is no sense of purpose that can be observed or even deduced in the growing organism. If the unborn child could speak, he would not say, "I must become a human being"—that is what an adult might say when he has strayed from the chosen path. The unborn child would be more likely to say, "I am now, a human being trying to adjust to the situation as I find it from moment to moment. I'm not concerned with the future. I'm only concerned with what I must do now."

Giving the growing organism a sense of purpose, Blechschmidt held, is teleological thinking, which might be all right in philosophy or art or in studying human relationships, but is not scientific. It is the sort of thinking that is present in so-called "functional anatomy", which has resurrected a medieval form of systematization in describing some organs as useful—as if there were any useless organs! "In reality", said Blechschmidt, "there are no suitable or unsuitable organs, only functional organs. . . . There is no doubt about the indispensability of many organs for the preservation of health, but the recognition of their significance, and perhaps of their great importance, does not explain their appearance"—their continuance, yes, but not their appearance.

What Blechschmidt found was that there was nothing at any stage of embryonic development that did not have its function. Nothing developed that could be said to be intended for future use. When the child is born, there are no useless cells, tissues, or organs that have been lying dormant in the womb, waiting for the moment of birth. The child is born with many skills developed as functions of growth in the womb, so any skill developed after birth is an adaptation of one developed before birth.

This is very important in understanding what follows: how all that we are now is made up of all that we have been from the moment of conception; that memory of what has gone before is incorporated in what we do. But such memory is, for the most part, unconscious.

d.   From fetus to child to adult

As this memory normally remains in the unconscious, people seldom remember anything of their birth; as a result, it was assumed that we could have no consciousness at birth. How do we know that a child is normally conscious at birth? Quite often parents and professionals in child health recognize that up until the age of 3 children are spontaneously referring to their birth, but not after that age.

How is it that they remember up to that age, but then lose the memory? It is to do with the order in which the different brain regions develop. The three main regions of the brain develop at different stages, which are along the lines of evolution: first the brainstem, the lower brain, which was new in the reptilian age; second the midbrain, the limbic system, which was new in the mammalian age; and last the neocortex, which was new in the age of hominids. The older two have become well integrated—the limbic system with the earlier brainstem. The newest in evolution, the neocortex, also the latest to develop in the child, is less well integrated with the other two. As the child develops in the womb and the time of birth arrives, the elements of the neocortex are in place and still growing rapidly, but until the age of 3–5 years they are not yet "wired up" and functioning. In the 2-year-old consciousness is still in the midbrain, the limbic system, as is the memory of birth.

Then, as the neocortex develops, its greater power of consciousness overwhelms the limbic system, whose memory becomes part of the "unconscious"—Freud's term. The unconscious memory can replay sequences, yet it senses everything in present time. It cannot discern when its process is of the past; it has no facility to do so. The limbic system has no sense of past or future, of history; this is sensed only in the neocortex. So when a limbic system memory is triggered, it seems to be relevant "NOW", even though its relevance is, in fact, long past. This is described as "the remembered present". But it is a memory that may well trigger an action that may be as irrelevant to the present as is the memory. Its value has been in its very rapid reaction for evasive or aggressive action, rooted in memory and necessary for survival in the wild (Panksepp, 1998).

And that is how it is with birth memories or the flashbacks of posttraumatic stress syndrome, which may come upon us unwanted and detrimentally. With guidance we can access them deliberately. Skilful psychotherapy can enable an altered state of consciousness within warm and loving attention. This can bring about the healing of these memories. Altering consciousness through drugs can be harmful.

A natural form of altered state of consciousness is dreams—Freud's "royal road to the unconscious" and Perls's "royal road to integration" (Clarkson, 1989). This is the subject of part B.

DREAMS, FEELINGS, AND RELEASING DISTRESS

CHAPTER THREE

Dream-images of womb
and self-healing responses

".. . go to sleep!
You will wake, and remember, and understand."

Robert Browning, *Evelyn Hope*

"The basic principle involved in most forms of complementary
medicine is 'learn to listen to yourself'. But by the time the balancing
or self-regulating instinct has to speak to us through physical
symptoms, this generally means other messages in a gentler language
have failed to reach our consciousness.

How does it speak to us, this law of our own nature, if not
by means of disease, accident and despair? Its main line of
communication is the dream. Night after night it begs to pay attention
to the images it sends; to honour our feelings no less than our
thoughts; to befriend the world of the senses and heed the promptings
of intuition; to be our many-faceted selves as fully as we can."

Ean Begg, *Myth and Today's Consciousness* (1984)

a.   *Images and meaning: Nandor Fodor*

A woman dreams *she is scraping away the sand that covers the
entrance of a cave. As she is scraping it away, she says to her son, "You cannot come in." Inside she finds a rolled-up parchment, yellow with age. She*

unrolls it and finds the writing is in a language she cannot understand. She asks David to read it. But at that moment the parchment suddenly becomes brittle, and then crumbles away. In the cave a horrible smell of fungus assails the woman.

The woman was a patient of New York psychoanalyst Nandor Fodor, who interprets the dream as follows (Fodor, 1949):

Cave: the womb

Parchment inscribed with a foreign language: the meaning of life. The woman asks her son to read it. If she has failed to understand, perhaps he will and will then be able to fulfil her dreams, the destiny she has missed.

The parchment crumbling away: You must find the meaning yourself. You cannot expect someone else, a son, to fulfil your destiny for you. When you search for the meaning of life from others, the meaning crumbles away. Only you know. You can find the answer within you.

The smell of fungus: The smell of death. "Birth and death mean the same to me", the woman tells Nandor Fodor. "The smell of fungus suggests to me everything nasty, damp and buried. I remember smelling it in some place where I had gone to sleep."

The place where she had gone to sleep, Fodor explains, was the womb, where she first came to life. The smell of death brings back the memory of birth.

A man in his early youth, also a patient of Fodor's, has a recurring dream of swimming pools. In one dream *the swimming pool is in a park where he used to go. It is filled with people, but there is a wall separating him from the swimming pool.*

His dream, says Fodor, is about a block he has of returning to his source of happiness; he feels guilty about being happy and secure, close to his mother again, inside his mother.

He also dreams *a lifeguard is in a small boat by a pier. Two men are swimming nearby. One disappears under the water and doesn't come up again. Is he playing or has he drowned? The dreamer sees him being pulled out of the water. He is wading in shallow water, and he's in a terrible rage, swearing at his rescuer. The lifeguard tells him that drowning people always swore and cursed at lifeguards after they had been rescued. He didn't understand it.*

The patient was being psychoanalysed because he said he had suffered from unreasonable attacks of rage throughout his life. His dream, said Fodor, provided the answer. He had resented being born, had hated being pulled out of the uterus, and this hatred had survived through the years without the patient having any knowledge of its obscure origin.

These are just a few of many dreams collected by Nandor Fodor that seem almost certainly to represent memories of birth and intrauterine experiences. He also produced a list of symbols related to birth that frequently occurred in patients' dreams: eggs, seeds, germs, fruit, things that grow or move underground, were symbols for the fetus. The uterus was represented by gardens, parks, islands, boats; amniotic fluid by seas, lakes, rivers, and so on. Obvious dreams of birth were of a boat floating down a river or plunging over rapids; being in a cave with the walls closing in; being sucked into a whirlpool; being trapped in small places; or falling.

The Dutch psychoanalyst, Lietaert Peerbolte, who came under the influence of Nandor Fodor, said that analysis of prenatal psychodynamics often succeeded where an exclusively classical approach failed (Peerbolte, 1954). Many of his patients, he said, had birth dreams. One example is of a woman who dreamt of a barrel organ:

"There is this barrel organ and there is someone coming up from behind me. . . . There is the sensation of a shutter falling. I'm extremely anxious. I'm in a creepy house . . . there are grimacing corpses."

The woman who had the dream interpreted it herself for Peerbolte. The "someone" coming up from behind is not a person at all, but a "natural force": the contraction of the uterine muscles. The barrel organ is the uterus, the falling shutter, the starting point of birth. She does not mention the creepy house or the corpses, but no doubt these are expressions of her anxiety.

The patient's problems—her fears and frigidity—were solved by bringing unconscious memories—mainly of birth traumas—into full consciousness, and this was facilitated by interpreting dreams in terms of prenatal psychodynamics. Dreams can provide unique clues to human functioning. In our waking lives there are things that are vaguely disturbing, things that on one level we are aware of but cannot explain; we dismiss them as irrational, but they come up again in our dreams.

Premonitions of miscarriage: R. D. Laing

In *The Facts of Life*, R. D. Laing gives examples of two dreams that seem to warn the dreamers of an impending miscarriage (Laing, 1976):

> A woman dreamt *she was wandering through Jerusalem*. "*All is in ruins and crumbling*", she said. "*There is nothing to grip, no house to enter.*" Two hours after waking from the dream she had a miscarriage.

> The woman said that it wasn't her dream, but the embryo's; and, in a sense, this was true: it was the movement of the embryo breaking away from the lining of the uterus that produced the dream. The woman must have felt this disturbance. Maybe she didn't want to believe it, but her dream told her the truth.

Another woman's dream was similar. She told Laing:

> "*I'm in a sealed car at the centre of a crossroads at dead of night. The traffic lights are not working. There are cars travelling back and forth, up and down. I am terrified. I am trying to get out of the car, but can't.*"

In the morning the woman had a miscarriage. She, too, was convinced that the dream was the embryo's. She was also convinced that the embryo was a girl. "I just knew it", she said. "The girl wanted to get out and got out. I don't blame her."

An even more remarkable dream, described in Laing's book, was that of a woman of 30. She told Laing that she had dreamt of *a piece of gum going down an escalator, the steps of which were not moving, to a garage*. The woman had been keeping a dream book. The dream of over a year back had occurred, she subsequently calculated, two nights after she had conceived. She had not "dreamt" she had conceived until she "missed" her next period. The way she saw the dream, on re-reading it in her dream book, was that it was the representation of a zygote, which is the single cell resulting from the union of ovum and sperm (in the dream, a piece of gum) going along the uterine tube (escalator that did not move) to the uterus (garage).

She must have been aware, before she missed her period, that she had conceived. Something in her must have told her what was happening; but possibly the feeling was blocked and came up again in her dream. If it is true that every dream-image is a feeling, as the Gestalt psychotherapist Fritz Perls claimed, then what she was feeling in her dream was, indeed, the feeling of the zygote.

Dr Thomas Verny believes that many of the dreams of pregnant women express their unconscious conflicts about the unborn child (Verny, 1982b). These dreams, he says, have beneficial effects, often resulting in shorter labours and smoother births. Dreams, he says, help pregnant women to deal with their anxieties. Most women have such dreams at some time during pregnancy, but they ignore or forget them because they are afraid of being regarded as scatty and superstitious.

One night before one of Verny's patients had a spontaneous abortion, she found herself screaming, "I want to get out! Let me out!" The patient was convinced that it was her unborn child speaking to her, and she unconsciously obliged by creating the conditions in the uterus to allow the child to break away.

A bonding problem: healing through a dream: David Kay

Dr David Kay, a London physician and Jungian analyst, told the story of a patient, whom he called Mrs J, who one day brought her 6-week-old baby daughter to his surgery, saying that she was extremely anxious about her because she never stopped screaming, vomited frequently, and had painful attacks of colic (Kay, 1984).

This case, said David Kay, marked the starting point of what he called an investigative psychological journey that led him eventually to a deeper understanding of the nature of neonatal and prenatal psychic life. On examining the child, Kay could find no physical abnormality. He suggested, however, that the mother might try changing the brand of milk, feeding on demand, and giving the child glucose water to relieve the colic. But nothing worked, and the mother became extremely angry with Kay, complaining that her daughter's health was steadily deteriorating. The child's behaviour, she said, was more like that of a "limp rag-doll" than of a baby.

"I confronted Mrs J directly with the situation as I saw it", said Kay, "by telling her that there was nothing whatsoever wrong with her baby, but that it was she herself who felt ill and troubled inside." The mother's reaction to this diagnosis was extraordinary. She collapsed and started sobbing uncontrollably. Kay left his desk to comfort her and to support the baby, who was, he said, in danger of being dropped on the floor. The mother went on weeping, and it was some considerable time before she was able to talk coherently. Then she told a very sad story about how emotional pressures had been building up throughout her life. Her parents were divorced when she was 11 years old. Her 4-year-old brother stayed with her mother, while she went to live with her father, who set up home with another woman and her three children.

From then on there was very little contact between the two split family groups, mainly because her divorced mother travelled around the world a great deal. She suffered prolonged periods of depression, culminating in her suicide four years before Mrs J had her baby.

Mrs J felt she had never really had a mother. At about the time her mother died and before she met her husband, she had conceived. She had subsequently arranged an abortion when she was three months pregnant, and this may well have been connected with her mother's death. When she later gave birth to a baby daughter, all her feelings of maternal deprivation came to the surface. She said she had no memory of a good mothering experience to draw on and felt she had no adequate maternal resources of her own.

The baby seemed to sense her problems. There was no warmth between them, and the child never once looked into the mother's eyes when she was being fed. Mrs J's feelings of inadequacy were exacerbated when she saw how relaxed the baby was when her husband was feeding her. She was, she said, very pleased that her husband was able to take care of the baby when she was being particularly difficult, but at the same time she felt depressed and resentful towards him because she felt she was failing in her maternal role.

David Kay (1984) found, as others have, that postnatal depression is often relieved when hostile elements are brought into consciousness. It was when he skilfully drew Mrs J's attention to her own troubles, enabling her to release her own pain through her uncontrollable sobbing, that the bond between herself and her baby began to heal:

> Towards the end of our interview, she and I became aware that there had been a dramatic change. It was quite simple—the baby was looking directly into her mother's eyes and seemed totally relaxed. It is difficult to find words to describe how deeply Mrs J was affected by this response, except to say that the relationship between the two reminded me of lovers who are sharing feelings of mutual adoration while being oblivious of the outside world.

Mrs J seemed incredulous and ecstatically happy; she felt she had "got her baby back again and the nightmare was over".

What had happened to make such a small baby react with such hostility towards the mother? It was the experience of the sudden reconciliation that made Dr Kay wonder when the bonding between mother and child had been disrupted. "I felt it was important to understand more about the nature of that crucial link", said Kay, "whose restoration I had witnessed."

Even before he had read any of the literature on prenatal psychology, he suspected that communication must begin before birth. His investigation took him into areas already discussed in this book. He was impressed with what Thomas Verny (1982a) has written about the complexity of the interactions of mother and child even before birth and about how important it was, above all else, that the mother should show positive feelings of love and respect for her unborn child. Loving feelings, said Verny, were capable of acting as a shield against a stressful environment.

Discerning different kinds of stress: Gerhard Rottman

David Kay also referred to the research of Gerhard Rottman at the University of Salzburg (in Graber, 1974), who found that the fetus could discriminate between various forms of stress. Rottman divided mothers into four main types, each type influencing the development of the unborn child in a different way (quoted in Verny, 1982b):

1. "Ideal Mothers" (who consciously and unconsciously wanted their unborn child) consistently produced the healthiest offspring, physically and emotionally;

2. "Catastrophic Mothers" (who had a rejecting attitude towards motherhood coupled with serious medical problems during pregnancy) had the highest rate of premature, low-weight, emotionally disturbed infants;

3. "Ambivalent Mothers" (outwardly accepting but inwardly doubtful) produced infants with behavioural and gastro-intestinal problems;

4. "Cool Mothers" (whose jobs and financial security were threatened by the pregnancy and who felt emotionally unprepared yet subconsciously desired and welcomed their baby) produced

apathetic, lethargic babies who behaved as if they were confused.

Kay subscribed to the view that touching is vital to human development and to the maintenance of psychic health. Many now believe
that it is the sense of touch that first establishes, in the womb, a
boundary between what is perceived as "me" and "not me". We discover ourselves, our separate identity, by touching or grasping hold
of something. And the object that we touch—or the external noise,
sight or smell that we experience—that is not some thing originating
within ourselves is described by Winnicott (1972) as a "transitional
object" or "transitional phenomenon". This object, the thing grasped
or sensed, is important in the intermediate stage between subjectivity
and an objectively perceived environment.

The need to hold or grasp, said Kay, probably first expresses itself
when the fetus holds its cord or a limb or grasps onto the womb
boundary. Does this need for a transitional object continue throughout life? Is it an essential part of the creative process? Is it our way
of discovering the world, our way of finding out about anything, of
expanding our knowledge?

The answer, said Kay, is yes, we do go on having this need to hold
onto something when we go out to explore the unknown. We have to
touch something to find our way in the dark. In the cinema we grip
our seats when we see something terrifying on the screen. But there
are more subtle objects we carry around with us or hold onto in our
minds: religious symbols, charms, mantras. There is the symbol of the
mandala, which usually appears at moments of stress that threaten to
disrupt psychic wholeness: its presence usually promotes a feeling of
wholeness or tranquillity.

M. Fordham (1977) wrote of the "need for creative illusion in
the discovery of reality"; Kay (1984) suggested that this "creative
illusion" could be regarded as the transitional object. We need our
dreams, our fantasies, our hunches and theories to take us into the
future. It could be argued that we also need our problems to project
us into the future. For many they are illusory problems, something to
solve, handed down to us from the past, giving us a sense of continuity. In the analytic situation, Kay found that patients satisfied their
need for a transitional object in a variety of ways. Two female patients
regularly and repeatedly held, caressed, or played with the woollen

tasselled fringe of the rug on Kay's couch. Another patient stubbornly picked at the counterpane until she "created" a thread, which she then held on to during the entire session with Kay.

If the child in the womb suffers from a loss of contact with the mother or feels rejected or poisoned or threatened by her, or cannot reach out to the mother, has nothing to hold on to, no feeling that in spite of a hostile environment there is the mother's love always present—if these things are lacking, then after birth the child will behave like someone living in a vacuum, suspended, all links severed, as lifeless as a limp rag-doll.

"The tiny infant in my consulting-room", said Kay, "was disoriented and failing to thrive because she had lost visual—and, to some extent, tactile—contact with a mother who was filled with fear and anger. Once this situation was resolved, she could look once again and start to touch and play with her mother's face and body. An atmosphere of calm was restored in which the normal maturational processes could proceed. I followed up the case of Mrs J and her baby for two years: all seemed to be going well, and they remained good friends."

b.   *Responses to children: William Emerson*

A difficult birth can be deeply traumatic, but the right kind of childhood can do much to compensate: a mother's love can more than make up for the negative things: the fears and failures. Lots of things can go wrong, but if you hold on to love, that is enough: it is the most powerful force there is.

Many people, alas, never get over their traumatic births. They are people who have been damaged through alcohol, drug abuse, the anxieties of parents, or perhaps the violence of a hospital birth—a forceps delivery, for instance.

Dr William Emerson is a psychotherapist who specializes in what he calls "infant birth re-facilitation", which means helping children to relive painful birth experiences. The object is to sort out the problems arising from birth, which can be dealt with before they develop into serious behavioural problems that will go on troubling the child and his parents and later the adult (1984).

The way Emerson does this for infants is through massage, touching, and re-creation of the physical pressures of birth. In addition to this, he plays tapes of heartbeat and what he calls "birth music", which can be anything from rock to classical music.

Emerson's approach is based on one basic premise: the infant's world is simply a continuation of life in the womb. Almost everything he does and thinks and dreams about can be related to prenatal experiences. For the infant there are two major psycho-historical inputs: intrauterine events and birth experiences. This is clear from bodily action and reaction, breathing patterns, and basic emotional responses. (Both authors of this volume have found such early memories impinging on their lives.)

Emerson found that birth issues were rampant in the art, fantasies, and dreams of children, especially before the age of 8. Birth and play were temperamentally related: the moodier the child, the greater the likelihood that play would be birth-oriented. Such play might include climbing through tunnels or trapping other children under beds.

Emerson mentioned the case of an infant called Rowan, who would push herself to the corner of her cot and lodge her head sharply and uncomfortably against the bars. The parents said that they were aware that the second stage of labour had been very difficult for the child. The total length of labour was 18 hours, with Rowan being stuck during the last four-and-a-half hours of pushing. Her head was crowning for two to two and-a-half hours, with a great deal of pressure in a band around the top of her ears and eyebrows, where there seemed to be some broken capillaries. In the end she had to be delivered with the help of forceps.

At weekend seminars for parents and their children Emerson collected the dreams and artwork of the children. This, he said, yielded several interesting findings:

1. Of the dreams of the children, 95% involved animals and objects but no humans.

2. Dream processes and dream content were underwater mammals, fish, caverns, prisons, tunnels, distant lights, distant voices, impenetrable or unclimbable walls, gigantic and crushing rocks, fragile eggs, egg yolks, water, caves, quicksand, darkness and shadows. In many of the dreams there were themes related to

entrapment, death, suffocation, denial, exhaustion, retaliation, resignation, withdrawal, hiding, procrastination, betrayal, and abandonment.

3.   Children with the greatest difficulties tended to have a greater percentage of prenatal and birth trauma in their dreams and artwork. For example, one girl, diagnosed as having a learning disability, had repetitive dreams of herself pushing against a brick wall, trying to get through. Sometimes the wall had ivy and hedges round it, sometimes it was stark. Sometimes a hole developed through which she could crawl, and sometimes there would be no way through at all. Her dreams were often accompanied by a high degree of anxiety, and she would wake up disturbed. Her drawings were of little girls or animals penned up or in chains. When she was asked to comment on the little girl in her drawings, she would say, "No one's there. She's all alone. She's waiting for her Mommy."

Memory in the organism: Professor Jerome Lejeune

The biologist and doctor Professor Jerome Lejeune, famous for his discovery of the extra chromosome in Down's Syndrome, gives an extraordinary example of what is sometimes called an organismic memory (in Sassone, 1977). He tells the story of an identical twin, a girl, who at the age of 18 seemed to have some awareness of a rare accident that had happened to her during the separation process in the fertilized egg. What happened was that from an XY chromosome, which was bound to be a boy, two cells were produced; but the Y chromosome was lost from one of the cells during the separation process, leaving a single X chromosome, which produced an imperfect girl.

The 18-year-old girl was the first case of this kind that Professor Lejeune had come across. "The girl complained", he said, "of a strange trouble. She was afraid of looking at herself in the mirror because whenever she did so, she imagined she was looking at her brother."

Professor Lejeune described this as an "extraordinary intuition" of a very complex situation that at that time he had not detected medically. The girl knew nothing about it, but she had sensed the truth about herself. Through loss of the Y chromosomes, she saw herself as incomplete, as just a part of her brother.

Peerbolte also reported dreams of lost twins—for instance, a dream of a young man who was being treated for alcoholism and drug addiction (Peerbolte, 1954):

I am on a roof of a school with my brother. It is foggy and I can't see very clearly. My brother suddenly falls from the roof and is lost.

The brother was the lost twin, the fog the mother's highly toxic condition during the early months of pregnancy, when the twin was aborted. The mother was admitted to hospital with renal toxicity. It was the sort of condition that in a later stage of pregnancy would call for induction to save the lives of the mother and child. The surviving twin was always complaining of feeling poisoned.

Dreams as fairy stories

Fairy stories are like myths, like dreams—they touch something deep in ourselves. They are often about small creatures, miraculous events, countries off the map, about sleep and being awakened by love: and much of the symbolism seems to relate to our prenatal life.

Professor Lejeune mentions Tom Thumb and compares him with the fetus at 2 months old. At this age the human being is less than a thumb's length from head to rump. He would fit neatly into a nutshell. Everything is there—hands, feet, head, organs, brain—all are in place. If you looked very closely, you would be able to see the palm creases; and, looking still closer, with a microscope, you could detect the fingerprints. Professor Lejeune believes that it was out of this knowledge that the story of Tom Thumb was invented. The reason why it has always enchanted children, and may even grip the imagination of adults, is that buried in all of us is the memory of Tom Thumb in the womb.

Tom Thumb is one of those stories that have universal appeal: they turn up in many different countries, they have been told in different languages, and they go back to antiquity. A writer has only to hit upon some theme with a prenatal connection or allusion, not too obvious, but with the sort of feeling of being small but powerful and living in a kind of dream or a secret place, and his story will be read everywhere. Fairyland, the land of the unborn, is full of small creatures: goblins, dwarfs, sprites, genii in bottles. The theme is sometimes the small person versus the giant—the David and Goliath story.

Many well-known books seem to draw on similar memories: J. M. Barrie's famous story of Peter Pan, the boy who never grows up, is about a child who remains in the womb; he flies everywhere, floats about as he did in the womb, with a delightful freedom of movement.

Another famous children's story, some parts of which seem to have been inspired by an "organismic" memory of the womb, is Lewis Carroll's *Alice in Wonderland*. There is Alice falling down a rabbit hole (the birth canal?). It is scary, but she comes to no harm. Alice is reduced in size (the size of a fetus?) and swims in a pool (amniotic fluid?). And there is Alice growing larger and larger in a room—"there seemed to be no chance of ever getting out of the room again"—which is a graphic illustration of the "no exit" feeling of the second clinical stage of delivery (described in ch. 5[b]. Certainly, the profound and constant fascination such books exercise on us suggests that they re-activate feelings from the earliest and deepest parts of our psyches.

CHAPTER FOUR

Recalling past distress and releasing it

"There's a memory of the body, a visceral memory in the blood, in the muscles . . ."

Otto Rank, *The Trauma of Birth* (1929)

a.   *Early prenatal psychology: Otto Rank*

For decades prenatal psychologists were neglected by the general public and even mainstream psychologists. Then from the 1950s their views were taken up by psychotherapists such as R. D. Laing, Frank Lake, and members of societies such as the Association of Birth Psychology in New York, the Association for Pre- and Perinatal Psychology and Health of North America, and the International Society of Prenatal and Perinatal Psychology and Medicine, based in Heidelberg. Some understanding of their theories helps to understand the regression techniques in use today.

Perhaps the most famous of the early prenatal psychologists was Otto Rank, whose name is associated with the birth trauma. An Austrian, he was at one time a favourite pupil of Freud's. Like his master, he noticed that severe attacks of anxiety were often accompanied by physiological features similar to those seen in babies at the moment

66

of birth. This observation led him to the development of his theory that all neurosis originates in the trauma of birth.

In substance, his theory is that separation from the mother at birth produces feelings of anxiety that are often reactivated later in life as a result of threatened or actual separation from someone or something. The most obvious separation occurs when someone you love walks away. Then a memory stirs in you, and you start feeling anxious: will I be lost without her... will she fall under a bus . . . will her plane crash . . . will she be killed on the motorway? "In every parting there is a glimpse of death", said George Eliot. That glimpse of death, according to Rank, is a memory of birth. It felt like death when you came to the end of your life in the womb. It was the first of those life events—first day at school, first day at a new job, unemployment, retirement, bereavement—that produce feelings of anxiety. Anxiety is expressed in various ways, but it is usually concerned with the loss of something: status, people, property, money, health, eyesight, hearing, a limb or limbs, or life itself.

If birth is often experienced as a kind of death, the idea that death is a return to the primal state of bliss in the womb, the pleasurable Nirvana, "no-thing" as distinct from nothingness, is an ancient one, still believed in some parts of the world. According to this view, the womb is a kind of lost paradise, while human life is just a vale of tears. In Buddhism, the penalty for living blindly—without awareness—is being born again: reincarnation.

For Rank, these views were not merely primitive superstitions: we all experience a desire, usually unconscious, to return to the womb, and this desire often came to the surface during therapy and in his patients' dreams. Furthermore, Rank seems to have believed that life in the womb was paradisal (a view revised through research); more important, he explicitly stated, quoting the views of Schopenhauer, the great German pessimist philosopher, and of Sophocles and other ancient Greek writers, that it is better for humans never to have been born, that life is a vale of tears—sorrow and suffering all the way from birth to death. In his extreme pessimism Rank differs from most subsequent prenatal psychologists. He did, however, sketch out some ways of overcoming neuroses. We had to accept that life is tragic, but a way of overcoming tragedy and suffering was strange and paradoxical: it meant going back to the prenatal state and trauma of birth. The reliving of anguish conquered anguish.

Today *The Trauma of Birth,* first published in 1929 (English edition 1934), with some Freudian jargon, is not all easy reading, but you will come across some fascinating material. In many respects the book was ahead of its time. For instance, Rank points out how theories concerning psychoanalysis are male-orientated, completely neglecting the woman's point of view. Even sexual relations are approached by the psychoanalyst only from the male point of view. Rank attributes this partly to the male psychoanalyst's abysmal ignorance of the woman's sexual life, but also to an unconscious fear of women's superiority as bearers of children, with their power to inflict pain. This he sees as an unconscious fear associated with the birth trauma.

He also offers intriguing explanations of sadism and masochism. The former expresses hatred of someone who feels rejected, expelled from the womb; and his pleasure is to force his way back there. In extreme cases you get the Ripper tearing open the abdomen from whence he came. In most cases, it means taming the woman who has the power to inflict pain; it is, in a sense, identifying with the woman and experiencing the supreme pleasure of inflicting pain at birth.

Rank's book also offers some interesting glimpses of his clinical practice. Sometimes his patients dreamt of their expulsion from paradise, and what they described was a reproduction of the birth trauma in all its painful details. The patient had an unconscious wish to return to the womb, but his way was blocked by the memory of a painful birth.

Patients also sometimes talked of experiencing a regression to the fetal stage in the womb. One patient said: "I feel that I am getting younger and smaller all the time; now I am four years old, then I shall come to the swaddling-clothes stage, and finally back into the mother."

According to Rank, it is common for people suffering from some psychotic or neurotic illness to have fantasies of returning to the womb. No help, he says, can be given to the psychotic: he "loses his way in the labyrinth of the womb". But the neurotic "finds his way back to health . . . by threads of remembrance thrown to him by the analyst".

Rank sees many neurotic problems as the expression of a conflict between wanting to return to the womb and being afraid to do so. The same sort of struggle goes on in the mind of the epileptic, says Rank. The epileptic probably suffered a very painful birth: "The aura preceding the great epileptic attack, with its feeling of blessedness described so wonderfully by Dostoevsky, corresponds to the prenatal libido gratification, while the convulsions themselves reproduce the act of birth."

b.   "First primal therapist": Donald Winnicott

Although Rank's name became mud among most mainstream psychoanalysts, there were some who did edge a little closer to his position. The London paediatrician and psychoanalyst, Donald W. Winnicott, was one of the first to recognize that from conception onwards the body and psyche developed together. He saw the development of the sense of self as a reaction to what he called "impingements" in intrauterine life, and these he regarded as part of the normal preparation of the fetus for life after birth.

He has been described by William Swartley, who founded the International Primal Association, as the first primal therapist (Swartley & Maurice, 1978). "His importance", said Swartley, "to our primal community stands out in three major respects:

- He was not afraid to allow patients, children or adults, to manifest physically their "body memories" of birth experience and was thus able immediately to recognize them as such.
- He was not afraid to touch his patients, male or female.
- He was not afraid to cultivate and communicate his own ideas, however much in defiance of accepted psychoanalytic views they might be. Indeed, his determination only thrived on disapproval from his less secure fellow analysts.

Winnicott regarded the principle of "non-interference" as one of the most important aspects of Freudian psychoanalytic technique. As an example, during the Second World War one of Winnicott's patients curled up on his couch in the fetal position. Winnicott allowed him to do this, and he did not interfere later when the patient began to push towards the top of the couch with his head and shoulders in what seemed like the movements of a child during delivery, or even when the patient pushed himself over the top of the couch and fell to the floor. This and various other similar scenes, said Swartley, are the first accounts of "birth primals" of which he was aware.

Writing of a middle-aged woman patient who had had several years of classical analysis without any effect and who was suicidal, Winnicott said that "she must make a very severe regression". He also said that he would "follow the regressive tendency wherever it led". Winnicott went on:

> In the patient's previous analysis there had been incidents in which the patient had thrown herself off the couch in an hysterical way. . . . Eventually I recognized how this patient's unconscious need to relive the birth process underlay what had previously been an hysterical falling off the couch. [Winnicott, 1949]

Winnicott described how, when the patient did relive the birth process, every detail of it was retained: "not only that, but the details had been retained in the exact sequence of the original experience". The patient acted out the sucking of the thumb in the womb, the constriction passing down the birth passage, the pressure on the head, and also "the extreme awfulness of the release of pressure on the head; during which phase, unless her head were held, she could not have endured the re-enactment". When the regression reached what Winnicott called "the limit of the patient's need", there was a natural progression, "with the true self instead of a false self in action".

Winnicott also noted certain odd behaviour among children which he associated with the birth experience. In a paper, "Birth Memories, Birth Trauma and Anxiety", Winnicott (1954) described a boy of 5 whose play showed signs of birth trauma. He was deeply disturbed. His mother had rejected him, and Winnicott spent a lot of time with him, trying to win his confidence. The boy came repeatedly towards him and then backed away nervously. This went on for some time, but eventually the boy climbed onto Winnicott's lap. Then something rather bizarre happened. The boy got inside Winnicott's coat, turned upside down, and slid down between the legs. He did this again and again. Winnicott did not, however, say anything more about the child, except that he was psychotic.

Winnicott felt that most births were normal and could not be described as traumatic in any sense of the word. Birth, of course, was a separation—"a break in the continuity of the infant's going on being"—but trauma only occurred, in his view, if there were a severe disturbance at birth that prevented ego development.

Fathoming anxiety—Phyllis Greenacre

The New York psychoanalyst Phyllis Greenacre, who was a contemporary of Winnicott's, also took an interest in pre- and perinatal
experiences and discussed the possibility that they were sometimes
responsible for what she described as "the predisposition to anxiety".

She described anxiety as the sense that something unpleasant or
positively painful would happen:

> Different people react to anxiety in different ways—one person
> has creepy sensations in the skin, another weakness in the legs, a
> third with a headache, a fourth with diarrhoea. . . . From a careful
> scrutiny of reconstructed material from analytic patients it seems
> that such patterning of the anxiety reaction always represents
> the genetic constitutional elements fused with birth experiences.
> [Greenacre, 1978]

In other words, each person reacted in a different way, according to
his nature. What is now called "trait" anxiety, either a genetic trait—
that is to say, inborn—or anxious behaviour developed in the womb
can add to the normal anxiety of birth. Dr Greenacre puts it the other
way round: birth changes the genetic pattern of anxiety.

Greenacre discusses fetal behaviour in her book, *Trauma, Growth
and Personality* (1978): "The fetus moves, kicks, turns around, reacts to
some external stimuli by increased motion. It swallows and traces of
its own hair are found in the meconium. It excretes urine and sometimes passes stool." She points out that the fetal heart rate and fetal
movements are increased by loud noises, maternal nervousness and
other stimuli. Can they be taken as signs of anxiety, she asks, as they
can in a child or adult?

She suspected, however, that to talk of fetal behaviour as expressing anxiety was merely "projecting backwards". She was persuaded
by Freud—after his break with Rank—that the fetus and the newborn
child behaved in ways that had "no psychic content". She neverthe-
less believed that the anxiety-like responses that were observable in
the fetus were responsible for a predisposition to anxiety. She did not,
however, pursue this line of enquiry: "I run the risk of encroaching
on the domain of neurology and reflex reactions, and on the field
of biology, which describes anxiety-like (frantic) behaviour in lower
animals and even insects."

How misguided this attitude seems to be now! You cannot separate human life from the whole of life on this planet. Psychology, neurology, and biology are becoming one, and we now have our neuro-psychologists and bio-sociologists.

c.   An integral universe: Francis Mott

"If the doors of perception were cleansed, everything would appear as it is, infinite.
To see a world in a Grain of Sand,
And Heaven in a Wild Flower,
Hold Infinity in the palm of the hand
And Eternity in an hour."

William Blake, *Auguries of Innocence*

Francis Mott was another psychoanalyst who, like Rank, ploughed a lonely furrow. He was totally ignored by mainstream psychoanalysts. Mott did, however, win the approval of a number of poets and scientists for his theory about a universal design in the universe, which explained the creation of human life and the creation of the solar system. That was the huge and confident claim. Mott (1964) held that the same forces were at work everywhere you looked.

He set out to prove his theory, which someone described—when he had worked it out—as "the basic marching orders for the organization of the universe". He published the results of his research in a large tome (1964) financed by a trust established by one of his friends. Mott's work impressed Jung and was hailed by one eminent scientist, Dr Gustav Stromberg, as "a world picture of logical consistency and great beauty".

Briefly, Mott's theory was that the universal design that governed all creation, from atom to mind, was very simple, with a "paternal" focus linked by a constant back-and-forth flow with a "maternal" periphery. He saw the human mind as the response of the human organism to the all-pervading influence that underlies all material forms. This response, he maintained, began specifically in intrauterine life. The two-way flow of blood to and from the placenta through the umbilical cord is the origin of feelings of aggression and submission, emptiness and fullness, giving and taking—a pattern that is to be seen everywhere in the universe.

The mind, he said, was the topmost level in a hierarchy of levels: "The mind which knows has the same formative basis as the phenomena which it knows." There is an interplay between body and mind like the two-way flow of uterine blood. The brain that controls was created by the system it controls. It is sensitive to that system and responds to its needs, more a servant than a master.

Mott's theory brings to mind certain mystical sayings: for example, sayings about the One in all things, the one universal design. "There are not many different designs for many different things. Embracing multiplicity", says Eckhart, "is blindness."

In his analytic work Francis Mott said that he had unearthed what he believed to be a fundamental principle—namely, that every psychological feeling derives from an older physical feeling.

We use the word "feeling" in two different ways, as in, say, "I feel hot" (which describes a physical feeling) and "I feel sad" (which describes a psychological feeling). We may put this down to a looseness that some words have in the English language, but Mott thought that the use of the word "feeling" as applied to an emotion was quite justified.

Mott illustrates what he means with the case of one of his patients, a man who could not accept help or advice: he shied away, almost with a feeling of revulsion, from anyone who offered him help. One either regards this as inexplicable, says Mott, or one traces it back to some emotional feeling such as the rejection of a dominating father. "But", he writes, "I have found that if the feeling is traced back still further it will in the end derive from something much more physical, such as an infancy rejection of the thrust of the mother's nipple into the newborn mouth."

Mott goes back even further in tracing the sense of "I" to the primary physical feeling of contact between the fetal skin and its surround. This prenatal physical feeling, he says, is transferred to the eyes after birth. In his sessions with patients, he said, dreams not infrequently presented the symbolic figure of a man who had eyes all over his skin or of an animal skin covered with eyes. He also points out that the symbol of the eye-covered skin is a familiar one in mythology.

d.   *The Growth Movement: Abraham Maslow*

In the 1950s and 1960s there was a move away from classical Freudian psychoanalysis to a more humanistic approach. The movement, which was called the Growth Movement, had its flowering in California at the time of the counterculture revolution, when so many other things came together: an interest in Zen and other Eastern religions, meditation, altered states of consciousness, the Hippy movement, student power, a new openness to sexuality, a great creative upsurge in pop art and pop music.

Existentialism had a tremendous influence at the time. God is dead, said the Existentialists, quoting Nietzsche. Man can invent himself. He is his own product. Therefore, there is no one to blame. Man must take responsibility for himself.

There was also a revolt against analytical, mechanistic psychology, treating people who were disturbed as machines to be repaired. Rollo May, the existentialist psychotherapist, gave expression to the main complaint, against a view of people that is merely mechanistic. Such qualities as care and joy spring from our state of being (May, 1983).

Abraham Maslow (1968), who founded what he called the psychology of Being, said that psychology had hitherto concerned itself with deficiency needs—needs that were repressed or denied. In future he would concentrate on Being needs. What does it mean to be a human being? What does it mean to be healthy, successful, to be fully functioning as a human being? How much does this depend on ourselves and how much on the environment? The problem, as always, concerns the relationship of inside to outside.

In this context Frank Lake and Stanislav Grof were practising abreactive LSD therapy and getting some surprising results from their patients, who sometimes seemed to be regressing back to the womb. Said Frank Lake:

> In 1954 people began to tell me not only the things Freud wrote about—about babies having bad disappointments at the breast and so on—they began to tell me that they were reliving their births—and they looked as if they were and I didn't know what to make of it. I wrote down everything they said and I found it very difficult to accept any of it. Then I went to an international conference and was told that yes, people were reliving their births and it was the neurologist's job to explain how it happened. [Lake, 1980b]

e.   Gestalt therapy: Fritz Perls

There was Fritz Perls's Gestalt Therapy (1969) and the Encounter Movement, which was about people helping people by being open and honest with one another, not running away or hiding behind their talk. They had had enough of talk therapy, lying on a couch and drooling about their hang-ups. They wanted action, or, if it had to be talk, real talk—not what Fritz Perls called "aboutisms". It had to be here-and-now talk, about feelings in the present, about owning them and not blaming them on someone or some situation in the past. Knowing how it happened, yes, but making changes in the present.

As Roy Ridgway portrays a session, "Existence is now", the Gestalt therapist would say. "It's experiencing what's going on now. It may be an itch on the nose or the sound of a car backfiring or a book I'm reading or a memory of a childhood experience that's still bothering me. It's what's happening now that's important. How the past is affecting me now. I don't have to go back because the things that are troubling me are troubling me now. I can sort out all my problems in the here and now."

A patient would say: "I'm in a street in New York. I hate going down this street. It's too narrow and the buildings on either side are too tall. They make me feel giddy, I feel hemmed in . . . and I can't bear looking up or down. I'm stuck. I must run. I must get out of this street. Fast! I've got a blinding headache. I can't see where I'm going. But there's a bar at the end of the street . . . I'll go there, have a drink: then I'll be OK."

—"Tell me more about the narrow street . . .

—"It's horrible. It's scary. It reminds me of something. Yeah, running along it is like some dim memory. It's like being born."

—"Go into that. You're being born . . .

—"Hell!" (He screams, lies flat on the floor, curls up.) "I don't want it! I don't want to be born! My mother doesn't want me! She doesn't care! She's hating me because I'm giving her so much pain. She can't stand it. She doesn't want . . .

—"Change places with your mother. Be your mother."

—"I don't want this child. I never wanted it. My husband didn't want it either. He's not interested. He only married me because his mother forced him to because the child was on the way. She's strict. And he's still tied to her. He cared more for her than for me."

—"Play the role of your grandmother . . ." [Ridgway, 1987]

And so on. It was a new way of dealing with emotional problems—bringing them into the present; and having a dialogue mainly with yourself, with different parts of yourself. Bringing everything together.

"The insights just flowed", said a woman taking part, "the good feelings just flowed, the catharsis, the euphoria, the understanding—I mean, it was just so clear that this was one hundred times better than any therapy we'd ever had."

CHAPTER FIVE

Recalling of birth memories with LSD

"When we return to the root we gain the meaning."

Kanchi Sosan (Chien-chih Seng-ts'an), *On Believing in Mind*

a. LSD therapy: Frank Lake

It was the Swiss chemist, Albert Hofmann, who discovered the potent psychoactive properties of lysergic acid diethylamide 25 (LSD25), when he was accidentally affected by a minute quantity of the substance in 1943:

> Last Friday, April 16, 1943, I was forced to interrupt my work in the laboratory in the middle of the afternoon and proceed home, being affected by a remarkable restlessness, combined with a slight dizziness. At home I lay down and sank into a not un-pleasant intoxicated-like condition, characterized by an extremely stimulated imagination. In a dreamlike state, with eyes closed (I found the daylight to be unpleasantly glaring), I perceived an uninterrupted stream of fantastic pictures, extraordinary shapes with intense, kaleidoscopic play of colors. After some two hours this condition faded away. [Hofmann, 1980]

Shortly afterwards LSD25 became the subject of considerable controversy, which has not diminished over the years. Welcomed by a small band of scientists interested in the nature of consciousness, it was later feared and denounced along with other psychedelic drugs for poisoning the minds of young people during the counterculture movement of the 1960s.

What the drug did was to make people realize that their perception of reality was largely conditioned by social needs and goals: in other words, it gave them an insight into the distinction between social reality and a reality that transcended their ordinary, everyday perception of the world, or, as some would say, a spiritual reality.

The effect of LSD was to loosen up the organization of the normal state of consciousness and bring into awareness a vast amount of subconscious or unconscious functioning. For many during the psychedelic revolution it was a short cut to Enlightenment.

Not everyone, of course, came out of an LSD trip with the feeling that they had gained much from the experience—there were good and bad trips. But, for some at least, there was an awareness that the ego, or everyday self, was like a switchboard operator plugging into what was permitted by parents, teachers, and society as a whole.

During LSD sessions, under professional guidance, just enough of the observer remained to report, though usually in a very feeble way. It was like a nightmare with just one part of the brain holding on while the rest was being drawn into a whirlpool of sensations.

The authorities in the United States became alarmed, and understandably so, by the widespread and irresponsible use of LSD—in 1967 it was estimated that between one and three million Americans had taken the drug—and highly restrictive legislation was enacted on a Federal level and by a number of states. Jail sentences were imposed for the mere possession of LSD. This was perhaps necessary in the circumstances, but it was most unfortunate for serious researchers, who were not able to obtain supplies of LSD because they were severely restricted. For research workers the carefully controlled use of the drug was not a threat to health or an incitement to lawlessness, as the press made out in their sensational reports; on the contrary, it was a very useful tool in loosening the associative processes of the mind and thereby freeing people from their obsessions, anxieties, and other mental disturbances and making them more, not less, responsible for themselves and others. To know that you are the product of your environment and to choose to be the person you are is better than not knowing what you are doing and living mostly out of fear rather than choice.

One of the professionals who became interested in LSD was the Czechoslovakian psychiatrist, Dr Stanislav Grof. For ten years Grof (1975) carried out the most extensive, carefully controlled scientific research into the effects of LSD. He did this work in Prague, where the drug was freely available to professionals for therapeutic use. It was listed in the official medical pharmacopoeia along with reputable drugs such as penicillin, insulin, and digitalis. Grof had amassed an enormous amount of data from many hundreds of LSD sessions and was in the process of sifting and analysing it when he was invited to the United States to take part in a research project in Baltimore.

When he arrived in the United States in 1967 with the intention of continuing his research, he found, to his dismay, that the country was in a state of hysteria over LSD and other psychedelic drugs. He was not therefore able to continue along the lines he had planned; he decided, instead, that he could be more usefully employed in trying to meet the need to provide honest and objective information concerning psychedelic drugs.

Grof worked for decades with LSD and other psychedelic drugs. In 1975 he published the first of a series of books in which he planned to summarize and condense, in a systematic and comprehensive way, his observations and experiences during those years. What he has attempted to do, in his own words, is to produce "the first maps of new, unknown and uncharted territories of the mind". "The material from serial LSD sessions, even in its present form", he writes, "is of crucial theoretical significance and represents a serious challenge to the existing concepts of contemporary science."

During the two decades that LSD was legal, a huge number of researchers and professionals—psychologists, psychiatrists, theologians, psychic consultants, and so on—were looking into LSD. Hofmann was so cross about his discovery being outlawed that he took a photographer around the world and photographed every mind-altering herb, bark, fungus, and so on, and he wrote them up in his splendid book, *LSD, My Problem Child* (1981).

It is not within the scope of this book to discuss this in any great detail, but a review of what is known and conjectured in prenatal psychology would not be complete without some mention of Grof's research and of the work of another researcher, the Englishman, Dr Frank Lake, who also used LSD as a therapeutic agent.

Frank Lake founded the Clinical Theology Association and trained over 12,000 men and women in the study and practice of pastoral counselling (Lake, 1981). He became convinced that the origins of most of the afflictions from which people suffered could be traced back to pre- and perinatal experiences. An understanding of these experiences, he said, was necessary to gain "a fuller sense of what it is to be human and what is promised to those who are 'in Christ". He quoted St John of the Cross:

> My sickness fills me so completely
> That I die because I do not die.
>
> [Lake, 1980a]

The "sickness" is an attachment to self, to the ego. The cure of this sickness that so completely fills the mind of the neurotic is not the one offered by psychoanalysts, which is the strengthening of the ego, but dropping the ego in order to discover the true Self. Then "I die so that I may live". Frank Lake wrote:

> Our problems of living derive from the fact that our "strength and prosperity" are usually expressive of our repressed defences. Strong character is the expression, not so much, or so often, of an integrated, whole humanness, as of a strong sustained reaction against a painful early experience which we refuse to integrate because we fear its recurrence. . . . Before any truth or wholeness can return to our persons, our masks, that is our personality defences, must be dismantled. [Lake, 1980a]

Lake saw pain and the experience and suffering of weakness—the dark night of the soul—as the way to God and truth. The pain came through a relaxing of the defences: the giving up of the ego; and this is not unlike the teaching of Buddhist psychology and the teaching of Christian mystics such as St John of the Cross—namely, that the loss of the socially conditioned ego brought about the strengthening of the true Self.

In the 1950s and 1960s Frank Lake said he found that LSD25 was able to abolish repression in a selective way, so that traumatic material, returning to consciousness, could be dealt with by association and acceptance, which, he said, was the basis of therapy. In his book *Clinical Theology* (1966) he gives a number of examples of how this worked.

One of Lake's patients was a clergyman whose problem was his schizoid fear of intimacy. He said he hated his mother, and bound up with this hatred was an inability to respond to love and a fear of marriage. He explained how he wanted to get close to people and moved towards them, but as soon as they responded, he moved away.

The clergyman described how in a number of LSD sessions he went down into his "deepest self". It was all pain and misery and death. "But I have lived through it now—and that is the great thing", he said. He had "let death out and let life in. . . . Pain let out is health let in." In conjunction with LSD, Lake gave his patient 12 mg of methedrine intravenously. This precipitated a very early abreaction.

The clergyman said:

> I am small, tiny and shrivelled, a small baby, a few inches in length—a little wizened baby. My mouth is dry . . . hands clammy, trembling. . . . My hands are tiny just like a bab's. I'm dried up like a fetus, almost. They are taking stuff out of my mouth. My legs feel bigger, like balloons. I am trying to swallow, but can't. All I am aware of is my little penis, wanting to pass water. I am struggling to find something smooth and soft to rub. . . . Oh, I'm bigger now; I'm in my cot. There's father and mother and nurse. The nurse says something to scare me. Now I am in another room—scared of loneliness, trying to pretend someone is there and holding on to my penis.
>
> Then father, doctor, nurse, mother come to me, want to find out why I had been hysterical. I couldn't tell her. I can tell you now, but I am detached from it all now, and I can tell you. Things are going so pinpoint and small. . . . I was scared of mother. [Lake, 1966]

Frank Lake did not know what to make of all this material that he was recovering through LSD, and he was not at all sure that it was of prenatal origin. He reported the following, saying that the reader could make of it whatever he chose:

> Father putting himself into mother. I was in the womb. I know what it feels like, with dry stuff in the mouth. I came to life in the womb—months before I was born. Coming to out of nothing, being inside a house. Had to grow up and get out, came down the channel—inside it—your mouth is all bunged up. Things taken out of your mouth. You came out straight—crying bath and slapping. [Lake, 1966]

The clergyman then knelt up on the couch and curled up in the fetal position. He began to writhe and groan and turn, as if going through the movements of the head passing through the birth passage. This, explains Frank Lake, is a common phenomenon under LSD. After going through these contortions for some time, he lay still without breathing. Then he began to pant in very short breaths, like a dog exhausted after a very long run. After a period of relaxation, when his breathing was very shallow, he suddenly looked terrified, and he started hissing through his teeth, which were clenched. Several waves of extreme violence went over him, his head rolling loosely as if it was out of control. Then, in a final paroxysm, there was almost a glottal spasm, as if each expiration had to be forced.

A week later, in another LSD session, he had the same respiratory distress. He said that some part of him, deep down, recognized this as something that had happened to him at the time of birth. During a series of abreactions of a similar nature, the only problem for him was to stay alive; he had the feeling that he was going to be suffocated. But tied up with this experience, he said, was a sense of painful aloneness: "You're on your own now, for the first time, at birth."

It seems from this that the clergyman's traumatic birth had produced in him the double fear that Otto Rank (1929) described: the fear both of going forward and of going backward, the fear of intimacy and the fear of loneliness, the fear of separation from the mother, "the all", and the fear of returning to "the all". The neurotic, as Otto Rank said, refuses the loan (life) in order to avoid the payment of the debt (death). The asthma—a suspension of life accompanied by a fear of dying, wanting and yet not wanting to die—is an expression of the double fear: "I'm afraid of living because I'm afraid of dying."

As early as 1966 Frank Lake acknowledged that his patients were reliving not only their birth trauma but also their anguish at being set aside in a cot, their bond with the mother damaged at this crucial moment following birth. To this double trauma, of restriction then abandonment, he attributed the cause of their lasting affliction in *Clinical Theology*.

Lake later became convinced that asthma and various other allergies had their origin in intrauterine life. The struggles and running battles that took place before birth, he said, entered into the emotional and perceptual life of adults as profoundly distorting factors. The allergy theory fits in with what Mott said about an emotional disturbance. A feeling of loneliness and rejection, whenever it occurs, could reactivate the physical struggle of birth.

b.   *Four stages relating to birth: Stanislav Grof*

Stanislav Grof also recognized among birth memories what Otto Rank had said about the similarity between birth and death. Subjects were brought face to face with the reality of physical pain and the suffering decrepitude of old age, dying, and death. This encounter with human finitude could have a devastating effect on the person, but Grof found that it was often the occasion of inner transformation. Terrifying experiences could alternate with more positive experiences of a tension-free state of bliss, a sense of merging with the environment: everything appears perfect, everything is as it should be.

Habitual emotional disturbances would relate to particular moments in early life, very likely a relating to biological birth. Each stage of birth had a physical, emotional, and spiritual content forming psychological blueprints recognizable as a guide in the way we experience our lives. Grof (1990) discerned four such perinatal stages:

Stage1.   The undisturbed intrauterine existence. The feeling of supreme bliss—the "good womb"—or the experience of rejection or of being poisoned by hatred or by alcohol, tobacco, or some other drug—the "bad womb". The child in union with the mother feels all her positive and negative emotions: a sense of elation or of depression. Love leads to self-esteem, self-respect, creativity, the feeling of self-fulfilment; hatred leads to self-disgust, self-abuse, the feeling of being in a cruel environment.

The experience of life in the womb can lead to a variety of experiences later in life. Frank Lake mentions psychotic paranoid delusions where people feel they are being poisoned by some unknown outside agent and they may be labelled insane: "Yet this can be an accurate but time-dislocated statement regarding the mother's smoking and drinking habits."

Grof mentions feelings of mystical union, encounter with metaphysical evil forces, bewitchment, possession; hypochondria, based on strange and bizarre physical sensations. On the other hand, the "good-womb" experience could contribute to many happy moments in life, the joy of being in beautiful natural settings, the intense pleasure of swimming in the ocean or a clear lake.

Stage 2.   The first clinical stage of delivery, the contractions in the enclosed uterine system, corresponded with the experience of "no exit" (which Grof named after Sartre's *Huis Clos*) or hell.

There is a feeling of helplessness, of being stuck, unable to move. Gone is the sense of freedom, in which the fetus was able to make himself comfortable, to kick and push. There is nowhere to turn: an unbearable and inescapable situation that will never end.

Grof mentions situations in life that reactivate these feelings: war experiences, accidents, operations, near drowning, imprisonment, interrogation, physical abuse.

Stage 3.   The propulsion through the birth canal in the second stage of delivery corresponded with the spiritual experience of the death–rebirth struggle.

It is recalled in LSD sessions as a titanic struggle, at times of volcanic ecstasy. Later in life the feelings inevitably come back in battle, revolution, storms at sea; also, according to Grof, in highly sensual activities: sexual orgies and the like. "We see the sadomasochistic element rooted in this matrix", says Frank Lake. "The vigorous forward and backward thrust of the pelvis is an essential and characteristic movement of the active fetus. If this adult function is paralysed by unknown fears—as it often is in frigidity and impotence—it is to these intrauterine antecedents that we can most profitably look for the pathological link up and therefore for the therapeutic key."

Stage 4.   The termination of the birth process and of the events in the third clinical stage of delivery corresponded with the metaphysical experiences of ego death and rebirth.

It is recalled in LSD sessions as enormous decompression, expansion of space, visions of gigantic halls, radiant light, and beautiful colour; feelings of rebirth and redemption; pleasant feelings can also be interrupted by umbilical crisis: sharp pain in the navel, loss of breath, fear of death. (These four stages Grof termed "Basic Perinatal Matrices" or "BPM 1–4").

Frank Lake mentions a fascinating illustration of the way this fourth matrix can affect people later in life. He was working with a paediatrician who later became a child psychiatrist. She told Lake that she could never stay in the delivery-room when a child was being born—she had to go outside. Lake describes what happened when she was reliving her birth:

> Just as she was born, evidently the placenta became detached and came out straight after her. There she was, lying in her own blood "with this great thing dead alongside me". This companion, which she had associated with life, movement and pulsation, was lying there dead alongside her, indelibly associated with "the smell of blood and death". She had repressed this awful moment when she couldn't get free from the placenta and from the smell of blood and death. Another severe difficulty had focused on intimacy. Whenever she tried to make relationships she was overcome by terror of emitting a bad smell. To offset this she customarily perfumed herself heavily. But whenever a man came close to her she felt: "He will smell death." She relived the origin of both these terrors, that of being present at a birth and of emitting a bad smell, on the one and only occasion she used her turn at the workshop to go back into her own birth. She has been totally freed of both terrors. [Lake, 1980b]

It should be mentioned that on this occasion LSD was not used. Another regression technique was used, as described in the next chapter.

c.   Turning point: rediscovery of cosmic unity

Grof describes the LSD training session of a psychiatrist who had some remarkable experiences that changed the direction of his scientific thinking. At first, he reported experiencing the feelings of a fetus suffering some strange toxic effects during the intrauterine existence. He had the sensation of being greatly reduced in size, with his head bigger than the rest of his body and extremities. He felt suspended in a liquid milieu. He felt as if harmful chemicals were being channelled into his body through the umbilical area, and, using some unknown receptors, he was detecting these as noxious and hostile. he could also perceive the offending quality of the intruding substances in his gustatory buds—the sensation seemed to combine the taste of iodine with that of decomposing blood and old bouillon.

He was aware that the poisonous substances had something to do with the condition and activity of the maternal organism. Some of these substances he could distinguish as the ingestion of alcohol, inappropriate food, or nicotine; others he perceived as chemical mediators of his mother's emotions: anxieties, nervousness, anger, conflicting feelings about pregnancy, and even sexual arousal.

The psychiatrist said that the "scientist" in him could not at first accept the reality of these experiences; but just when he was rejecting them as some sort of fantasy of no real scientific importance, he said, it became clear to him that it would be more appropriate to consider revising accepted scientific beliefs—something that had happened many times in the history of science—than to question the relevance of his own experience.

When he was able to give up his analytical thinking and accept the experience for what it was, there was a dramatic change in the nature of the session: the feelings of sickness and indigestion disappeared, and he was experiencing an ever-increasing state of ecstasy. It was as if multiple layers of thick, dirty cobwebs were being magically torn and dissolved, or a poor-quality film projection or television broadcast were being focused and rectified by an invisible cosmic technician.

He talks of the fetus experiencing, on one level, the ultimate perfection and bliss of a good womb and, on another level, he "becomes the entire universe", reflecting Mott's sense of universal design, the mind having "the same formative basis as the phenomena which it knows". He was witnessing, he said, the spectacle of the macrocosm, with countless pulsating and vibrating galaxies; but at the same time as he felt that this was going on outside himself, he also knew that he was the spectacle he was witnessing. Although many of these experiences sound incompatible with common sense, he did not himself feel that they were outside the realm of science (Grof, 1975).

And they were not, according to neurologist Karl Pribram and quantum physicist David Bohm. As they see it, there are two juxtaposed ways of knowing, for which they use the terms "explicate" and "implicate":

> One means of talking about the perceiver–perceived interaction has been agreed upon by both Pribram and quantum physicist David Bohm with their use of the terms explicate and implicate. Each theorist notes that analysis explicates extrinsic properties of the physical world—for example, the scientific laws of gravity. Juxtaposed to this way of knowing is the implicate study, which seeks to understand intrinsic or subjective psychological

properties. Each sphere is knowable according to its own rules of observation, and the interactions of the two govern the dynamics of an individual's perceptions. In other words, we cannot account for one's construction of reality until both these ways of knowing are taken into account. [Pelletier, 1978]

The psychiatrist, who, in Grof's example, was taken back to perinatal experiences could not at first accept what he experienced as authentic, because it did not fit into any system of thought that science had devised. As soon as he was able to accept the authenticity of his experience, he was on the way to creating a new paradigm to take in his experience, pushing out the boundaries of science.

The psychiatrist's experience, according to Grof, belongs to the undisturbed stage of intrauterine existence, Perinatal Stage 1, which is the experience of cosmic unity. Grof goes on to describe other experiences that, he believes, belong to stages of birth.

A good example was that of a social scientist who, in a training session, had what Grof calls the "no-exit" experience. After an initial feeling of nausea and tension, he was suddenly overwhelmed with feelings of impending disaster and emergency and an excruciating pain, which seemed to last for eternity. "I had the fantasy of lying in a bath of warm water with blood flowing out of my veins", he writes. He felt at that moment there was no way out except to commit suicide. "And, like life, the absurdity of it all, the exhaustion of carrying my pain-filled body through days, years, decades, a lifetime, seemed insane to me."

The situation seemed a familiar one to him; it was a state he had experienced before in various forms; but the form in which he was experiencing it, under LSD, as "an amplified hell", had, he said, an important lesson for him. "It was as though I was a prisoner in a concentration camp, and the harder I tried to get out, the more I was beaten, the more I struggled to free myself, the tighter the bonds would become. And yet I knew somewhere deep inside that I had to fight, that I had to escape, and that I would, but how?"

The "no-exit" experience is followed by Perinatal Stage 3, the propulsion through the birth canal, which manifests itself in LSD sessions as an enormous pressure on the head and body and the sensation of choking. Grof describes the experience of a clinical psychologist and psychotherapist during a training session. He had the sensation of being pushed and crushed and "wildly confused". At first he felt he was immersed in slime that was all over him and in his mouth, choking him. One of the major moments of release in the session, he said, was when he got rid of the filth and spat it out, clearing the mouth and throat with a huge scream. This was followed by an experience that he described as "tremendously erotic". The filth of the earlier session became the divine lubricant that made it possible for him to be "pushed and guided". It was pleasurable, he said, when he let go, and he didn't fight the process but simply allowed himself to be pushed. It was a revelation to him. It was so incredibly simple. You simply let go, and life pushes you and guides you through the journey (Grof, 1972).

The experience confirms the rightness of Fritz Perls's injunction: "Don't push the river: it flows by itself" (Perls, 1969).

Subjects come out of their experiences, according to Grof, with a deeper understanding of their lives. For a clergyman who experienced the transition between Stage 3, the propulsion through the birth canal, and Stage 4, the clinical stage of delivery, it was the experience of the suffering and death of Christ on the cross, and the resurrection. He described his experience in terms of music. At first the music sounded distorted, moving very rapidly, until a "wild symphony" took over.

He had a sensation of being on the top of a roller-coaster, losing control and unable to arrest the downward plunge. As the roller coaster was going down, the music sounded "as though it came from a million earphones. . . . My head was enormous at this time, and I had a thousand ears, each one with a different headset on, each earphone bringing in a different music."

He felt as if he was dying, an experience of intense agony and pain, panic, terror, and horror. He felt he was experiencing the passion of Christ. Then, "we moved towards Golgotha, and there in agony greater than I have ever experienced: I was crucified with Christ and all men on the cross. I was Christ and I was crucified and I died."

This experience of Christ's death on the cross was accompanied by "the most heavenly music I have ever heard . . . the voice of angels singing. . . . There were great processions in enormous cathedrals—candles and light and gold and incense." He had no sense of his personal existence; he was every man rising from the dead, all the people in the processions. The music was soaring, everyone was singing. He had a vision of "looking down through the earth to the foundations of the universe . . . in the depths of the universe the light can be seen. In the depths of the universe there are many prison cells; as I went through these cells, the cell doors opened, and the prisoners came forth praising God." The clergyman said that when his symphony came to an end, he was "filled with awe and humility and peace".

In a paper on "Varieties of Transpersonal Experiences: Observations from LSD Psychotherapy" (1972), Stanislav Grof gives a vivid description of the death-birth experience, which I think is worth quoting in full:

> After an individual has experienced the very depth of total annihilation and "hit the cosmic bottom", he is struck by visions of blinding white or golden light and experiences freeing decompression and expansion of space. The Universe is perceived as indescribably beautiful and radiant; the general atmosphere is that of liberation, redemption, salvation, love and forgiveness. The subject feels cleansed and purged and talks about having disposed of an incredible amount of "garbage", guilt, aggression, and anxiety. He feels overwhelming love for other fellowmen, appreciation of warm human relations, friendship and love. Irrational and exaggerated ambitions as well as cravings for money, status, prestige, and power appear in this state absurd and irrelevant. The appreciation of natural beauties is enormously enhanced, and an uncomplicated and simple way of life in close contact and harmony with nature seems to be the most desirable of all alternatives. Anything of natural origin is experienced with utmost zest by all the widely opened sensory pathways. Brotherly feelings for all fellowmen are accompanied by feelings of humility and a tendency to engage in service and charitable activities.
>
> The experience of rebirth is frequently followed by what is usually described as an experience of "cosmic unity" and seems to be closely related to the "good womb" and "good breast" experience and happy childhood memories. The individual tuned in to this experiential area usually discovers within himself genuinely positive values, such as a sense of justice, appreciation of beauty, feelings of love, self-respect and respect for others. These values, as well as the motivations to pursue them and act in accordance with them, seem to be on this level an intrinsic part of the human personality. They cannot be satisfactorily explained in terms of reaction formations to opposite tendencies or as sublimations of primitive instinctual drives. The individual experiences them as intrinsic parts of the universal order. [Grof, 1972]

There is a similarity between the pharmacological reactivation of an early memory and results obtained through electrical stimulation of the cortex. The most remarkable neurological discovery of recent times, I think, has been the fact that a person carries around with him a vivid memory of the past that is not just a photographic or phonographic reproduction of past scenes and events, but is an actual feeling that the past is still happening now: it can, in fact, be recovered by electrical means and re-experienced as if it were a present reality. The patient feels—in experiments carried out by Penfield while working with epileptic subjects—hears and sees everything he experienced at a particular time in the past. At the same time he is fully aware that he is living in the present. It is as if two parts of the brain had become disconnected and one was observing the other. The patient feels himself to be both the observer and observed (Penfield, 1952).

There are other regression techniques, which merely require the cooperation of the subject—there is no stimulation by chemical or electrical means—that have the same results. Some of these techniques are described in the next chapter.

CHAPTER SIX

Echoes of womb-life:
bliss and distress

"see all, nor be afraid."

Robert Browning, *Rabbi ben Ezra*

a. Fantasy and reality

The French dramatist and critic Jean Cocteau described in his diary an interesting experience he had when he revisited his childhood home in 1953 (Cocteau, 1988). He was interested to see whether by going back he could recover some of the feelings he had when he lived there. Could he relive his childhood?

The man who lived at his old home would not let him in. Cocteau looked around at the street and the houses and found that everything had changed; he wondered if it was at all possible to bring back his childhood memories without going into the house.

Cocteau then recalled how as a child he would walk close to the houses in the road and trail his finger along the wall. He did this again, hoping that memories would come flooding back. But they did not. There were a few memories, but they were thin and pale.

Suddenly, he remembered that as a child his hand had trailed along the wall at a different level. He was, of course, much smaller at that time. So, bending down and closing his eyes, he again moved his finger along the wall. The result was remarkable:

Just as the needle picks up the melody from the record, I obtained the melody of the past with my hand. I found everything: my cape, the leather of my satchel, the names of my friends and of my teachers, certain expressions I had used, the sound of my grandfather's voice, the smell of his beard, the smell of my sister's dresses, and of my mother's gown. [Cocteau, 1988]

Basically, this is the technique Frank Lake employed at his workshops. He had begun using LSD25 in psychotherapy in 1954 (Lake, 1981), Stanislav Grof in 1956 (Grof, 1990). In 1969 Lake gave it up because "for some reason it causes excessive symbolization and it gets you away from the actual physical suffering and adumbrates it as a myth". Janov's view concurs: "What LSD does not do is allow connections to be made solidly. And only connection accounts for lasting change" (1973). He also avoided the use of LSD, as did Konrad Stettbacher (1991), primal therapist to author Alice Miller (House, 1999; Miller, 1991), in Switzerland.

Influenced by Reichian technique and bioenergetics (Reich, 1933), Lake found that a "pattern of deep breathing we stumbled on" surpassed the effects of LSD. It left the patient more able to recognize their powerful physical experience as reliving their birth or, in the womb, their devastating feeling of rejection.

During the late 1960s and early 1970s people, mostly helped by facilitators trained by Frank Lake, began using such techniques in growth centres to relive past experiences and, particularly, to bring about what they called "rebirthing". A woman, say, in her mid-twenties would lie curled up on the floor in the fetal position. There would be cushions piled up around her, and four or five people would press hard on the cushions as she struggled to free herself without using her arms. It would take perhaps half an hour for her to push her way out of the symbolic womb. Then she might cuddle up to an older woman, who would put her arms around her. And she would stay there for some time—exhausted.

Frank Lake would also sometimes use what he called the deep-sea fantasy. Taking the client, in imagination, to some cave deep in the sea, said Lake, would set the tone of the session, giving it a feeling context: "The person lying relaxed on the floor as he visualized his watery descent will suddenly begin to pick up primal images, very faint at first, but becoming stronger and stronger."

There were those, of course, who said it was nothing more than a fantasy trip, with absolutely no basis in fact. Elizabeth Fehr, who began to practise what she called "natal therapy" in New York in 1969, has something to say about this (Feher, 1980). Fehr (not to be confused with Feher, who wrote about her) commented that fantasy was not to be ignored, however illogical or unbelievable, because its effects were real. It is the physical or emotional effects that are important.

A neurotic patient would sometimes come to her with some quite outrageous and unbelievable fantasy, which, he would say, was making a misery of his life. He felt it—so it was real to him. Fehr would encourage and help the patient to work through the fantasy until, as she put it, it was "completed"—that is, carried to a conclusion. The fantasy was the patient's problem; being stuck in the fantasy was being stuck in the problem. It was not, of course, the real problem, but its projection: an imaginative projection. In the case of many of her patients the problem, or the origin of the problem, predated speech, so there were no words to describe it: nothing but feelings and images.

> One day a patient came to Fehr complaining that he had the fantasy experience of being stuck in a manhole. He felt he would never get out unless someone helped to pull him through. Fehr obliged. She didn't intellectualize about his situation, but pushed and pushed until in the end the patient did actually feel free of the manhole. The fantasy had been completed.

> Only afterwards did they talk about birth. The patient's contortions, as Fehr was pushing, and his relief afterwards identified the fantasy as a birth fantasy. In the therapy sessions that followed, emotions and anxieties related to the patient's birth, which had been blocked off, began to surface: "Memories unfolded, sensations and feelings were experienced that had previously been unknown. With each subsequent session new associations were formed and repressions lifted".

Later, instead of waiting for patients to come with their birth fantasies, Elizabeth Fehr began to induce birth memories, just as Frank Lake did. Fantasy was a very useful tool in taking a patient back to his birth. To describe what goes on, Lake used Pelletier's (1978) term, "controlled free association". It has also been called "open passivity". In the first place, there has to be some direction to get the patient into the right feeling context; then a patient has to work through it all himself, within a fantasy. It is a subtle but well-recognized technique, used in relaxation exercises, or to help to reduce blood pressure or control unconscious processes. Thinking about the problem, whatever it is, does not help. You must be put in touch with unconscious processes and stay with them in a sort of twilight world. This can be done using fantasy or by simply re-enacting the birth process.

A rebirthing group session at the Elizabeth Fehr Natal Therapy Institute in New York was described by a Swedish woman journalist:

> At the rebirth there were some other observers: a couple of psychologists and social workers—all sceptical. Those being reborn were an actor and his wife, a teacher, an academic and a psychohistorian.
>
> We are all sitting on the floor in the basement room, mattresses around the walls, burning candles here and there on the floor. One person at a time is made to lie down in the fetus position. In a soft suggestive voice Leslie Feher brings the person's thoughts backwards to the time of birth.
>
> One helper is holding the feet with all his might. Another is pushing the head.
>
> One cannot believe what one sees. As in a wild trance the child starts pushing forward, working round the room in a long passage on the mattresses.
>
> The four I observed were born with quite different temperaments. All, with the exception of the actor who seemed dutifully to pretend, had orgasm-like outbreaks . . .
>
> We observers were shaken, fascinated, embarrassed—but not sceptical. We got involved in that moment, we believed it to be a genuine experience. The babies were very different from one another. One was born with enormous vitality and energy. The teacher moved exactly as a jerking infant but did not want to be born, had to be pulled out. The academic screamed in a way I will never forget. Our hair literally stood on end, one left the room pale. [Feher, 1980]

b.   Inducing recall: alternatives to LSD

In addition to the deep-sea fantasy, Frank Lake used Reichian deep breathing—Reich had been a student of Freud. The way it works is as follows: the client is told to "breathe up into your strength. Wait. ... Now down into your weakness—or whatever else emerges of primal joy or grief. Wait. Now up again. . . ." As you breathe out, you make a deep sound resonating downwards. You take the stream of attention down into your belly and observe what is coming in, and, whatever it is—good or bad, just a feeling—you give it a voice.

At that moment, in a group of six people, some might say: "This is beautiful. She's so warm. She doesn't know I'm here, but she's such a loving, warm person." Others might say: "It's very cold in here." The words, of course, are not the memory. It is the adult talking, trying to express the feelings that come to the surface during the exercise. The fetus is given a voice in the here and now; connections are made between early physical feelings and later emotional states—"it's warm": I feel loved; "it's cold": I feel unloved, rejected. The adult does the talking, and behind the talk the unborn child is there, afraid, unloved, inarticulate, just a sound—which may break out in the course of the session—a scream in the darkness.

This breathing brought the brain into theta-rhythm. Theta-rhythm is more prominent in very young children than in adults. It appears to link conscious and subconscious minds (Lake, 1981; Pelletier, 1978). Theta-rhythm is associated with drowsiness and hypnagogic imagery, while alpha-rhythm is associated with meditation and mysticism (Johnston, 1974). Lake (1981) said:

> In the twelve years that we have used deep breathing, in prefer-
> ence to the LSD we administered for the fifteen years before that,
> the more natural method has proved superior. LSD acts beyond
> the conscious control of the subject, sometimes throwing up mate-
> rial he or she is not ready to deal with. By contrast, breathing is
> a self-regulated act with a built-in control. Also, in so far as pre-
> natal memories are concerned, under LSD the subject avoids the
> actual terrors or joys of the fetus itself and evades the recognition
> that this is happening to them in the context of their mother's
> womb. Deep breathing, however, promotes a faithful owning and
> "contextualizing" of the intrauterine experience. Under LSD the
> actual experiences of the individual were removed to the realm of
> myths and to dream-like sequences which occur in symbolically
> stated religious conflicts and deliverances. Stanislav Grof's work
> confirms this observation.

Grof moved into past-life therapy, whereas Lake remained intent to the end on the person relating a regressive experience to the original experience within this life's cells, however early, even before conception.

The roaring sounds, sounds of hatred, fear, anxiety, or terror that people sometimes made at his workshops, were, Frank Lake (1980b) said, the sounds of the suffering small person in the womb—the only language he had available with which to draw attention to "his injured and trapped presence within us". It is the past talking to the present—an organismic memory that has stayed around and will not go away. It troubles us; but we do not understand what it is. It is a feeling of distress. It is the "bad" mother, says Frank Lake, entering into us, which we cannot accept. It is the "good" mother we want to remember: "My mother was good, good, good . . . she wasn't bad. It's a lie, she wasn't bad!" Our life depends on her. In the womb it does. We can't live without her. To reject her is to die.

The sounds are cries of help. Frank Lake's comment was:

> We do not run away from cries of help from babies and chil dren. Or do we? This therapeutic journey is to listen to, go to, feel with and help that small person to bear and express that pain. Being encouraged to do this, and finding it shared with love, he casts out the fear of it. The terrified child from which the adult had been in flight, feels himself calmed and cared for. [Lake, 1980b]

c.   Primal integration experience

Simon House witnessed powerful responses in a primal integration group:

> In 1978, while co-counselling with a patient of Lake's, I recounted some strange experiences that I had had 20 years previously. She exclaimed that I had worked through an entire primal program in one night by myself. At once I signed up for a primal integration group. I was glad it was on a smaller scale than Lake's own—a group of 8 plus two therapists trained by Lake—and did not use guided journeys or any suggestive methods. The therapists were warm and humorous, and respectfully ready to discuss any aspect. We met one evening a week for 3 hours. A little bioenergetics—such as axing an imaginary tree—an introduction, then we assembled on mattresses and whoever was first in the ring worked, just one at a time. If the patient recalling distress triggered off a second person, a neighbour, would support them. So the patient would be receiving loving attention and physical containment from at least 7 people. 10 in all is a good number. As

a group further enlarges it becomes harder for the members all to keep close physical contact and focus on the patient.

People seldom took long to start. I was impressed at each stage by the therapist's questions and directions: "How are you now?"... "Stay with the feeling" (emotional or physical) . . . "Does it remind you of anything in your childhood?". "Stay with that feeling" . . . "Let the sound out." . . . "Keep breathing, deeply. Breathe into that: give it a sound" . . . "Where are you now?" Meanwhile the patient's posture would often indicate "where they were". Everything was to come from the patient. Low key questions or guidance with breathing were enough to help the patient to stay with the original experience.

If appropriate, we would recreate the womb using huge cushions. If the patient seemed tightly constricted, for instance near birth, we would increase the pressure. If they seemed free floating, at the stage of ovum or second trimester, we would give them space. Holding or touching was used mainly as a carefully timed response to replicate the patient's original situation as closely as possible—even as far as holding up by the legs a "newborn" man 2-meters tall! It was used for reassurance of present caring and safety. In John Older's words, "To touch is not a technique: not touching is a technique" (Older, 1982). The approach in this small group could be more fully supportive and containing than seems possible in Lake's larger workshops. Week by week, people working were being released from primal distress, making significant recovery of natural feelings, finding freedom from phobias and violent tendencies, becoming more fully themselves.

In our group I remember vividly the first person to move into the ring. The therapist asked him "How are you now?" "My boss is on my back! He's been there all day. . . . But I know it's not his fault. It's me!" "What does he feel like?" "Heavy!" "Stay with the feeling. Let yourself breathe." Long pauses throughout this dialogue. "Does this feeling remind you of anything?" "I'm nine, sheltering from an air raid, back in that underground station. It's caving in on me." Contained by our large cushions he was thrashing around. This chap sweated and shook and yelled. He then emerged from it looking relaxed and a lot happier. Only in the conversation following did we recognize that he had been reliving his birth. His had been a difficult birth. He had lived ever since with this terrifying claustrophobic sensation, ever ready for restimulation by constriction, physical or emotional. Now, in the loving safety of the group, he could storm like a child and release this long pent up distress. Subsequently the problem with his boss diminished.

Another man in the group, in his late twenties, suffered attacks of acute agoraphobia and compulsive violence. One night he had to yell to his father, "Get my mother out of the house before I kill her". He was turning green and we could smell the fear coming off him. "This is the laying on of hands."—not that theology was thrust at anyone—"Put your hands over him, and feel." The cold seemed to come off him like ice. Soon after that he was moving house, a vulnerable moment, but it was now no problem to stay with his parents.

This way of recreating a perinatal situation is echoed by Emerson, who used "massage, touching and re-creation of the physical pressures of birth" (Ridgway, 1987). The therapist made sure that each patient made the connection between their chronic feeling—oppression, depression, rejection or whatever—with the prenatal or perinatal experience; that they "contextualised" the origin of the feeling. When a patient had finished working they might rest, held by one or two others. Before leaving, the therapist ensured their safe return to a normal, grounded state of consciousness.

Experience in this group radically changed the way I counselled people, individually or in groups. One day a 28-year-old French schoolteacher arrived looking drawn and tense. She soon set herself amongst the huge coloured cushions, surrounded by eight of us in the group. She threw herself down on the mattress and so surprised all of us by immediately flailing around, that the group spontaneously closed in to "en-womb" her. Uncertain, I put a hand on her shoulder saying, "You know it has to come spontaneously from within?" She looked puzzled. "How do you feel?" I asked her gently. "Confused", came her answer. As I nodded, she rolled onto her front again and we softly cushioned her. She thrashed violently needing us to contain her more firmly. From time to time she kept signing to me to press on the back of her head. I did so firmly, keeping her head forwards. After some forty minutes she thrust hard and her head twisted sideways, just like a baby's at the point of birth. Then she began to calm down. After a while I caught sight of her face and said "Look at yourself in the glass." She stood up and laughed to see her changed face. She was flushed, relaxed and radiant—"the face of an angel". I commented on her need for pressure on her head, and a woman in the group, a midwife, said, "Oh, we often press babies' heads forwards during birth. If their heads go back they present a broader front, making birth more difficult." Later that summer I called on this patient in France. She had her mother staying, and told me; "For the first time in my life I've had a real conversation with my mother."

I do not want to leave the impression that everyone responds well. Lake carried out a post-workshop survey and percentages were recorded. Most had gained greatly. There were a few negatives. Using the more intimate style, for a much smaller number, I am sure that there were no negative experiences of primal integration therapy in the few groups I have run. Judging by feedback comments I think at least 7 out of 10 gained, even if the others were not able to benefit. The reasons I prefer the style developed by our group therapist trained by Lake are these: it is non-suggestive, less contrived, more strongly supportive both physically and through group attention. It uses the optimum group number for a sense of safety, and for group energy and physical containment. Lake would I believe have had a higher proportion benefiting, had he kept his work on this scale, but it would have taken his association far longer to achieve the widespread influence that he has had, despite resistance and modest acclaim. [House, 1999]

It became evident that much of the problem had come from the mother's distress. Francis Mott (1964) called the invasion of maternal distress the "negative umbilical affect". In his prenatal integrative work Lake found that a lot of the "badness"—the mother's distress—had been dealt with by displacement to different parts of the body, even sometimes to the eyes. Lake told Roy Ridgway of a woman whose negative umbilical input went into the feet. The woman, who was a nursing sister on an obstetrics ward, consulted Lake because, for no accountable reason, she was constantly ripping skin off her feet:

When she went into this she said, "I don't understand. My mother loves me. She has always loved me." She was convulsed with weeping as she pushed all the "badness" into her feet. She always felt that her thighs were ugly, and heavy and painful, but as a matter of fact she's got beautiful, shapely thighs. Symbolically she was carrying all the distress from the umbilical input.

"But what was this weeping for?" asked Dr Lake. "She couldn't believe that her mother could be responsible for it." Then she recalled that three months before she was conceived, her maternal grandfather was diagnosed as suffering from an incurable cancer. The mother nursed him throughout his illness until he died at the end of the first three months of her pregnancy. The fetus was invaded by the mother's grief; hence the weeping, the sadness that was pushed into the feet.

When the "badness" is pushed into the skin, the central core of the self and its organs are preserved, according to Lake. But there are others who retain the "badness" of the influx from the distressed mother in the internal organs. They feel that the inner abdominal organs, at times the heart and lungs, but more frequently the uterus and pelvis, have been given over to "badness". These people, said Lake, kept their skin as good, attractive, fresh and "deceptively" young looking. [Lake, 1980b]

Giving birth can trigger rebirth

The psychotherapist William Emerson (1978) points out that mothers who are giving birth may re-experience aspects of their own birth. He gives an example of a mother who, while giving birth, was taken back to her own birth. Both during her own birth and during the birth of her daughter she had a feeling of "being crushed, bound, imprisoned, and left to die". The latter birth, in fact, gave no trouble: it was easy, and labour was short. Yet when the daughter was later rebirthed, she had the same experience of being crushed. It is the mother's strong identification with her baby that brings back her own birth experiences. In this way, anxiety traits, for instance, can be transmitted from one generation to the next.

Another woman found herself being taken back to the seventh month of intrauterine life during her rebirthing. She experienced extreme shock and anxiety and felt that she and her mother were in extreme danger of losing their lives. This woman's grandmother, while she was carrying her mother in the seventh month of pregnancy, had been arrested and thrown into a concentration camp. The grandchild had never been told this: but it had obviously been a terrible shock to her mother while she was in the womb, and this shock had been transmitted to her during the seventh month of her own life in the womb.

d.   *Rebirth: interpretations right and wrong*

Emerson describes how the subjective experience can interpret wrongly what happened at birth (Emerson, 1978). He cites the case of a rebirthed girl whose actual birth was full of complications. The doctors and nurses had been very busy on the ward attending to a number of other births at the time, and the mother felt she had been neglected. The cord was twisted round the neck, and the child had to be delivered by forceps. According to Emerson, the cord was experienced as an attempt by the mother to hold on to her, and the forceps were seen as an attempt by "others" to make her comply with "their way of doing things". She was referred to Emerson because she was difficult and rebellious—which is hardly surprising after what she had been through! After her rebirth experience, said Emerson, her subjective perception of coercion softened, and she improved rapidly during therapy. "Most people's subjective experiences of birth are highly consistent with reality", says Emerson, "but where reality and subjectivism differ, it is the subjective experience which forms the basis of psychotherapy."

William Emerson worked with Frank Lake for five years, but even at the age of 16 he had already recognized the elements of primal head-movements in a woman whom he had rushed to help in a car accident. Recognizing movements in a patient, he would position their body accordingly and induce discharge of early stress. He learnt to recognize typical movement of various stages of development in the womb or during birth. He describes this "somatotropic therapy":

> Somatotropic therapy evolved from twenty years of practice and experimental follow-up done in Europe and the United States. In the late 1970s in England, I [Emerson] collaborated in workshops with Frank Lake and shared research findings with him. It was at this time that I developed my initial somatic approaches to uncover primal trauma. Focusing on the time from conception and working through implantation and gestation to birth, I discovered ways to access the deepest and earliest pre- and perinatal traumas. Gradually, I found a precise methodology for working with infants and children to access and discharge an astonishingly wide array of traumas. In the course of my work, a way of reading the face and posture as a cartography of the client's specific pre- and perinatal trauma began to emerge. Using these physical and gestural traces as indicators of the temporal origins of disturbance, I have developed ways of inducing these experiences in the therapeutic context, and thus the means to discharge the compulsive control they exert on characterological behavior. I have also perceived that in moments of somatic disclosure during therapy, the body will take particular shapes that recapitulate embryonic development. These perceptions enable the therapist to ascertain with a great deal of precision the moment of disturbance in the

client's pre-natal life. I have also determined that the birth process tends to re-enact the traumas that occur from conception through implantation and gestation, and that the resolution of these earliest traumas dissipates the effects of the traumas that occur at birth. [Emerson, 2002]

On his website he gives a marvellous picture of how primal therapy has developed and branched out in recent years, with an integral perception in detail of psychological with physiological development over the entire lifespan.

Emerson collected material from five years' work in "one-to-one rebirthing", as he described his sessions with individual clients. He followed up all these sessions by questioning mothers, fathers, and others who had been present at the birth to see whether there were correspondences; and he found that in most cases yes, indeed, the relationship between the rebirth and the actual birth was consistent. He was aware that some clients might have been told by parents or others what had taken place at their birth and that this could be what they were remembering rather than their own actual experience; but, said Emerson,

Taking cases where the birth facts were not likely to be conveyed directly to the child (thereby biasing the rebirth experience) the correspondences are amazingly accurate. Low bias situations are cases where: (a) both parents had died shortly after the birth, (b) where the parents denied ever mentioning the birth facts or (c) where the mother was unaware of certain occurrences at birth (e.g. cord around neck) and which were experienced by the rebirthed person and written in medical records. [Emerson, 1978]

Emerson told the story of a man who resisted conventional treatment for a condition diagnosed as "schizoid with strong paranoid tendencies", but was quite happy to be taken back to his birth experience. During rebirthing he said he felt that "those of the outside" were pursuing him and that he was being "invaded by toxic substances and poisoned by the dark ones". Following enquiries made about his actual birth, he was told, much to his amazement, that he had been delivered by Caesarean section and that his mother had attempted suicide by taking a drug overdose during the last three months of pregnancy. His life patterns followed these themes. He worked as a detective, was obsessed with following and being followed, and was regarded by co-workers as over-zealous in drug cases.

Birth and behaviour—correlation

Leslie Feher, director of the Elizabeth Fehr Natal Therapy Institute, New York, says that the frequency in which correlations between behavioural problems and birth problems occur cannot be ignored (Feher, 1980). At the moment studies of such correlations lack scientific method, but she believes that further studies will confirm her own findings:

- A great many babies born with the help of instruments grow up with the need to lean on others. They have difficulty in coping where a situation calls for individual initiative. They tend to be humourless and academic.

- The "Caesarean personality" needs a lot of help in achieving goals. He dislikes the trials on the way and tends to blame any failure on others not giving him their full support. On the plus side, the Caesarean personality is enthusiastic, spontaneous, and artistic.

- "Breech birth personality" traits include over-reacting to environmental demands and aggressiveness. The reason for this, Feher says, is the pressure put on the baby by violent contractions during the breech birth. Head pressure, however, is reduced in these births where the baby is not turned round but is born feet first. They grow up, says Feher, to undervalue cognition. They have an expectation to be "pulled through" difficult life situations, exams, and so forth, by others; they have high expectations of others, although they do not usually communicate them and are often disappointed.

- The premature baby grows up to be "clinging", feels pushed into things, resists change, tends to avoid responsibility, and fears growing up. Because he is often taken away from his mother, he suffers from contact deprivation, which later hampers emotional development. He may come to lack social skills. Thomas Verny, in *The Secret Life of the Unborn Child*, said that many of his prematurely born patients tended to feel rushed and harried all the time. "I suspect the feeling that they will never, ever catch up is a direct result of their prematurity. They began life rushed and now, many years later, they still feel that way." Verny points out that psychological damage to the premature baby varies in degree, according to whether it is a few days, a few weeks or a few months premature.

Abortion attempt — a convincing cause

Sometimes Lake's subjects relived an attempted or failed abortion; there existed an awareness, feelings that came back, of a mother's rejection of her child, and, according to Lake, the fetus "relives its own near-murder with quite shocking accuracy and overwhelming terror". He mentioned the case of a successful businessman who was born in the East End of London to a mother whom he adored (1980b). The mother, like many women in the East End before the war, had been through very hard times but had faced her troubles with great courage. The businessman was proud of her, so he did not think that his troubles could have anything to do with her. But he was puzzled. Throughout his married life, he said, he had lived in terror of a sudden attack on his life—sometimes it took the form of a fear of being poisoned. He felt threatened by those close to him, people he loved; and he just could not understand it. He was often cruel and unjust to them (Lake, 1981).

He went to see Lake and joined one of the primal integration groups. There, in the safety of the group, he re-experienced feelings of love and then, to his surprise, rejection by his mother; and these feelings, he was convinced, belonged to his life in the womb. At first, he said, he felt nothing but joy, but this was followed by a sudden feeling of great disturbance in his mother's life, and then he felt he was being poisoned.

"He was convinced", Lake said, "that it was an attempted abortion in which he nearly died, after suffering a long anguish of toxic wretchedness". Then he was astounded at what he described as a distinct sense of his mother's guilt feelings (he did not expect this): she was appalled at what she had done and was trying to forget it. The rest of the nine months were uneventful, though he had an increasing sense of how greatly he was loved. This reliving of the trauma of an attempted abortion, followed by feelings of guilt in his mother and the knowledge that she loved him, explained everything to him; and it is a measure of the authenticity of the experience that it put an end to his fear. It explained everything, especially his distrust and fear of people he loved. It also explained a memory he had of a neighbour coming to his mother, in her later years, and confiding to her that she was pregnant again—she had a very large family—and was going to have an abortion. His mother, said the businessman, hit the roof and threatened to go to the police. This memory had made him feel that under no circumstances would his mother contemplate an abortion. But after his session with Frank Lake he understood why she had overreacted to her neighbour: it had brought back all her guilt feelings, which had never been resolved. But although the mother had never been able to forgive herself for what she had tried to do, the son did; after a temporary setback in his feelings for her, be began to think of her again as a loving, caring person.

In this particular case there is no evidence, apart from what the businessman experienced in the rebirthing session, that the mother did actually attempt an abortion; she was no longer alive when the businessman went to see Lake. But Lake found, in general—as do most people who work in this field—that the experience of the re-birthed person did correspond with what had actually happened at birth. At least, the objective facts were usually true ("She wanted to have an abortion; father was not present"). The subjective experience, however, might not be true ("she didn't love me"). Lake, however, had no doubt at all that the businessman's experience was a re-enactment of a real attempted abortion.

e.   Conception and the first trimester

After 1969 the focus of psychotherapy shifted, for Lake and his colleagues, from birth to the first trimester of intrauterine life. These first three months after conception, Lake said, held more ups and downs, more ecstasies and devastations, than he had ever imagined when he was working with LSD in the 1950s and 1960s. By 1978, fresh evidence again overwhelmed his scepticism. He became convinced that his patients were regressing much further back, and that they were reliving their first trimester in the womb and even conception itself. In the new book he had begun, *Tight Corners in Pastoral Counselling*, he wrote:

> What we . . . have become firmly convinced about, is the vulnerability of the fetus to all that is going on in the mother, particularly in the first trimester. Affliction in its worst forms strikes in the first three months after conception. . . . Any severe maternal distress, whatever its cause, imprints itself on the fetus. These damaging experiences are now accessible to consciousness without undue difficulty. [Lake, 1981]

This, Frank Lake's outstanding contribution, has been much over-looked. What he reveals is the stage of the most powerful imprinting for life, and what he pioneers is the most direct means of accessing the root cause for the purpose of primal healing.

"In our sessions now", Lake said in an interview in 1980, "we begin at conception, through to the blastocystic stage, to implantation and the events of the first trimester. It is here, in the first three months of life in the womb, that we have encountered the origins of the main personality disorders and the psychosomatic stress conditions" Ridgway, 1987

Others were beginning to say the same sort of thing in the late 1970s. They talked of "conception shock" and "implantation trauma". The late Dr W. Swartley said that the first sensations on the surface of the zygote (the fertilized egg) and the subsequent splitting of the cells and development of the organs, kidneys, eyes, brain, and genitals—the whole generation process—are remembered in significant detail and are available through dreams and other altered states of consciousness. In an interview Swartley said:

> We've had a number of people who remember their conception, and that gets very interesting because some people identify with the egg and some with the sperm and some with both—but apparently conception can be remembered. Even more mysterious is one case where someone remembered their conception, they saw the seduction of their mother and they saw events which happened before their conception. And they saw details, labels on dresses and we've tried to confirm these details and they do correspond so far as we can check. . . . It appears there are two things, neurology and consciousness, and those two things interface with each other in a totally mysterious way. As if consciousness is independent of neurology and integrates with it as it develops. [Swartley, 1977]

Swartley talked about the difference between what he called a Birth Primal (re-experiencing birth) and an Implantation Primal. The characteristic movement of a Birth Primal, he said, was "a pushing, to find a hole and get through". Implantation was completely different. It was a "searching, an attempt to adhere, to find the right spot to attach, usually with the forehead. Implantation is centred round the Third Eye. An Implantation Primal just looks quite different."

"Just looks quite different"! Swartley was a very intelligent and sensitive man, and he was not just talking about one or two crazy people who had perhaps had a history of mental disturbance, but of a large number of quite ordinary people who had these extraordinary experiences, which were so common that an Implantation Primal could be distinguished from a Birth Primal.

But it is not only recently that people have been talking about pre-natal memories going back to implantation. Dr Isidor Izaak Sadger, another student of Freud and devoted follower (Sadger, 2005), wrote about some of his patients who, he said, "brought the embryonic period into the sphere of their associations" (Sadger, 1941). He said neurotic symptoms disappeared when that embryonic period was penetrated. The results of such delving were so impressive, Sadger said, that after a certain amount of scepticism and long hesitation, he was compelled "to follow the patient into the psychic primeval forest".

Most of his patients, he said, were uneducated and had never in their lives heard of embryos or spermatozoa, but they described events that were biologically accurate. Later, some of them began to talk of "embryonic feelings of guilt". He writes:

> Experience teaches that very few mothers conceive their children with great joy at the start. . . . [The event] disturbs them in so many different ways . . . they try either deliberately or unconsciously to rid themselves of the fetus. Many a fall or accident is an attempt at abortion. . . . When nothing works and the child is born there is a transition from too little love or even hatred to overflowing affection. . . . The mother feels a strong sense of guilt which is, in the later stages of pregnancy (where there is an acceptance of the child), communicated to the fetus. [Sadger, 1941]

The fetus, of course, can have no conception of wrong; but he can feel discomfort or pain; such feelings in the child are referred back to the earlier physical feelings, which, in the memory, become feelings of guilt. Sadger quotes some of the things patients said to him:

> "Birth is a withdrawal of love which I don't understand. Therefore I am always wanting to return to my mother's womb."
> "Most embryos should have had the feeling of being loved without stint. If this is not the case, they suffer injury all their lives."
> [Sadger, 1941]

Sadger educated his patients in the fundamentals of biology so that they could talk about the different stages of embryonic development. Sessions with Sadger were concerned with such Freudian interpretations of neurotic symptoms as fear of castration and the Oedipus complex, but in a sense "Every spermatozoon is ultimately castrated by the ovum." There were feelings of guilt when one made its entrance with particular force and violence. "I forced myself through", a patient confessed, "and pressed with great pleasure into the ovum. But when in doing so I lost the caudal filament (tail), a downright sexual pleasure occurred." Difficult to believe, but others have had similar experiences, and they are not memories people willingly talk about for fear of being ridiculed. The jargon made them more acceptable.

In the group experiences of the 1960s and 1970s there was a much more direct approach to these problems. Freudian jargon was out. There was no discussion of unconscious mechanisms. People reported their experiences, however bizarre, honestly and in plain English—although not always in the clear grammatical terms used by patients in the heyday of psychoanalysis. And not all experiences were unpleasant.

Glyn Seaborn-Jones had founded his Intensive Rhythm Therapy. He replied in answer to the question "How far back do you think the fetus is conscious?":

> I have always hesitated to talk about this. . . . I have definitely had an experience which I can only explain as the spermatozoon swimming through some fluid and coming up against a soft resistance and pushing right into it with the head first relaxing and then the shoulders and then right through the body and eventually only the feet swimming. And then the feet going quiet. And I was in. And it was bliss and it was one of the most blissful experiences of my life.
>
> Well, that really sounds very far-fetched. It sounded far-fetched when I thought about it. I objected, "I'm not a spermatozoon, I'm the result of the fusion of a spermatozoon with an ovum!" And so you have the problem of what "I" means.
>
> But there's no doubt about the experience, whatever the explanation, and no doubt that the whole womb is psychologically recorded, including all the shocks that may happen in the womb. But the only experience of womb life I have had before the trauma of birth was completely blissful—absolute perfect peace. No problem, no effort, nothing at all. And no awareness of anything lacking or missing. And certainly no sense of being imprisoned, because you have no experience of what it is like not to be enfolded. There is nothing that one's adult mind might associate with

and find to be uncomfortable or distressing. There is no distress at all. And that is why I have this feeling that perhaps the whole of our conscious lives on this planet are a kind of anti-climax after the good months in the womb. I think what is sometimes referred to as a death wish is not a death wish at all—it's a womb wish! This is the core of the theory I am now working on.

I'm hoping to shift the emphasis now from reliving the birth trauma to reliving the birth experience, from reliving pain [Janov] to reliving bliss. In other words, if people realize vividly enough that it's possible to recapture not only the pain of birth, but also the bliss of prebirth, here will be an experience where people can gather strength for the pain of rebirth. They had all that strength from the good womb experience to face this trauma in the first place. [Seaborn-Jones, 1977]

Although Seaborn-Jones talks of the bliss of the womb, it is doubtful if an implantation memory, assuming it can be retrieved, can be anything but traumatic. After all, the mother's body is regarding the tiny organism that is you as an intruder, and the endometrium is bringing white blood cells into the battle to throw off the foreign body. That is not bliss! Although somewhere it is recorded as an experience of winning, overcoming tough opposition, like Jacob wrestling with the angel (Genesis 32.24). Thomas Verny suggests that events in the womb serve as a template for postnatal experience:

They may serve as a template for the feeling of pleasure associated with pushing in, getting ahead, diving fearlessly into things, exploring new territories with confidence or trepidation, always moving cautiously ahead (putting feelers out—chorionic villi?). Many people spend their lives trying to get into a club, a fraternity, a university, a group of friends they see as desirable to belong to. Often they fail at it. They have dreams of quicksand, swamps, storms, winds, shipwrecks, breaking into pieces. They may complain of an inability to get into what they are doing, suffering unexplainable fatigue, lack of willpower and intellectual impotence.

In other words the kind of reception one receives from the primitive germ cell onwards begins a subliminal chain of programming that eventually leads to definite and discernible personality traits. [Verny, 1982]

Many people will not be able to accept some of the accounts given above of prenatal memories, but everyone has had the sort of feelings Thomas Verny mentions. Is it not possible, even likely, that many of our pleasures originated in biological processes? Erich Blechschmidt believed it possible. What we are dealing with here is what Blechschmidt (1977) called the "living knowledge" of the body. People who understand what is going on and can go back to early feelings or sensations that are not really translatable into words will equate them with what they know about impregnation, implantation, and so on. How else could they communicate what they know—what, in fact, we all know—in a non-verbal sense, about ourselves and our origins?

Hearing of such memories for many people clicks into place a familiar but unexplained sense:

> I have a taste that sometimes comes back to me, and it's nothing like any taste I know now. I talked about this to Frank Lake. "Could it be the taste of amniotic fluid?" I asked him. "It could", he said, "but it could also be the taste of your mother's milk. Only you can know." There are really no words to describe that taste. And even if there were, the words are not the taste, although people are always confusing words with feelings. [Ridgway, 1987]

Even Freud, who largely lived in his head and invented a lot of new words, knew that. He once confessed that at first he thought that a disturbed patient suffered from "a sort of ignorance" and that the removal of the ignorance would lead to recovery. But, he said, "such measures have as much influence on the symptoms of nervous illness as a distribution of menu cards in a time of famine upon hunger" (Freud, 1910). People have to experience something, not just know about it; they have to re-experience the past, the things that went wrong, if they want to give a new direction to the present: otherwise they will go on repeating old patterns. And, according to Lake and others, the most devastating things that happened to you, colouring the whole of your life, often happened in the first trimester.

Cellular memory

When Roy Ridgway visited Frank Lake in Nottingham in 1980, he talked to the latter about prenatal memory:

> "Fact or fiction?" I asked. It was difficult for me at the time to accept some of the stories I had heard, particularly about conception memories. But Dr Lake said he was in no doubt at all that

there were what he called cellular memories. He hadn't, however, come up with a satisfactory theory to account for their existence. He didn't like the way some of his colleagues regarded him as eccentric and gullible. He never forgot his scientific training, first in tropical medicine in Liverpool and then in psychiatry. He was anxious to demonstrate to the medical profession that he was a serious scientific investigator and was disappointed when orthodox medical journals, such as the *British Medical Journal*, failed to recognize his work and even ignored him. He was keen to impress me at the time because I was executive editor of an establishment journal, *BMA News Review*. He said he had spent the first 13 years of his medical life as a parasitologist studying the behaviour of amoebae and other single-celled organisms under the microscope. "I don't find it difficult as others might", he said, "to attribute a sharp and discriminating, even learned reactivity to the single cell." [Ridgway, 1987]

Lake mentioned Richard Dryden's (1978) contention that the cytoplasm of the fertilized egg contained information that was essential to at least the early stages of development. There were several sites where cytoplasmic information could be stored. The abundant free ribosomes could carry developmental information. The mechanism of protein synthesis leant itself to analysis by information theory, with the ribosomes helping to convert the coded message into a protein molecule.

There was also Karl Pribram's holographic theory of memory. According to Pribram, memory functions in a two-step process. A stimulus, such as a sound, smell, or image, triggers an individual short-term memory, which then resonates through the infinite complexity of the brain's stored holograms until an association is triggered in long-term memory:

> The holograms of cellular memory are still broadcasting from infinitesimally small, but collectively audible transmitting stations. These minute radio stations belong to successive periods of development, from conception to implantation and the developmental stages of pregnancy. It seems they are still transmitting and it is possible to tune into them. [Pribram, 1971]

"By these means" commented Lake, "you can distinguish what typically belongs to the first trimester or the second with its free-floating movement, and what belongs to the gradual closing that occurs in the last three months before birth takes place" (Lake, 1981). Though all this is theory and there is still uncertainty about how long-term memory could work to bring back prenatal memories, Frank Lake was in no doubt about the authenticity of the prenatal memories of many of his clients:

> My interest in the possible biological bases of pre-natal memories is not to demonstrate the legitimate existence of our findings but to indicate their biological feasibility and to guard against dismissive criticism based on antiquated neurology when they are reviewed. [Lake, 1981]

In keeping with Lake's conviction that the impact of the mother's emotions were greatest in the first trimester, Curt Sandman told us at the APPPAH Congress in San Francisco in 1999 that this is a time before the child is sheltered from effects of shock by a hormone subsequently supplied by the placenta. The placenta secretes a shock suppressant, corticotrophin-releasing hormone (CRH), but this scarcely begins before the second trimester. The CRH level then rises steadily until near the due birth-date. And, in keeping with this steady rise, was the effect of stress in pregnancy recorded following the tragic 1995 earthquake in California—memorable for its image of a collapsed motorway. Sandman's team surveyed the effect on women in the area who had been pregnant during the quake. Significantly more of those women who had been shocked by the quake in their *first trimester* had delivered prematurely—a *sign of stress*—than of those who had experienced the quake in their second or third trimester (Glynn, Sandman, & Wadhwa, 2000). As the CRH level rises, it helps to bring on delivery, but it also has a lasting effect on the fetus: higher level of CRH correlates with reduced sensitivity of a particular kind (Glynn, Sandman, & Wadhwa, 2000). It may seem contradictory that a similar survey following the Twin Towers atrocity showed the opposite—that women in the area in their third trimester had a preponderance of stressed children over those earlier in pregnancy. It was doubtless a different kind of shock, with different effects of bereavement and raising of fears.

At the same congress, Bruce Lipton showed us how genes are being switched on or off by environmental factors. They read the environment, nutritional, hormonal, and so on. They are not rigidly set for life, as confirmed by the Genome Project in 2001 (Human Genome Project, 1990–2003; see also ch. 9[a] on objectivity). The embryo/fetus reads its own environment, the mother, and through her the external environment with its variations.

Recognizing the roots of pains and fears

Lake and his colleagues argued that you do not have to know the cause of a pain to know you have a pain. You feel it, experience it—and that is enough. Many people went to Frank Lake because they could not understand why they were behaving in the irrational way they did, and mostly they were able to trace back their behaviour to what Lake called the negative umbilical affect—the result of maternal distress—or the maternal–fetal distress syndrome. The recovery of the prenatal memory, said Lake, healed the wound. It was a memory of a physical feeling that had become a part of their adult nature: a physical fear had become a psychological fear, which was no longer appropriate in the adult. Simon House writes:

> Lake himself liked the big scale so responded to the widespread urgent need for pastoral counselling. In some twenty years over 20,000 people attended the 1500 seminars run by his trained tutors (Lake, 1966). It was these seminars that led to his huge tome *Clinical Theology*, declaring his conviction that the birth trauma and separation anxiety were the root of neurosis. [House, 1999]

By 1976, living quite near Lake, I knew from friends and fellow-counsellors of his remarkably effective work. Lake would lead a "research group" of 20 members with 4 staff. He spent a day or two helping people to get to know and trust each other. He took notes on their life stories and why they had come, listening for any resonance with life in the womb. Throughout the day, even at mealtimes, he was describing the physiology of life in the womb, while on the walls were numerous pictures of the reproductive journey. He also had an imaginative repertoire of fantasy journeys: deep-sea dives, rocks and caves, and moving creatures. Thus prepared, one person at a time "worked" in each group of 4 or 5 people. One staff facilitated; one person tape-recorded, noting down body movements. Those working lay down on mattresses and cushions. Lake invited them to imagine themselves at the beginning of life and led them through the journey of sperm and ovum through conception to the womb and on through each stage to birth and sudden change in environment. As he established the validity of yet earlier memories, he began these journeys at an ever earlier stage.

Over 1,000 subjects had worked with Frank Lake on residential courses of three to six days in the United Kingdom, the United States,

Finland, Sweden, Australia, India, and Brazil. All the evidence he had gathered at these workshops, said Lake, pointed firmly to the first trimester as the time and place of origin of the common personality disorders as well as psychosomatic reactions, allergies, to food in particular, asthma, and migraine.

In *Migraine: Evolution of a Common Disorder* (1970), Oliver Sacks describes the primary role of migraine as a particular form of reaction to stress (Lake, 1966). Lake saw the reaction as originating in the negative umbilical affect. This negative affect accords with Sacks's other description of migraine as "a withdrawal from a noxious or endangering stimulus". The noxious stimulus could be a drug, such as alcohol, as well as the mother's distress.

Lake also describes irritable bowel and irritable bladder syndromes with ulcerative colitis as probably "displacements of negative umbilical affect". He even went so far as to attribute many present-day social problems to the rejection and violence experienced during the first trimester:

> You sometimes get the fetus trying to rip off the umbilical cord. And this may account for the violence of many young people who rip up trees, slash tyres, rip out telephones—the telephone wire is a marvellous umbilical cord.
>
> A number of probation and prison officers say, "The more I work with you, the more I see what's going on with people I've got in my care." Some of the violence that lands people in prison may well be an offloading of the violence experienced in the womb. [Lake, 1980b; cf. 1981 p. 131]

Lake extended this hypothesis of the maternal–fetal distress syndrome to sociology, anthropology, business administration, and every kind of leadership and membership of groups. He saw institutions that moved into constricting circumstances, with tight boundaries, guarded exits, confused internal states, as reaching down to similar patterns at the beginning of life. The "tight" group, afraid of invasion from outside, anxious to remain intact, created the "fetal trance state"—that is, living inside itself, refusing to communicate openly with the outside world through fear of negative feedback: their boundary was "the bad womb".

The health of the individual and that of the groups to which he belongs—the family, school, factory, and so on—greatly depends on the way we treat the pregnant woman and her unborn child.

f.   A word of caution

Just as no one should practise medicine without an appropri-ately skilled medical practitioner, so no one should attempt methods of psychotherapy without an appropriately skilled practitioner. The person seeking therapy should realize that they are likely to work at a deep level of the psyche. They need time before leaving the therapist to return to the here-and-now state of mind, with their attention out on their surroundings and alert to everyone's safety, and to be able to maintain that state of mind until a further session.

GENERATING HEALTHY, NON-VIOLENT PEOPLE

CHAPTER SEVEN

Preventing the imprint of violence

a.   The search for peace

The sense of peace, well-being, and prosperity is combined in the word *"salaam"* or *"shalom"*, which are basically the same. The spiritual quality most needed to achieve *shalom/salaam* is compassion, or empathy—terms that are central to religions. Destroying and negating these qualities are violence, depression, and degrading poverty. The great religions are often the first to work against these negatives, keeping to their original purpose of inducing *salaam/shalom* by enlightening people. Not that they are not alone in this; and religious elements have often notoriously shown themselves distinctly devoid of compassion or empathy, even exhibiting atrocious violence, however remote that may have been from the intentions their founders and true leaders.

Science, though no alternative to religion, has contributed to health and prosperity, although its record in drugs for mental disorders is mixed. Yet scientific evidence is now clarifying the effects of specific nutrients on a person's feelings and behaviour. This will help us to safeguard the qualities of *shalom/salaam* and empathy/compassion in the human make-up. Attention to both nutritional and emotional needs can contribute powerfully to peace and reduce personal violence.

There is nothing new about the idea that social and global peace need to spring from the hearts and minds of individuals. Raising the level of mental health will, in time, benefit the world as a whole.

Mental ill health often underlies violence, with its knock-on effect that knows no limit—we know that violence begets violence. Imprinting belongs primarily to early life. This may be by abuse, but often it happens unwittingly, for instance through forceps delivery or other intervention, combined with early separation from the mother. Nor is the "insult" switching to a violent tendency necessarily physical. It may be hormonal or nutritional; too much stress, toxins, or inadequate nutrients. Moreover, mental disorder is closely related cardiovascular disorder, and both to perinatal disorders. All three are forecast to be top of the global burden-of-disease list by 2020 (Global Forum for Health, 1998) (see ch. 8[c]), and each of them will cost more than HIV/AIDS or the other communicable diseases.

The human brain and the environment affect each other. Change of our environment by technology is accelerating, increasing dangers to the brain. We are capable of enhancing the globe with culture and comfort, or wrecking it with wars and waste, harmful processes and products. Currently the environment is deteriorating, in terms of nutrient depletion and pollution. In such adverse circumstances the brain demands our prime protection, most particularly during development.

b.   Safeguarding children's primal state

The tendency to violent behaviour is often imprinted though child-abuse, yet it can arise through difficulties at birth (see ch. 5[b] and ch. 6), an early operation or accident, or from poor nutrition or toxins. The more we know about such imprints, the more possible becomes their prevention during childbearing, and the better and better can they be healed, or at least the person can develop control. Frank Lake reminds us that few people are free from violent tendencies, either towards others or, hidden, towards themselves. About violence and restraint, he writes:

> When once the violence has been painfully and ruthlessly imprinted, the dynamics of retaliation are established and fixated. They

lurk in the shadows. The least hint of injustice in contemporary life can trigger off the primal violence. . . . The remedial structures are in emotionally costly . . . parenting, schooling, befriending and community caring backed up by just laws justly administered. . . . Restraint, however, is not the cure. Nothing radical has been done to heal the memories of violent assault and vile penetration, by promulgating ordinary law or even extraordinary love. [Lake, 1981]

There seems no better way to heal imprinted violence than through sensitive and loving guidance, as directly as safely possible, to recall of the moment of imprinting with emotional release of the original distress—that is, according to therapy described (see ch. 6). Lake, Janov, Stettbacher, and Miller relate violence on every scale—including torture and war—to violence in early life (House, 1999). None of them underrates the social and even global effects (Lake, 1981). Alice Miller, working with Stettbacher on her own childhood abuse, achieved integration. Having widely researched tyrannical dictators, she states:

The principle—"I am beating you for your own good: one day you will thank me for it"—can thus be found in the careers of all dictators, regardless of religion or culture. They call themselves the redeemers and saviours of their people, causing their subjects immense, unnecessary suffering apparently in order to help them. In reality, they are seeking to ward off the humiliations, threats, and anxieties of their own childhood. By holding hostage the world around them, by humiliating, blackmailing, and torturing their fellow human beings, they attempt to turn the tables on their past: they now perpetrate the terror, disguising it as philanthropy, just as their parents once did. [Miller, 1991]

The way that individual and corporate violence contribute to each other is the subject of psychotherapists Ludwig Janus and Winifred Kurth's study of psychohistory (Janus & Kurth, 2000). Alice Miller (1991) has revealed that all notorious brutal dictators—Hitler, Stalin, Saddam Hussein, and the rest—had as children suffered imprinting of violence, giving rise to social and international violence. When a person, especially at a young age, represses an experience of being violated, it can easily induce a compulsion to violate oneself or others. Caring education is needed for everyone, for all ages.

Konrad Stettbacher wrote of damage at an earlier stage that, though unintended, was having the same kind of effect:

Imagine a doctor yanking an infant out of its crib by the feet, holding it upside down and slapping it. Even in our culture, such a person would be regarded as crazy and a public menace. But a few days earlier, at a birth, such behaviour is sanctioned by medical practice. And this, at a moment when the child's central nervous system is at its most sensitive and educable. [Stettbacher, 1991]

Stettbacher, a specialist in child abuse as well as primal work, describes psychosis as an attempt to ward off a murderous past. He writes of the emergence of the soul, which constitutes our powers of sensing, feeling, and thought, of the entirety of our experiences and all our memories. He considers the continuum of the person, from their origin, through birth and childhood, to their resultant state in adulthood. From the beginning "the progenitors must establish an affirmative, responsible and caring relationship" with the child, so endowing it "with the feeling of security, trust and vitality." We should not lose sight of the continuum: lasting damage can ensue from child-abuse, or from prenatal and perinatal affliction (Stettbacher, 1991).

Adrian Raine (1995; also in Moir & Jessel, 1996) has shown a correlation between criminal violence and birth intervention followed by parental deprivation. The likelihood of criminal violence by the age of 18 seems to be some five times as great.

Paula Ingalls presents psycho-neural findings that both environment and experience are the architects of the brain. They can, even at conception, affect the zygote in a way that will be affecting development of the brain, and so the mind of the person-to-be, for life. Ingalls refers to Ronald Kotulak's (1996) interviews with over 300 researchers in various neurosciences. The consensus is that violence is caused by external stimuli reshaping the neural response mechanisms, rather than by intrinsic biology. Ingalls (1997) points to the last 25 years' "doubling of the rates of depression, suicide, crimes of violence, drug and alcohol abuse at a time of the doubling in divorce rates, less parenting time, poverty, mobility of the population, and an increase in technological pre- and perinatal care and birthing practices".

We can at least begin with children and the unborn. Parents and carers can help in children's primal healing, particularly if they know how best to cope with violent tendencies. Kernberg offers an invaluable guide on holding a child in a tantrum, together with a "time-out" procedure (Kernberg & Chazan, 1991; and see ch. 8[h]). This model can be used to heal while a child is still small enough for an adult physically to contain with gentleness. On the unborn, Lake writes very significantly:

> There is evidence to show that violence done to the mother, of whatever kind and degree, will distress her. Her distress is shared by the fetus. This maternal-fetal distress, both the impact on the fetus of being "marinated" in her miseries, and the fetal reactions which are so varied, tend to become the self's way of experiencing itself and perceiving both its cosmos and its core for the rest of its life. It affects most powerfully what can be believed, at heart and in the "guts", about justice in the universe, about God and man, as well as about institutions. It affects all groups in which individuals can be "homogenized". It projects onto the family and pervades all intimate relationships.
>
> Non-violence *then*, ensured by a priority given to the love and care of pregnant women, to providing understanding, expressive, genuine, and respectful relationships, would, I believe, be the best preventive we know of, to cut back on our present monstrous production of violent young persons. [Lake, 1981]

A 1970s leader in *The Times*, "Paranoia at the Kremlin", discussed the fear induced by atomic warheads trained on one's city, one's nation. It raised the feeling that, at a critical moment, the choice whether or not to "press the button" would depend on the cumulative level of *primal* paranoia in the members of government. Doubtless we can all recognize the symptoms Lake describes:

> If for political and economic reasons, recession bites into a school, reducing all manner of supplies and support, recognition and reward, the teacher with a record of prenatal deprivation can be plunged into the whole welter of primal feelings of persecutory loss, of placental deficiency, even of despair of survival. . . . As institutions move into constricting circumstances . . . the resonance reaches right down to similar patterns at the beginning of life . . . in the impersonal confusions of intrauterine existence. [Lake, 1981]

By safeguarding children's primal state, we can reduce society's root-cause of violence.

c.   *The sociological value of primal care*

Sheila Kitzinger is a social anthropologist and birth educator. Her research into midwifery around the world complements Lake's views. No one would deny that some births should happen in hospital, nor the need to have "high-tech" medical support reasonably near in case of emergency. But Kitzinger writes:

> Having a baby is one of the most important passages in your life. You feel the child develop and move inside you; in labour you swim with contractions that are like tidal waves sweeping through your body; as you push the baby down you know the intensity and passion, and then reach out with eager hands to welcome your baby and cradle this new life in your arms. To see love made flesh is to witness a miracle. [Kitzinger, 1991]

Nature has re-inspired industrial society. Watching African women giving birth vertically, in a secluded shady place, or by a river, first inspired Michel Odent. He notes: "When the anthropologist Marcelle Geber went to Kenya and Uganda to study the effects of malnutrition on newborn babies and infants, she was astounded to find that these babies were more advanced and smiled more than babies she had seen before in industrialized countries." The Ugandan baby was able to pick up a toy outside its field of vision at 6 or 7 months, compared with 15 months for American and European babies. This advanced development was credited to "a culture in which the period of dependence on the mother is not disturbed" (Odent, 1986).

In the South American Yequana tribe, the continuum of care experienced throughout the life cycle, in gestation and infancy especially, affect the people's whole wellbeing and healing, their harmony with nature and perception of death. In *The Continuum Concept* Jean Liedloff observes, during her three-year stay there, the Yequana's similar ease in raising children.

In a different context, comparing the effects of morphine with our own similar endomorphins (endorphins), Liedloff notes that those few addicts who survive for a long time while on hard drugs eventually attain their fill of what seems like the "in-arms" experience. This brings them a new sense of security, with a spontaneous freedom from the habit (Liedloff, 1975). With a new sense of security comes a new sense of values. Therapy at a profound level often brings such a change, a greater sense of being loved and of the ability to love, a reverence for life, empathy for other species, and ecological sensitivity (see ch. 11[c]).

Recalling memories from the limbic system of the brain can be disturbing. There can be contrasting moments, acute affliction, yet a sense of the infinite, even of bliss. Oskar Sahlberg (1999), extending Graber's (1974) view, believes that "ego boundaries" of the mystic are "strong enough to encompass and contain the energies of the prenatal dimension. But if these boundaries are not strong enough they will break and the result is a psychotic."

When people come to confront "the shadow", to face "the wilderness" in a search for their true selves, and perhaps to reconsider society and its ways, most people need a safe holding group. Francis of Assisi, like the man he followed, seems to be an outstanding exception. He surely was not psychotic. Even during his conversion and extraordinary perceptions of visions and voices, he could "manage his own ego boundaries". He did not offensively exceed the behavioural boundaries of local society, however seriously he exceeded those of his father (A. R. House, 2000). Francis's profound security was due primarily, no doubt, to exceptional mother–son bonding. His own remarkable transformation led spontaneously to the assembly of his own "holding group", in the safety of which his friends could manage their transformation.

Insight into the Franciscan transformation, personal and social, is clarified by today's psychology. And such transformations can, in turn, inform our work. We can see that Frank Lake, who, on the one hand, focused his attention on the single-cell human zygote, was equally passionate about transforming society:

> *Counselling, if it is not to be a flash in the pan, must have an institutional, socially validated group base, growing in relational caring and skills along with the individuals who are learning to care for their own hurt child with advancing skills.* The individual and the group must grow together. [Lake, 1981; emphasis in original]

And not only for therapy and growth, but for protection of coming generations, Lake urged those involved in childbearing:

> . . . *to give priority to the provision of a peaceful and harmonious environment for the mother.* [Lake, 1981; emphasis in original]

d.   *Psychological states relating to physiology of the brain*

We have already referred to the way psychotherapists have related psychological effects to physiological events in the womb, particularly Emerson (ch. 6[d]) and Lake (ch. 6[e]). In chapter 8 we look at the physiological development of the brain and its bearing on a person's psychological state. This is psychophysiology.

We have to look at the brain's physical sustenance and to see what it takes to feed a brain and keep this prime organ as healthy as possible. And that, of course, has a major bearing on keeping its owner psychologically healthy. Physical sustenance of the brain naturally takes us into the realm of nutrition—especially nutrition for development of the brain.

CHAPTER EIGHT

Nutrition to sustain the brain and mental health

> I know of nothing so potent in maintaining good health in laboratory animals as perfectly constituted food; I know of nothing so potent in producing ill-health as improperly constituted food. This, too, is the experience of stockbreeders. Is man an exception to the rule so universally applicable to the higher animals?
>
> Major General Sir Robert McCarrison, MA, MD, DSc, LLD, FRCP (1878–1960), Director of Research on Nutrition, India, *Nutrition and Health* (1953)

a.   *Mental health and diet: a global look*

Research studies are bringing to light the extent to which mental health is related to nutrition. National rates of mental illness and violence have been set against national levels of fish consumption, with remarkable results. Mental illness and violence are extraordinarily high where fish consumption is low. Homicide can be as much as three times as high. Depression can be 50 times as high (Hibbeln, 1998). We also find that nutritional supplements have a major impact on serious offences, including violence. This was demonstrated at a young persons' high-security institute, in a double-blind controlled trial (Gesch, Hammond, Hampson, Eves, & Crowder, 2002: see "Fifth window" in the following section). These are among many researches indicating the value of nutrition in keeping with our evolutionary environment and food selection.

As Sir Robert McCarrison—who was, incidentally, funded by the Medical Research Council—would remind people, nutrition is not just about diet: it includes the process of metabolism. Nutrition for healthy cell-life depends not only on diet but also on a good circulation of the blood, to deliver nutrients to the cells. So a poor cardiovascular system either of the baby or of the mother carrying him can mean poor nutrition of organs, including the brain. Moreover, heart and blood vessels require similar nutrition (Connor, 2000).

Sound nutrition is important, not only for building brain structure, but also as an appropriate setting for the various lifelong controls: genetic, metabolic, temperature, hormonal, allergenic, and immunal. The most significant effects of nutrient deficits and toxins throughout the reproductive process are outlined in "Generating Healthy People" (S. House, 2000).

Brain development does not proceed uniformly but in distinct stages, with varying degrees of need.

b.   *"Windows" in brain development*
      when nutrition is most significant

It is the rapid stages of development that are the most vulnerable to nutrient deficits and toxins (S. House, 2000). Accordingly, these stages are the most rewarding "windows of opportunity" for supplementation.

Conditions are needed to favour the brain's satisfactory development in respect of the brain regions and also the connections between them. Poor function of a region, or poor communication, will clearly affect the person's performance. Conditions also affect the setting of controls, which are like thermostats. They maintain stability, homeostasis, though not just of temperature, but also appetite, breathing, blood pressure, and mental as well as physical activity. Most controls are in the brain, and adverse conditions can affect their setting. From the time before conception, genetic controls are being set that adapt a child to the environment. As the brain and glands are being formed, more sophisticated controls begin to be set. Early life prepares the child for alternatives—for instance, either a safe and welcoming world with a feeling of being wanted, or a world of fear and struggle for survival; a world of plenty or one of scarcity; one of peace or one of violence.

Placental nourishment and breast-milk have specially evolved nutritional compositions. For this reason breast-milk is distinctly preferable to substitutes; better still if the baby receives it as part of the whole experience of breastfeeding and other touching, body sounds (Feldman & Eidelman, 2003). All these sensations, such as voices conveying emotions of adoration and playfulness, are setting the child's controls, to affect him all his life.

If the brain structures are poorly formed or if settings are not appropriate, the person can suffer a spectrum of disorders—"the metabolic syndrome"—including cardiovascular and mental disorders, diabetes and obesity. Obesity, the visible aspect of this burgeoning problem, has become a main target of Western governments. There is every reason that improved reproductive nurture could drastically reduce the problems of the metabolic syndrome.

A person's basic state of health comes from the effect on the genes of overall parental circumstances, especially the mother's. Protective nutrition ahead of rapid growth stages is best, building up stores for times of high demand, as with folic acid before conception. Since timing of conception is so unpredictable, a woman becoming at all open to pregnancy—and likewise a man at all likely to cause pregnancy—each need to establish and sustain a good state of nutrition and health for six months before conception.

The following are the *windows of opportunity* when optimal nutrition is most relevant for the brain:

1. *Before conception:* for sperm, ovum/follicle, and maternal body-stores.

2. *First trimester:* during neural tube development, at around 3 weeks of pregnancy.

3. *Third trimester & postnatal:* during rapid brain growth of the third trimester and after the birth.

4. *Puberty:* around puberty, during pruning and redevelopment of the brain.

5. *Late adolescence:* competing with heavy demands of late teenage body-growth.

First window of opportunity:
Sperm and ovum/follicle development,
building maternal body-stores

The first stage of high vulnerability is during the genesis of the sperm and the ovum-to-be (the oocyte). Sperm genesis and storage lasts some months. Sperm again seem to be extra vulnerable to nicotine, alcohol, and drugs taken during the last few days before being ejaculated.

The genesis of the oocyte has begun many years earlier, having taken place when the mother was still a fetus in *her* mother, the grandmother. All these oocytes lie dormant until a girl begins to ovulate. Then an oocyte, with its containing follicle, resumes its development, seven weeks ahead of ovulation, becoming vulnerable again, particularly in the two weeks before ovulation. The oocyte is now also accumulating food stores for its journey. Its surrounding follicle, too, must develop well, since it becomes the source of hormones to sustain a good pregnancy. Vulnerability peaks at fertilization, as ovum opens to sperm and sperm opens its contents to ovum, until the combination is sealed within this first cell of the new human being, the zygote.

This first cell, travelling on its eight-day journey down the fallopian tube to implant in the womb-wall, is dividing and multiplying, reliant on the stores built up before ovulation. Vulnerability remains high in the subsequent weeks, as the cells differentiate and the embryo's organs and limbs are defined. A full complement of nutrients is vital. To mention just a few of the many essential nutrients: magnesium is key in transferring energy for cell building; phosphorus in cell replication; zinc in DNA synthesis. Also needed in DNA synthesis is folate (or folic acid, vitamin B9). Folate's special importance in pregnancy is now widely recognized, yet generally people are still below the optimal level.

Throughout pregnancy and breastfeeding, the fetus draws on the mother's reserves, at a rate increasing with his growth. A reasonable restorative time for the mother, spacing of children by three years or so, is beneficial. Sufficient nourishment in advance, and constant replenishment, benefits the health of mother as well as of child and of any subsequent child. The gains to be made by pre-pregnancy care are exemplified by the convincing record of Foresight, an English group attending to couples in preparation, particularly to those with reproductive problems.

The Foresight approach recognizes that the future health status of a child starts at the preconceptual period. It addresses a basic plan for both partners, including family planning, awareness of dietary, environmental, and social factors as essential for both partners. It aims to correct or eliminate factors of imbalance in nutritional status, excessive smoking and/or alcohol consumption; genito-urinary infections, allergies, candida, and other intestinal infestation problems. They advise couples to continue with contraception until they achieve an acceptable state of health and nutrition and to choose contraception that avoids the undesirable effects of chemicals. It points out the danger of attempting to improve a woman's chances of pregnancy without establishing in advance her adequate nutritional state (Bradley & Bennett, 1995). Preconception care cannot be claimed as a new idea. Weston Price (1945) pointed out that the concept abounds in many traditions. To mention one, the African Masai tribe had specific times for marriage to ensure that the bride, and sometimes the bridegroom too, had had a few months on a highly nutritious diet.

We summarize below the analysis of Dr Neil Ward of Surrey University of Foresight's work with a particular group of couples. These results are not a controlled trial, but they do indicate that much can be achieved.

> A group of 367 couples attended a Foresight preconception program in 1990–92. It was monitored by Surrey University. Those regularly drinking alcohol amounted to 90% of males and 30% of females; those smoking, 45% of males, 57% of females.
>
> 59% of the couples had previous histories of reproductive problems (infertility, miscarriages, stillbirths, low birthweight, malformations, and sudden infant death syndrome).
>
> Follow-up in 1993 revealed that 89% (327) of the couples had given birth to healthy and well-developed babies, at 36 to 41 weeks, weight-range 23.68–41.45kg, with no multiple pregnancies.
>
> Because of couples' infertility, 42% of the men had semen tests, most indicating a reduction in sperm quality.
>
> For the 204 couples with infertility problems, success was only slightly lower than overall, 86%, and without any of the hazards of IVF (in-vitro fertilisation). [quoted in Bradley & Bennett, 1995, pp. 11–12]

Research shows the value both to fertility and to a child's lasting health of a well-nourished, toxin-free father as well as mother. Invaluable is the mother's build-up of her body-stores with the many nutrients for her child's major demands at various stages of development. Nutrition with toxin freedom is the earliest and most effective way to benefit the reproductive process and the child. A healthy body comes from a healthy sperm coming into a healthy ovum, to be implanted into a healthy womb of a particularly well-nourished mother. The younger the age that people learn this, the better the chances for their eventual childbearing. It may take the learning of a generation to appreciate and adopt such practice, but the effects are transgenerational.

The importance of bringing this home to people is highlighted in a report in *Pregnancy and Birth* magazine and relayed in the BBC News:

> The average age of those who responded was 29. While trying to conceive, 68% of all women said they continued to drink alcohol and two out of 10 admitted they drank "far too much". Of the 49% who were smokers, only 26% gave up the habit. Of the 47% of male partners who smoked, only 23% gave up.
>
> Unhealthy lifestyles—A third of the women and their male partners trying to conceive were overweight, according to the responses. [*Pregnancy and Birth*, 2005]

Those having difficulty can take heart from Foresight's success above, with the added realization that they are contributing not just to their chance of a child, but the likelihood of the healthiest child possible, contributing to the health of grandchildren too. Preparation well in advance will protect many a child from low birthweight and preterm birth. Foresight's practical work is complementary to that of the prenatal and perinatal societies. Coordination of insights can best benefit the lives of children to be conceived for generations to come.

The crucial alarm that alerted the world to the devastating effects of severe malnutrition on the unborn, even the unconceived, came from the Dutch hunger winter of 1944 (Stein, Susser, Saenger & Marolla, 1975; Wynn & Wynn, 1981). *The highest rate of mortality was among children* conceived *during the food shortage and in the four months following, rather than those* born *during the shortage* (see Figure 8.1). *Malformations* followed a similar pattern. Furthermore, those daughters who had been affected by the shortage subsequently had a high rate of problems with fertility, pregnancy, and offspring.

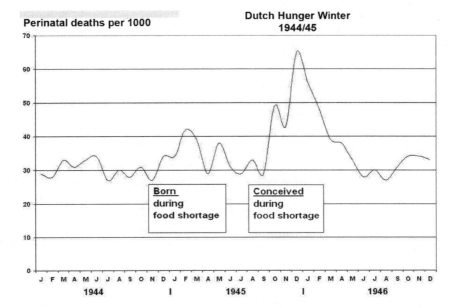

Figure 8.1.   Perinatal mortality highest when conception followed starvation.

Second window:
Neural tube development

At three weeks into gestation, the brain and nervous system are beginning to take shape. The embryo, an oval disc, curls around until the two edges meet and fuse, forming the "neural tube". If DNA growth is too slow, fusion along the neural tube will be imperfect. This can lead to lead to cerebral palsy, spina bifida, cleft palate, harelip, or other defects.

If there is incomplete fusion at end of the tube forming the rudimentary brain, it can affect the later development of connections between the left and right sides of the brain. Imperfect connections between regions will mean reduced signalling between, for instance, the brain's feeling right side and thinking left side. This would reduce a person's consciousness of their feelings, as in autism, and account for impulsiveness, compulsions, and reduced social skills.

Despite these connection difficulties, brain regions can develop well, and the brain's capacity for adaptation—"plasticity"—may lead to exceptional faculties: for instance, for memory, numbers, or drawing, as can happen with autism.

Autism was associated with damage from the drug thalidomide, which affected this stage of development (Rodier, 2000; Skoyles, 2002). It is also associated with genetic factors.

Simply as an anecdotal illustration, we mention a boy recently on television who at the age of 12 had already written a remarkable book, could speak splendidly in public, but had difficulties with close relationships, typical of Asperger's syndrome, and autistic spectrum disorder. This boy also had signs of a harelip and a wide mouth turning down at the sides, indications of too slow a fusion of the neural tube.

There are other formative signs at the neural tube stage: lines appear across the tube, visibly beginning demarcation of the spinal column and brain, doubtless into forebrain, brainstem, cerebellum, and so on (Hill, 1999). Again, if this demarcation is imperfect, presumably connections due across them between regions could be prejudiced, for instance between the rational neocortex on the one hand and feelings limbic system on the other. In this case there could be restriction of signals controlling conditioned reflexes, as in those liable to violence. Brain imaging of people with a tendency to violent behaviour does reveal poor signalling between regions. Given genetic susceptibility, there are, of course, other factors on the way to early childhood that may ameliorate or exacerbate autism: maternal emotions, the birth process, bonding, mental stimulation, and physical activity.

These neural tube problems are most often associated with deficient vitamin B9, folic acid—or folate—a shortage of which slows down DNA formation (S. House, 2000). The greatest reduction in malformations and complications was demonstrated in Hungary by Andrew Czeizel (1995), with folate at 0.8 mg/day and, notably, vitamin B12 and zinc, among other nutrients. Folate is said to be the most commonly deficient nutrient in the world, due primarily to inadequate diet. The name "folate" connects with foliage, being plentiful in leafy vegetables, spinach, broccoli, and asparagus (NIH, 2005). Meats and animal food—with the exception of liver—are poor sources of folic acid. Some cereal foods are fortified with folate. The United States fortifies bread, and now the United Kingdom also fortifies some breads.

Although preconception care is best, sometimes when a woman reports her pregnancy it may prompt the doctor to supplement her diet, which, even at this stage, can still reduce risks.

Many other vitamins and many minerals are essential to health. General demands on the mother naturally increase with the size of the fetus. Specific demands increase according to type of cell replicating rapidly. Toxins from smoking, drinking, drugs, or pollution can displace nutrients and damage cells. Conversely, plentiful minerals and vitamins can reduce some of the damage (Furst, 2002), as can pure water.

Third window:
Rapid brain growth in third trimester and postnatally

The reason for this third window is that the brain grows most rapidly in the third trimester—at double the body's rate—and continues to grow rapidly in early infancy. So the brain in particular is drawing more and more heavily on the mother's supplies. One essential nutrient is the omega-3 oil docosahexaenoic acid (DHA). It is indeed essential to the brain, of which it forms 10%. DHA is not always in good supply. The brain receives priority, yet there are other calls for DHA from the cardiovascular system and other organs, including the retina. In fact, the cell membranes of each of the trillion cells in the body need it. There are other omega-3 oils, and omega-6s, but we are focusing on DHA as the most important for the brain.

A fuller, more technical exposistion

The mother's supply for her baby, through the placenta, then the breast, is adapted for each stage to suit the child's needs. Preterm babies present a particular demand, being prematurely deprived of placental DHA; babies take all the DHA they can get through the placenta, so depleting their mother's supply, and she can make little DHA, and the baby less, if any at all (Crawford et al., 2003). For the preterm baby in his incubator, even the mother's expressed milk will not have reached its DHA potential before his *due* birth-date (Bitman, Wood, Hamosh, & Mehta, 1983; Leaf, Leighfield, Costelloe, & Crawford, 1992). During this gap the preterm baby critically needs supplementation, particularly with DHA. DHA is not only essential in cell-building but also affects genetic expression (Helland & Smith, 2003; Williams et al., 2001; Uauy, Hoffman, Peirano, Birch, & Birch, 2001). It appears from studies that birth prematurity itself may be reduced by fish oils supplementation.

A second essential oil, an omega-6, is arachidonic acid (AA). Protection of both DHA and AA levels, of either preterm or full-term infants, optimizes conditions for the development of membrane-rich systems, including the brain and nervous and vascular systems (Crawford, 1993). Formula milks specifically designed with both DHA and AA can achieve this (Crawford, 1993; Crawford et al., 1997; Farquharson et al., 1992; Makrides, Simmer, Goggin, & Gibson, 1993; Neuringer, Anderson, & Connor, 1988). Formula feeds may include the precursors of DHA and AA, but in these early months infants cannot convert them to DHA and AA.

We can gauge the importance of DHA in development through assessing children's levels of intelligence and eyesight:

- The Avon Longitudinal Study of Parents and Children (ALSPAC), ongoing, is publishing increasingly on this aspect (ALSPAC, 2006).

- Children's IQ and high-grade stereo-acuity correlate with their mother's DHA supplementation in pregnancy.

- Breast-fed one-week-olds demonstrate superior neurobehavioural organization (Hart, Boylan, Carroll, Musick, & Lampe, 2003).

- Children fed on (early-1990s) formula milk rather than breast milk were found to score significantly lower at one year in psychomotor performance (Bjerve et al., 1992; Ghebremeskel et al., 1999; Koukkou et al., 1997).

The effects of nutrition during the short postnatal period seem to be lasting:

- At 3 years, full-term babies on formula milk scored lower on visual and stereo-acuity and letter matching (Birch, Hoffman, Hale, Everett, & Uauy, 1993).

- At 8 years, preterm babies on formula milk had lower IQs than breast-fed babies. In contrast, at 4 months LC-PUFA-supplemented full-term infants, whether breast-fed or formula-fed, registered higher levels of neurodevelopmental response as well as raised blood levels of AA and DHA (Agostoni, Trojan, Bellu, Riva, & Giovanni, 1995); preterm infants could be expected to benefit even more.

- Levels were assessed of two groups of full-term infants' visual acuity and blood DHA. Both groups were on formula milk, but those supplemented with DHA sustained the same levels of visual acuity throughout their first year of life as those fed on human milk whereas those inadequately supplemented fell below (Birch, Hoffman, Uauy, Birch, & Prestidge, 1998).

The mother also can gain from supplementation. Postnatal depression correlates with low DHA in breast-milk, just as depression in general—and many disorders—correlate with low blood-level of DHA (Wang et al., 2003). A fetus or infant suffering this combination—DHA shortage and a depressed mother—is doubly unfortunate. Not that DHA is the only deficit with such results, which can be due to deficits of manganese or zinc (Bradley & Bennett, 1995), which in most if not all other mammals are boosted by consumption of the nutrient-rich placenta.

The potential contribution that these essential oils can make to our health is well summarized on the website of the US National Institutes of Health (NIH, 1998).

* * *

Every child-bearing woman should check that her supply of DHA is adequate. DHA status can be measured by a blood test. A swab of the cheek cells inside the mouth is also possible, although not so accurate as a small blood sample. Since Professor Michael Crawford's research group at the Institute of Brain Chemistry and Human Nutrition discovered the essentiality of DHA for brain development and function in 1972, they have pioneered these tests and given advice to many hundreds of people on how to respond to inadequacies (www. londonmet.ac.uk/ibchn_home).

Our understanding of priorities in infant feeding and weaning has benefited from a remarkable pioneer in maternity care a century ago. The meticulous record-keeping she instigated have, related in the last decade to the state of health of many of those babies who reached 60, indicated guidelines for long-term healthcare. In 1905 Miss Ethel Margaret Burnside, a vicar's daughter, was appointed Hertford County's first ever "Chief Health Visitor and Lady Inspector of Midwives", setting up an "army" of trained nurses to attend births and advise on babies' health. She established record-keeping that enabled the birth-weights of 60,000 people born between 1911 and 1944 to be stored. These were invaluably traced when babies had reached their sixties.

Professor D. J. P. Barker was able to check their cardiovascular health, health problems, and mortality against their having been breast- or bottle-fed and age of weaning. Barker, showing the effects of prenatal growth and infant diet on the cardiovascular health of men and women into their sixties, makes the all-important conclusion that cardiovascular disease originates in the womb and is related to infant feeding (Barker, 1998). Maternity and infant guidance is clearly a key way to tackle this and associated disorders. Imaginative and purposeful long-term recording schemes are clearly valuable.

(We should mention that a further window for supplementation may well be found at 3 to 5 years. During this stage the child's neocortex is becoming "wired up". By 5 years it is so powerful that it has become the seat of consciousness, leaving previous memories in the limbic system in "the unconscious".)

Fourth window:
Puberty—pruning and redevelopment of the brain

The reason for this fourth window is that puberty brings on a stage of pruning in the brain of the excitatory synapses. This we learn from the Norwegian neuroscientist Professor Letten Saugstad (2001, 2004). If the timing of puberty is near the norm, a brain will be less vulnerable to certain disorders. But if the timing of puberty is early, pruning happens more quickly and may be inadequate—and today's statistics of mental disorder doubtless reflect the younger maturing of children. Conversely, when timing of puberty is late, it lasts longer, and there can be excessive pruning. So early puberty leaves the brain more excitable, with possible swings between manic and depressive moods, while late puberty can leave the brain under-excitable, possibly prone to straight depression.

Treatment of these two problems—arising from early or late puberty—with antipsychotic drugs runs into difficulties: the two types of disorder require different drug types. On the other hand, a sufficient intake of marine oil "has a normalizing effect at both extremes of excitability". Part of the current dietary problem is sugar: it took Saugstad only two months "to demonstrate the malign effect of our high saturated-fat/sucrose diet". Marine oil, which is non-fattening, "may correct the altered brain activity in the obese". Saugstad finds it worth adding that in Norway their wartime switch from meat to fish "was accompanied by a significant decline in hospital admission for acute psychosis".

Fifth window:
Late adolescent brain competing with heavy demands of body growth

People often comment on the appetite of boys in late adolescence—"bottomless pits"—and they need plenty of the right nutrients. Although the brain receives priority for nutrients, it can suffer from the too-great demands of a large body growing rapidly. The problem is like that of the large mammals evolving on the savannah. For the rhinoceros, body enlargement was more advantageous than brain enlargement. Consequently, body competed successfully for DHA at the cost of brain—and the huge animal was left with a tiny brain. Boys in late adolescence, already large but still growing, have a similar internal competition for nutrients, restricting brain supplies of DHA and other EFAs (essential fatty acids) and of vitamins and minerals. Well-designed nutrition has now been demonstrated substantially to benefit the mood and behaviour of boys and young men.

A nutritional trial assessed the behaviour of boys in a high-security Young Offenders Institute (Gesch, 2002b; Gesch et al., 2002). "This is perhaps the only time when *the developed brain competes so strongly with the rest of the body for precious nutrients*", commented Professor Bernard Gesch, Oxford University, conducting the double-blind controlled trial. In the group supplemented with vitamins, minerals, and EFA, *serious offences, including violence, dropped by 35%* (Gesch, 2003). Gesch referred to nine other nutrition trials showing pronounced improvements in mood and behaviour. These feature in a UK Parliamentary report, *Diet and Behaviour* (Associate Parliamentary Food & Health Forum, 2003). Amazingly, the Prison Service decided against following up on Gesch's success. The research was sponsored by the charity, Natural Justice, a Trustee of which—General Sir David Ramsbotham, until 2001 Chief Inspector of HM Prisons—told BBC Radio 4 Food Programme that this is "totally infuriating as well as being extremely stupid"—especially when Tony Blair had famously promised to be *tough on the **causes** of crime* (Gesch, 2002b).

A combined programme for children promises even greater rewards than for late adolescents, says Gesch. Adrian Raine's studies are among those corroborating this (Raine, 2002; Raine, Brennan, & Mednick, 1994; Raine, Mellingen, Liu, Venables, & Mednick, 2003). A group of Mauritian 3-year-olds received a programme of enriched diet and exercise, in addition to being read to and having conversations. By the age of 11 they demonstrated increased brain activity on brain-scan read-outs, and by 23 they were 64% less likely than the control group to have criminal records. The most striking effects were in those most malnourished when they started the programme with its fish-rich diet (Raine et al., 2003).

The Chair of Natural Justice said of the Aylesbury study: "The study is of great importance not only to those who work inside prisons but also more widely in the community." In the second half of the last century offences in England and Wales rose by eight times. It is not genes that have changed in this time, but nutrition. It is becoming clearer and clearer that many behavioural problems have physiological origin in development, alongside those with a psychophysiological origin. Since heart and blood vessels are the route for nutrient supplies and waste, also for the brain, they are also of high priority, especially during development. The prime answer seems clear: do whatever possible to prevent the physiological problem in the first place and ameliorate any impairment possible, thereby stemming criminality at its roots.

c.   *Violence and depression correlate negatively with fish consumption and DHA*

Gesch's findings are corroborated by cross-nations studies showing powerful negative correlations of rates of violence and depression with fish consumption. To show us these remarkable statistics—symbolically, it seemed—within days of the suicide attacks on New York's Twin Towers, biochemist and psychiatrist Joseph Hibbeln, from Washington, flew in to London on a near-empty plane. Suicide, homicide, and depression, he demonstrated, are at much higher rates in nations eating little fish than those eating plenty. How do their rates of violence and depression compare? Low-fish-consuming nations can have rates of suicide that are twice as high, homicide six times as high, and depression some 50 times as high. Details are shown in the graphs and tables below.

Shocked by the drama and tragedy of the violent acts of 9/11 or other terrorist acts, we may overlook the intrinsic personal factors. In attempts to deal with such problems of aggression, we may fail to consider measures to tackle this root of the problem: the isolation, depression, and violent tendencies that underlie suicide pilots and bombers, warmongers, and brutal dictators. Without such a state of mind they may have looked for gentler solutions to their problems. Improving diet on the widest scale possible is clearly in the world's interest.

A child's brain may not develop fast enough, during the rapid growth stage of the third trimester and early months of feeding, if the mother's own cardiovascular system is poorly developed and not up to the heaviest demands. Plentiful DHA is vital, especially to the fetal brain and cardiovascular system.

The strong correlation of homicide with low national levels of fish consumption is clearly shown in Figure 8.2, assembled by Professor Joseph Hibbeln.

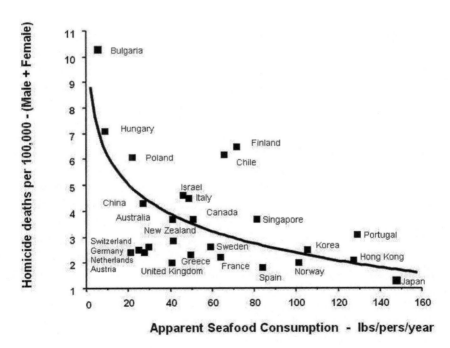

Figure 8.2.   Homicide rates (WHO, 1995) correlate inversely with consumption of seafood (Hibbeln, 2001a, 2001b).

To emphasize the remarkable degree of variation, these are a few examples, closely in keeping with the lines of the graphs:

- People in West Germany eat 1/5th as much seafood as those in Japan and have 40 times the rate of major depression.
- People in Central Europe eat 1/10th as much seafood as those in Iceland and have 20 times the Bipolar Depression.
- People in Central Europe eat 1/10th as much seafood as those in Portugal or Hong Kong and have 2 times the suicides.
- People in Eastern Europe eat 1/10th as much seafood as those in Japan and have 6 times the suicides.

Undoubtedly, if lake and river fish were included, the result would be largely similar. A relatively large seaboard has, at least in the past, clearly made fish more available, practically and financially. New Zealand, with its outstanding seaboard, has a remarkably low seafood consumption but as it "went overboard" on sheep, this is not so surprising.

Hibbeln's many graphs show similar curves and correlations of suicide and depression with the consumption of fish and DHA. In an upsurge in the inrush of suicide pilots and bombers into the Western world, these figures have acquired a heightened significance when we consider in such attacks the element of desperation and suicidal tendencies that must contribute to the attack. A further graph, particularly relevant considering the effects of mother on child, both physiologically and psychologically, is shown in Figure 8.3: the correlation of postnatal depression with low DHA in breast-milk.

The WHO Global Forum for Health (Global Forum for Health, 1998) portrays in Table 8.1 how important it is that we reverse these trends. In fact, the upper four diseases shown in the graph all have a bearing on each other. Nutrition of the brain, as of any part of the body, depends on a good blood-supply as well as food-supply, so mental health is related to cardiovascular health. Such "non-communicable diseases" worldwide are currently responsible for more deaths than the sum-total of all deaths from HIV/AIDS, malaria, tuberculosis, and all other infectious diseases, as Sir Kenneth Stuart (2004), previous chief medical advisor to the Commonwealth of Nations, told the Letten Symposium.

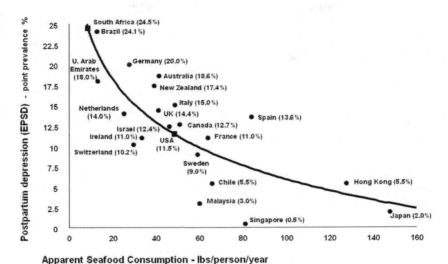

Figure 8.3.   Postnatal depression correlates inversely
with breast-milk DHA (Hibbeln, 2001a, 2002).

Table 8.1.   Mental, heart, and perinatal disorders rising to top
of disease burdens

Top Seven Global Burdens of Disease		
	1990 actual %	*2020 forecast %*
Coronary heart disease	3.4	5.9
Perinatal conditions	6.7	5.7
Depression	3.7	5.7
Cerebrovascular disease	2.8	4.4
Lower respiratory infections	8.2	3.1
Tuberculosis	2.8	3.1
Diarrhoeal disease	7.2	2.7

Source: Global Forum for Health (1998).

143

Tackling these diseases is of high priority, for economic reasons as well as human ones. Britain's two highest financial costs in ill health are heart disease and psychiatric disorders, counting workdays lost and medical costs (Rayner, 2004). "Scientists present the most powerful evidence yet that neuro-psychiatric disorders relate to inappropriate nutrition, costing 25% of NHS funds and 25% of national working capacity", as the McCarrison Society heard from the Director of the British Heart Foundation, Dr Mike Rayner (2004).

Likewise, the Food and Health Research spokesman (Winkler, 2004), echoed a *Lancet* (2004) editorial, maintaining that health policy failure was in large part due to a failure of food and nutrition policy to serve the interests of the human blood vessels, heart, and brain since the end of the Second World War, therefore affecting two generations.

Low maternal levels of DHA correlate with a child's subsequent poor brain acuity and attention-deficit hyperactivity disorder (ADHD) (Stevens et al., 1995). The prevalence of ADHD has risen rapidly in America, where fish consumption is low, and in Britain, where it is falling.

The low incidence of heart disease among Greenland Inuits, Japanese, and Icelanders is attributed to the high proportion of marine fish in their diet, Though the introduction of industrial-style marketing is beginning to tell on their health, and they would do well to take note. There is growing evidence that DHA plays an extremely important role in the prevention and treatment of atherosclerosis, thrombosis, and high blood pressure, of inflammatory conditions such as asthma, arthritis, migraine, headache, and psoriasis, and of cancers such as breast, colon, and prostate.

Despite omega-3 oils, classified as "fats", having featured prominently in research for a decade, some writers are still maligning fats indiscriminately, thus confusing the public. Owing to their importance in cell-building, these essential oils are termed *structural fats*, distinct from the more solid, saturated animal fats termed *storage fats*, which are dangerous in the amounts commonly consumed. It is essential that authorities make it clear that "highly unsaturated fats", including the omega-3s, have totally different effects from saturated fats, and that omega-3s (mainly algae/fish oils) and omega-6s (such as arachidonic acid) are vital and need to be in the right balance, preferably no more than 3 omega-6 to 1 omega-3.

d.   *Our unique brain evolved by seas, rivers, and lakes*

When we look at the brain's biochemical make-up and evolution, the correlations shown in the previous two sections ([c] and]d]) between an aquatic diet and mental health make sense. Some 10% of the large human brain is composed of docosahexaenoic acid (DHA). For most of us, our only plentiful supply of DHA is fish. Their rich source is algae, seaweed, and microbes. There is increasing evidence and agreement that we lived by the water's edge during the rapid development of our neocortex, from a 100,000 to 10,000 years ago—so we were close to fish, particularly easy-to-gather shellfish, so accessible to pregnant women in their greatest need of plentiful DHA.

The limitations of carbon dating had misled palaeontologists into believing that the remains of Homo sapiens found in East Africa's Rift Valley were 40,000 years old, and consequently they insisted that our ancestors had developed on the dry plains, the savannah. In the 1990s electron-spin dating revealed that these remains were not 40,000 but 100,000 years old—a time when the sea reached to the Rift Valley. Also, human remains have since been found from this age, accompanied by fish bones and shells.

Our ancestors spread along the shores of the world, by seas, rivers, and lakes. Meanwhile the savannah dwellers that grew much larger—lions, rhinoceros, and so on—were left with brains relatively smaller. Why? Their DHA supply on the savannah was strictly limited. As their bodies enlarged, they had to eke it out more sparsely throughout their system. The squirrel has a brain proportionately larger than ours, but only because its body has remained small. The only large mammals with brains comparable in size to ours are the marine mammals. Diet is the most significant aspect of environment, which drives a species' evolution and sustains it (Crawford & Marsh, 1995; Morgan, 1982). While our ancestors continued to live close to water and fish, their brains developed 30 times faster than Australopithecus, who went inland, having to make do with meat, and faster also than Neanderthal, who also went inland.

We can trace DHA further back through the evolutionary tree to the blue-green algae, 2.5 billion years ago in the primordial soup. These blue-greens became so prolific that they began poisoning themselves with the excessive gas they gave off. The gas was oxygen. This "poison" gas was to give rise to new life forms, becoming their very "breath of life". Fish emerged, who feed on the blue-greens and whose fertility depends on DHA. Our ancestors, descending from the trees to seashores, rivers, and lakes, relished the fish and shellfish. On their DHA our neocortex grew outstandingly, between 100,000 and 10,000 years ago. Our modern DHA intake is low. It has dropped in the last 10,000 years to a quarter of our mean intake over the previous 100,000 years. The need for such supplementation comes basically from our moving away from hunter-gatherer foods of the wild and the waterside to foods of farm and factory.

e.   *DHA: the exceptional molecule*

Of the essential oils, DHA is the longest chain and has the most double bonds. This makes it the crown of a range of omega-3 and omega-6 oils irreplaceable in our diet. On it depends our mind, our behaviour, our social well-being as a race. Not surprisingly, this is an intriguing molecule.

DHA = docosahexaenoic acid, from the Greek,
            indicating the structure:

     docosa   hexa   enoic   acid

     22 (carbons)   6 double-bonds

$$CH_3-CH_2-(CH=CH-CH_2)_6-CH_2-COOH$$

C: carbon atom;   H: hydrogen atom;   O: oxygen atom;
$-$: single bond; $=$: double bond

Of the great range of essential oils, including the omega-3 fish oils, DHA is the most elaborate—a long chain of 22 carbon atoms with a remarkable 6 double bonds, meaning 12 fewer attachments than if it were saturated. Being uncluttered, this molecule folds characteristically, rendering it a semiconductor with properties of controlling electron flow, which is important in signalling. This explains some of its importance to the brain, retina, heart, and so on. Arachidonic acid (AA) is an omega-6 oil that also has particular significance perinatally. Full-term, full-birthweight babies have remarkably high levels of AA. Low-birthweight or preterm babies only have a mere fraction of these levels, due to poor nutrition or having been born before full accumulation of AA could be achieved. Most probably the two factors operate together (Crawford, personal correspondence). It is also valuable in countering any cell damage in vessels.

f.   *Preventing criminality at its roots:*
      protecting and healing people young

"Genome studies have shown that the way a puffer-fish clots its blood in response to injury is exactly the same as in every vertebrate 'upwards' to man", said Professor of haematology Edward Tuddenham (2001). Without change, this blood-clotting system has sustained us through our evolution for nearly half a billion years. It is not the genes that have changed, it is diet and lifestyle; and we can correct them. Our cardiovascular problems include a huge thrombosis epidemic with high mortality, much of it caused by changes in blood-clotting. This epidemic has swept through economically advanced human populations in a mere 150 years. Since our blood-clotting system has not changed, says Tuddenham, "clearly some environmental change, soil or food production/consumption, has impacted our ancient genomic heritage in unexpected and deadly ways", including changes to the brain and behaviour. "The cure must lie in returning our diet towards its premodern state" (2001).

The rapidity of change is evident in the sharp rise in ischemic heart disease (IHD)—poor blood circulation to the heart. In a mere 45 years—1925 to 1970—the rate of IHD for men of 50 to 70 years has multiplied 700 times—to 700 per 100,000 (Morris, 1951, quoted in Tuddenham, 2001). This is due, no doubt, to the increasing popularity of smoking as well as changes in diet, including excess saturated fat, sugar, and salt. It was possibly aggravated by the drift from the 1950s onwards away from the celebrated "fish and chips" towards broiler "chicken and chips". This chicken had much more saturated fat than did fish and, not being wild, had lower nutrient levels. By 1990, nations that ate 900g of seafood/week/head retained cardiovascular mortality rate as low as 3 per 1,000. For nations where this was reduced to 110g of fish/week/head, the rate escalated to three times that level. In such places cardiovascular disorders seem bound to impact transgenerationally on brain development, and so on behaviour (Hibbeln, 1998).

g.   Truly "tough on the causes of crime"

Individual responsibility is an essential principle. Yet a criminal's behaviour is likely to result from psychological imprinting before the age of responsibility, making it all the more important to look for healing. A movement to replace the punitive justice system with one for healing and restitution is centred internationally at Simon Fraser University (*SF NEWS*, 1996). Their well-prepared document on trauma as mitigating evidence (International Justice Project, 2002) stresses the practicality of choosing healing over punishment. It discusses

- the prevalence of early trauma and abuse within those convicted of violent crime and specifically capital murder;
- the context in which such abuse should be both presented and understood;
- the emotional, psychological, physiological and neurological impact of such experiences upon a developing individual (Patterson, 2002a; see also 2002b):

  There are a lot of men like me on death row—good men—who fell to the same misguided emotions, but may not have recovered as I have. Give them a chance to do what's right. Give them a chance to undo their wrongs. A lot of them want to fix the mess they started but don't know how.

Early trauma, or insult from toxin or nutrient deficit, can have effects similar to those of abuse. Insult from a nutrient deficit or toxin can certainly predate conception and have a traumatic effect on the child. *The best way to be "tough on the causes of crime" is to prepare for the beginning of each life.*

Objective pre- and perinatal understanding can bring to millions the chance to benefit their own moods and behaviour and help in the protection and healing of others. Appropriate diet can heal some early damage and can prevent damage to those yet to be conceived.

Deficient nutrition is having devastating effects on our society and is likely to become worse. With 2 million children living in food poverty in the United Kingdom (Gesch, 2002a) and dietary standards that do not take brain development and behaviour into account, a potential social time-bomb is apparent. Sound diet and ready supplementation could transform society. In Professor Gesch's words, "*The brain needs to be nourished in two ways, the love, nurturing and education we all need, and also the nutrition to sustain our physical being.* We need to develop our understanding of the dosage and range of nutrients required to positively impact behaviour. *It may be a recipe for peace.*"

The objective information on depressive and violent behaviour is converging from many angles to build a watertight case for concerted action for protecting and healing. The world is calling for this. The World Health Organization's 2002 *World Report on Violence and Health* (WHO, 2002) is rooted in the conviction that we can prevent violent behaviour rather than simply accepting or reacting to violence. WHO is looking for an interdisciplinary science-based investigation of violence: its causes and correlates; its risk factors modifiable through interventions; the cost-effectiveness of implementation and dissemination. The Report recognizes that violence begets violence, particularly during gestation and delivery. Other early factors, for instance the roles of *bonding and nutrition* in preventing violent tendencies later, also need to be added to this Report (WHO, 2002, pp. 30–47).

The evidence for our approach is a strong case for WHO to apply it globally. It makes profound economic as well as humanitarian sense. Nelson Mandela introduced the WHO Report with these words:

> The twentieth century will be remembered as a century marked by violence. . . . Less visible . . . is the pain of children who are abused by people who should protect them, women injured or humiliated by violent partners, elderly persons maltreated by their caregivers, youths who are bullied by other youths, and people of all ages who inflict violence on themselves. This suffering . . . is a legacy that reproduces itself, as new generations learn from the violence of generations past, as victims learn from victimizers, and as the social conditions that nurture violence are allowed to continue. [Mandela, 2002, p. ix]

Action can protect us from generating people with violent tendencies, and there is all this evidence and far more that can be used. We can prevent damage that causes people to become a danger to themselves and to others—sometimes to others in their millions.

h.   Gently tough on misbehaviour

At some point we have to face the argument that we have to be tough, we have to discipline the criminal in society and the misbehaving member of the family; that the attempts of psychotherapy to release from anxiety and guilt are mistaken; that conscience needs strengthening, not weakening (Mowrer, 1961). Yes, if the person has been acting against an informed and just conscience, Mowrer would be right. True penance—perhaps costly—is needed, with a full apology to the appropriate person and due reparation, as opposed to what Dietrich Bonhoeffer (1937) termed that "cheap grace" that some presume in sacramental forgiveness. The essential basis is generating a right sense of conscience, in family life, in social groupings, and more extensively.

Yet each of us can recognize an undeserved sense of guilt. Children have much guilt put on them, particularly in cases of abuse, and Mowrer lived before the epidemic of abuse was recognized. Also, guilt feelings, being in the limbic system rather than the neocortex, are not so easily released. This usually takes psychotherapy.

Clearly, much can be done to combat compulsive misbehaviour, and the younger the better. Children in the same family can be so different: one so responsive, another so obstreperous. It is probably not their fault so much as luck, or bad luck. Boundaries are needed, and reward and penalty systems. A skilled consultant can be invaluable with an unusually difficult child, whose parents inevitably ask: "Why is this one so difficult, when the others are so easy?!"

Particularly for the child with violent tendencies, Paulina Kernberg and Saralea Chazan have a beautiful way of resolving a child's tantrums. One of the hardest tasks in a family is managing a compulsively violent child in a tantrum and discovering a form of discipline that benefits rather than damages. With most children punishment works, provided it is also related to a reward system. With a few, punishment is self-defeating. The child becomes desperate. He is losing, losing, it seems, his life, because he is into a primal memory—very probably a birth memory. And neither he nor his parents have any idea what is really affecting him. If punished, he feels "lost", as if his life is lost. There is no more to lose, so why submit? Just fight desperately.

Start early, says Kernberg, if possible when the child is small and less difficult to hold. In as friendly and comforting a way as possible you say: "I am holding you until you are calm and able to be quiet on your own." She calls this "time out"—on the stairs or in his bedroom. A large child may need two adults for restraint. Kernberg (Kernberg & Chazan, 1991) says: "It is most unusual for this holding procedure to require more than a few applications. Once the child has become accustomed to time-out procedures, he may initiate them on his own." Here is a way through an impasse with a compulsively violent person that heals, giving him an experience through which he can learn to hold himself. Her description sparked a memory of one day arriving on board ship when a man nearby suddenly fell writhing to the ground. He was simply saying *"tenez moi, tenez moi"* ["hold me, hold me"], so we all reached out and held him firmly, until gradually his fit—apparently epilepsy—subsided, and he got up and gratefully walked away. His uncontrollable movements were quite a different sort of disorder, and not damaging to anyone else. Yet some people subject to compulsive violence seem to enter a kind of nightmare world, a panic of rage, losing touch with the shared world of other people. If there is the strength to hold them in love, particularly as children, there seems to be hope that their fears are reduced, their instinct of trust of others and themselves increases, and they can gain in calmness and self-security.

Paulina Kernberg's concept of *holding* seems more than good practice. It offers a valuable icon of good holding, from the child's beginning; from holding the child psychologically in the womb, with loving and welcoming thoughts, to psychological holding of the distraught adolescent or adult with friendly, gentle firmness.

CHAPTER NINE

Protecting and regenerating our nutritional environment

a. *Soil regeneration is a must
for mineral and vitamin supplies*

We are discovering how rich and unpolluted we need the soil, sea, and air around us to be, and how precise the supply of nutrients has to be, to generate and sustain healthy people. Soil-science, marine studies, and human nutrition discern the drastic effects on our basic physiology of our failure to respect soils, crops, and animals; oceans, rivers, and fish. Medical and nutritional studies reveal the effects of ill-advised farming and food processing and presentation.

If our environmental base is to sustain us, we have to sustain our environment.

The farmer has long recognized how the quality of feeding his sheep, cattle, and other livestock affects the new offspring. For countless generations he kept his best fields and feed for the run-up to the mating season. His forbears had observed the advantages of preconception nutrition in large samples of newborns. At last we are beginning to catch up in the human field. In trials, scientists have now monitored thousands of women bearing children, confirming the farmer's reproductive wisdom, but, ironically, his best fields are no longer what they were. Soil minerals have on average dropped by half, over half a century. Soil minerals in North America have, indeed,

**Table 9.1.   Earth Summit mineral depletion analysis:
percentage drop 1939–1991.**

Minerals drop in soil		Minerals drop in fruit, vegetables, & meats			
Continent	Soil	Mineral	Fruit	Vegetables	Meats
North America	85	Sodium	29	49	30
South America	75	Potassium	19	16	16
Europe	72	Magnesium	16	24	10
Asia	76	Calcium	16	46	41
Africa	74	Iron	24	27	54
Australia	55	Copper	20	76	24
		Zinc	27	(59)*	n/a

Source: UNCED (1992).
*From 1978 only.

dropped by 85%, to a mere 15% of what they had been (Table 9.1).
We used to replenish soil by growing "green compost" crops such
as clover, or through crop rotation, sometimes leaving land fallow.
Now that replenishment is usually limited to chemical fertilizers, es-
sentials other than nitrogen, phosphate, and potash may be neglected.
Even the application of nitrogen can have adverse effects (Stockdale,
1992).

Here are a few examples of how soil mineral deficits are threatening populations. Magnesium is key in transferring energy for cell
building; magnesium deficiency before mating can damage male or
female germ cells. Phosphorus is key in cell replication. Zinc is essential to DNA synthesis (S. House, 2000). In practice, where conditions
are healthy and food plentiful, we can get these complex requirements
quite simply. Nature assembles many vitamins and minerals in fruit,
vegetables, meat, and fish, and particularly in reproductive cells,
seeds, nuts, roes, and so on. A mineral currently attracting attention
is selenium, relevant to cardiovascular disorders and mood-effects,
among other aspects (Guvenc et al., 1995: Rayman, 2002), Breast-
milk has been monitored in relation to selenium intake and supplementation. The soil in some countries in Europe, New Zealand, and
Australia has low levels of selenium, whereas that of North America
is high. Finland's high rate of cardiovascular disorders fell when the
Fins began applying selenium to their fields with the fertilizers. Since
selenium binds with mercury, it provides some protection against

any accumulation of mercury through currently low-risk amalgam tooth-fillings, immunizing injections with mercury-based preservative, or pollution.

b.   *Safeguarding DHA resources to sustain the brain*

Of the essential oils, DHA is the most complex. It is the longest chain with the most double bonds. We cannot readily constitute it ourselves (Spector, 2001). This has kept us dependent on oceans and inland waters. So far we have relied mainly on fish to collect DHA for us, but now the human species is in trouble. First many populations abandoned the waterside, but although cold-food transport expanded, few people realized the importance of fish to the health of our lifecycle. The dependence of the human brain on fish for healthy development and maintenance constitutes the prime reason for protecting fish-stocks for the future. There *are* signs of hope. Scotland is breeding shellfish as well as fish. The healthy Japanese appetite for quality fish drives fish-spawning. Brittany's coast has small companies marketing algae products. Tunisia's marine research is advanced.

Open restocking of waters is preferable to confined farming, which is more susceptible to disease and contamination of wild breeds. One valuable suggestion is to designate zones of the oceans to be guarded internationally from fishing or damage (Holmes, 2001; Channel 4 TV, UK, 2001). Meanwhile, as human populations industrialize and expand as never before, we are polluting the oceans and decimating fish-stocks, dragging their seabed habitats to death and in places illegally blasting them (Holmes, 2002). We have begun making fish a danger to ourselves with pollutants, dioxins, and mercury in particular. As well as eating more oily fish, many people are buying supplements, including omega-3 oils in capsules. These at least preclude mercury, which is not soluble in oil.

The effects of pollution on the marine food chain was discussed by Torger Børresen (2004) from SeaFoodPlus, Denmark. Despite some reports, lack of marine oils is a higher risk than that of toxins through fish, which is lower than through some other universal foods. Børresen was optimistic about the role aquaculture would play in the future, but policy makers need to act.

Japan, Hawaii, China, and the United States are among those counties where algae, chlorella at least, are farmed. Chlorella and spirulina have the added property of binding heavy metals, so cleansing the body of them, as well as recovering them industrially (Dubacq & Pham-Quoc, 1993; Hudson & Karis, 1974). A pioneer company in marine products, Irish Scientist, is selecting micro-algae for their EPA (eicosapentaenoic acid) and DHA content. "An alternative source of EPA and DHA will have to be found. The micro-algae would seem to be ideal" (*Irish Scientist*, 1999). Moreover, DHA is produced by photosynthesis, binding carbon to counteract the greenhouse effect.

Land-crops too can benefit from the sea by seaweed-spreading— the old practice of "wracking"—so replacing minerals and other nutrients. Meanwhile we could improve our soil, recycling our minerals more efficiently rather than diverting our nutrient-rich sewage to pollute our seas and inadequately replacing them with fertilizers too limited in range of minerals (Marsh, 2002).

The bulk components of organic matter are carbon, oxygen, and hydrogen, and there is plenty of those around in farming conditions, but they do not grow living cells without minerals, which, being elements, cannot be made by living things, only transferred. Unless they are already in the soil, they have to be added by livestock, birds, or man himself. Soils need monitoring. Nutrients that are not in soils or sea cannot reach our bodies. The toxins in them do. For continuing replenishment we have to harmonize with nature's symbiosis (Robertson, 2001).

c.   The danger of taste in a changing world

Taste has evolved at its own slow pace in relation to environment and survival. A sweet tooth was once an advantage when richly nutritious fruit and honey were scarce. A craving for sweetness spurred the hunter-gatherer into greater efforts for these rare nutrients, bringing fitness, fertility, and survival. No doubt salt and fat were less prolific too; again, a taste for them would favour those genes. But now a sweet tooth spurs children and adults alike to sugary sweets and drinks, and a taste for salt and fat for salty fries.

Alas, the food-chain operators are adept at low-cost simulations of the sweetness of fruit and honey, presented with every lure, the bright colours of berries, the gloss of freshness reflected in shiny packaging. The manufacturer may be unaware of the damage these substitutes do to consumers directly, or indirectly by diverting them from essential nutrients towards harmful counterfeits. On a faulty diet, the body continues is search for needed nutrients, which keeps the person feeling hungry, so inducing obesity and prejudicing healthy tissue. Then dieting too intensively has its dangers. The body's fat-stores reduce, but their breakdown products, for instance, may increase any cholesterol threat to the cardiovascular system, or stored fat-soluble pollutants released may threaten elsewhere. Hence the value of colon cleansing for those on a diet.

We cannot evolve our taste at the pace that we are changing our environment. But we can educate it. *We need expert guidance in educating our tastes; and in husbanding the soil and waters and air around us.*

d.   *A practicable approach out of complex research*

The market is not geared to nutritional quality for health but to consumer appeal and financial profit, with inadequate controls to protect the consumer's health. Education could enable the consumer to select a sound diet, avoiding harmful items, but food-labelling needs further clarification. Greatly improved health would be the priceless and cost-saving effect of these measures. The evidence is that savings in terms of workdays lost and health services would mean many times the expenditure, let alone gains from the improved educational results (Winkler, 2004).

How can producers meet these real consumer needs and appropriate legal requirements? By redirecting their animal breeding and feeding towards best nutritional values rather than sheer weight alone. This means returning breeding, rearing, and feeding closer to wild stock and conditions, which some farmers are now attempting. Compared with today's farmed meats, wild meats can have five to ten times the ratio of valuable nutrients to saturated fats. Cultivating a wider range of vegetables and herbs would provide a greater variety of nutrients, more akin to the hunter-gatherer's foraging in the wild. Informed consumer choice can help to drive the market, steering farmer and manufacturer towards more nutritious produce (Crawford & Marsh, 1995; Robertson, 2001).

The basic principle for optimum nutrition is that many nutrients are needed at particular levels of concentration. For instance selenium, which is toxic even at quite a low level, is an irreplaceable nutrient at trace level. The body's need of oxygen in plenty calls for protection of cell-tissue from an excess of oxygen ions. This is another role fulfilled by some essential oils and also vitamins, acting as antioxidants. The art is in keeping components of our environment, particularly our food and air and water, as close to optimum levels as possible.

Anything we can do to establish wild-type food production is most valuable, but for today's billions some supplementation is needed. Scientific guidance for the general population could be extended more specifically to accord with individual body dimensions, condition, stage of life, lifestyle, and activity, including exercise. The most essential time for specification is in the likelihood of fathering or conceiving a child and during pregnancy and breastfeeding.

Applying natural principles could remedy the main problems that complex science has revealed. Wild foods from the sea are falling short, though there is a wealth of fish we throw back dead because marketing has not caught up with its quality. For most of our food, farming land and sea being inevitable, we must employ the healthiest and most sustainable ways. Algae-farming could reduce malnutrition. A return to local growing and selling, even to home-growing, could produce healthier food and more exercise, as once achieved during the wartime "dig for victory" campaign when we maximized local use of land. Allotments, "farmers' markets", and many organic producers are, at least, on the right track.

CHAPTER TEN

Objectivity and action

a.   *The objectivity of the evidence is powerful*

Objective evidence has accumulated that violent behaviour arises from early psychological and physical conditions, having long remained merely anecdotal. We have seen that Freud himself, as well as Rank, Winnicott, Lake, and others, perceived psychological scarring as coming from birth and gestation. Qualitative analysis is being corroborated by quantitative analysis. Raine showed that obstetric forceps or other birth intervention, combined with separation from parents in their first year, correlates with increased criminal violence (Raine, Brennan, & Mednick, 1994).

Groundbreaking work in the *biochemistry of emotions* began in the 1980s. Candace Pert (1998) showed bliss, stress, and shock to be recognizable as molecules in the bloodstream and acting on receptors at nerve synapses. Biochemistry has become an objective common ground for understanding both nutritional and emotional imprints on a child from at least conception. At a time when Frank Lake was facing an early death in 1982, Pert and others were clarifying some of the biochemistry that underlies what Lake perceived: the ways that a child in the womb seems to experience his mother's emotions, and their lasting effect on him. Lake's conviction that the impact of the mother's emotions was greatest in the first trimester is objectively corroborated by Curt Sandman's studies (as explained in ch. 6[e]). Pert's work has also substantiated Michel Odent's (1986) findings that in the first hour from birth, natural closeness and tenderness can bring bliss to mother and child. All being well, she is flooded naturally with endorphins and oxytocin—"love hormones" that are essential to their *bonding*.

Lake (1981) was already clear from his own cell biology studies and those of his neuroscientist associate Karl Pribram (1971) that pre-natal and perinatal memories were scientifically feasible (as related in ch. 6[e]). They recognized that cells remember, and that they resonate with each other through radio vibrations, some having short-term memory, some long-term. Numerous experiences recounted through-out Part C corroborate these findings of Lake's, and verified instances of imprints originating from attempts to abort, or even from a desire to do so, as Ridgway (1987), Renggli (2003), and Piontelli (1992) record. Mothers are often shocked at finding themselves pregnant, and this tends to imprint on the child, who may have a tendency to depression or violence. If a mother's shock had been simply at her pregnancy, or telling her husband of it, her child's tendency to violence might be slight. If she had suffered violent abuse during pregnancy, her child's violent tendencies could be stronger.

For decades pioneers in nutrition, endocrinology, obstetrics, and psychotherapy had held that individual development was depend-ent on the immediate environment. This view was confirmed by the Genome Project's surprise count of a mere quarter of the human genes expected—some 35,000 against 150,000—showing the *flexibility of genes and nurture's powerful impact on nature*. In *Nurture and Human Development*, Bruce Lipton (2001) demonstrates how genetic expres-sion is highly susceptible to environment, corroborating Lake's con-clusion, and also Crawford's (Crawford & Marsh, 1995) that nutrition drives evolution. These scientists provide hard data of nutritional and emotional imprinting by maternal-fetal environment.

Darwin's theory has often been quoted as "survival of the fittest", which was, in fact, Herbert Spencer's interpretation that Darwin was never really happy with. Darwin had written about those "best fitted for their places in nature". Lipton, however, perceives, along with Darwin's view of natural selection, a process of "survival of the most loving". Scant nurture or other severe conditions will programme the new being for anxiety about survival: generous nurture will pro-gramme a child for trust, love, and creativity, for reproducing and nurturing (Lipton, 1998).

Despite theories of genes for violence, there seems no evidence of violent behaviour arising without it being imprinted or caused by damage. There is a mutation of the gene MAOA (metabolizing en-zyme monoamine oxidase A), which in children correlates only after maltreatment with nine times the risk of violent behaviour (Caspi et al., 2002). This version of the gene, with a lower level of expression, is associated with a slower rate of breakdown of the biochemicals of anger. When a spell of anger lasts longer, there is an increased chance of its breaking into violence.

The general recognition of the ways in which nutrients and toxins affect brain development and subsequent behaviour is quite new. DHA's vital role in brain evolution, related to our ancestral waterside life, did not start to gain wide credibility until the 1990s. Pioneer-ing views, such as Michael Crawford's (Crawford & Marsh, 1995) affirmed Darwin's much-overlooked "Law of Unity of Type and of the Conditions of Existence Embraced by the Theory of Natural Selection" (Darwin, 1842, 1859). And among conditions of existence, nutrition is key. The way we attend to human brain development and evolution from now on could scarcely be more important to the future of our species and our planet.

This increasing objectivity of prenatal and perinatal psychology and medicine will increase the power of conviction. We deal with two kinds of evidence: on the one hand, hard scientific evidence such as double-blind controlled trials, and molecular evidence, such as biochemical interactions; on the other hand, subjective evidence from experience of life, particularly in psychotherapy. As we integrate the various aspects, we need to distinguish anecdotal evidence from scientific, not to undervalue qualitative analysis but to support it with quantitative analysis and hard evidence.

Objective evidence has accumulated on the physical effects of nutrient deficits or toxins on the embryo or fetus. Inevitably any psy-chological effects are less objective, but chapters 1–6 reveal the sheer weight of evidence, despite its being anecdotal, accumulated by large numbers of people through recall during regression. We have to con-sider what may be psychological effects of acute hunger in the womb? For some years now scans have revealed intense reactions of babies in the womb against toxins, nicotine, or alcohol. The emotions of the hungry baby, yelling for the next feed, are plain for all to see and hear. The bliss of the well-fed baby is visible. It is naturally hard to imagine a tiny embryo suffering such pangs or enjoying such satisfaction—at least, it was hard until thousands of adults were individually convinced by their own experience that they were recalling their sense in the womb of feeling hungry, poisoned, unwanted, or, alternatively, of bliss. Cumulative evidence is now overwhelming that somehow early cell memory can later arise powerfully into consciousness, revealing sometimes a sense of well-being, but sometimes a psychological scar (House, 1999; Wilheim, 2002).

Objective evidence confirms that nutrient deficits, or toxins, at such early stages can be physically more damaging to the individual than at any subsequent stage. We now know some of the effects on a child's physical health from adverse conditions as early as oogenesis and spermatogenesis. Fetal demand is a hugely powerful drive. The embryo or fetus has many times the mother's power to draw certain nutrients from her, partly thanks to his "placental pump", which intensifies concentrations of nutrients in his favour. We know that until the third week of gestation, there is no functional placenta, and even then the placenta is far less effective at screening toxins than once believed. Much of the process of gestation is biochemical, electrochemical, and electronic. Even though we cannot yet prove the psychological manifestations of the physical processes, it would seem unscientific to ignore their possibility, if not their likelihood, in the face of the evidence.

Altogether, the findings contribute to a growing impression, from the moment of fusion of sperm and ovum, of the embryo's psychosomatic unity: that body and mind develop as one. Memory is not confined to the brain. Cell memory operates throughout the system. What is happening to the embryo or fetus physically is registering in memory and can later, at least, be recalled at a conscious level. Any good or any harm, physical or emotional, that comes to this small person, is to the lasting good or harm of the whole person, body and mind—good that can be passed on down the family and out into society.

Until recent decades, there had been a block in human consciousness blinding us to the life, memory, and awareness of the unborn child and to the power of events imprinting him or her for life. We are at least now realizing the huge effects on the unborn child's mind of the mother's diet, as well as her emotions. Nutrition and emotions

impact on structure and memory—on "hardware and software"—
profoundly affecting later moods and behaviour.

* * *

We have reached a stage when so much of the evidence is objective, showing the way to a healthier, more peaceful life. How are we
to project it? We have been involved with a London Metropolitan
University team for research and publications, and networking internationally. We have had many conferences, some international, and
regular publications. One small initiative, for example, is educational,
in some London schools. Another in newly independent Wales is
political.

b.   *In schools: healthy eating, exercise, and lifestyle—
practice and education*

We visited a London school where the healthy breakfast club
is the head teacher's focus for improving the children's health. They
also have occasional healthy eating events, sharing foods from their
50 different cultures. In the United Kingdom schoolchildren up to the
age of 7 receive fresh fruit every day. In this school the children do not
just eat the daily fruit given, they are told why it is so important for
themselves, and also for the health of any children they may have one
day. Some grow food in pots and on allotments, and they are given
more opportunity for exercise and games. The school has a grant to
convert part of its large playground into a new garden for fruit and
vegetables, and to create their model of ecology. These children eat
and drink more of the right things and less of the wrong ones, and
they are learning and choosing a healthier lifestyle. This marks the
start of an ongoing process of transgenerational learning, for healthy
children promoting a healthy world.

In this way we can begin to achieve life-cycle health, safeguarding generation by generation. At any stage in the life-cycle, education
focusing on the reproductive process can contribute to the health of
subsequent generations. It can prevent the most serious damage and
achieve gains in intelligence and behaviour (Crawford & Marsh, 1995;
S. House, 2000; Marsh, 2001). The most cost-effective way is surely to
set girls and boys in the way of *sound nutrition and understanding of its*

importance before conception as early as possible in life. This means that more couples will already be in a healthier state before they conceive. Educational programmes as they become more likely to conceive will find them too preoccupied. Margaret and Arthur Wynn (Wynn & Wynn, 2001), who have written prolifically on nutritional care from before conception, deem *free school-meals of quality for every child the most cost-effective means to improve the health of a population.* It is a good way, for one thing, of catching future parents young, especially the children in greatest need. The message has at last got through to professionals and the public that nutritious meals improve behaviour and learning. Good school-meals not only nourish children; they are the basis of their education in healthy eating—a point that the provisioners hopefully grasp.

c.   *In politics: action on the food-chain of a small nation*

Our science-based advice has been valued by the newly independent Government of Wales mainly through the Food Alliance of Wales. Wales is working towards policy integration between health, nutrition, agriculture, fisheries, ecology, and tourism. The country has idyllic aspects: traditional hill-farming, sheep among mountain streams, green fields, woods and rivers, long coastline with splendid fishing potential, all in need of protection. Much of Wales is still farmed freely, rather than intensively, helping to conserve quality. This is hugely important when you consider the drastic drop in soil minerals over recent decades (UNCED, 1992; US Senate, 1936). At the Earth Summit in Rio in 1992, the US Senate presented the figures for soil mineral contents and resultant depletion in fruit and vegetables (UNCED, 1992; see Table 9.1).

The Welsh policies may avoid some of the modern farming methods that deplete and pollute the soil. Impacting of the land by the heaviest machinery would be reduced with modified machines, in order to destroy fewer earthworms and other valuable organisms. The Welsh Food Alliance has been standing out against genetically modified (GM) crops. The new upsurge of organic farming and the public's avid uptake of organic foods could possibly herald a realistic future for the land. Costs for such care will be high in the first place, but not as high as ruining our agricultural base; and in the long term conserved soils will contribute to human health. Already some rewards are being recognized. Welsh research has just shown that organic (*biologique*) milk contains three times as much omega-3 oil, raising it to about one-third the level of breast milk.

Along the beautiful coastline of Wales, with cliffs and rocks, birds and beaches, you will yet find shellfish and fish, though her waters are not pollution-free and are over-fished with catchall nets slung between boats. Not far away monk-fish are taken at half-size, half the age for fertility. Protecting young fish and re-stocking the oceans— rather than intensive fish-farming—is vital, and the health of the human brain depends on it!

d.   *Coordinating insights for action*

Everything is registered electromagnetically and biochemically in molecules, genes, and tissue-cells in the hardware and software throughout the system (Lipton, 1998; Odent, 1984). But our detailed understanding of human nature is like a fragmented mirror. It fails to reflect a complete image (Odent, 1999). If we can integrate the many specialist views, we shall have a truer reflection of human nature's strengths and flaws, a more complete vision of ways to protect and heal, and the best hope for generating healthy and peaceful people. Convey this vision to as many professions and people as possible, and we shall have a healthier, more peaceful world.

We urgently need a cultural re-evaluation of childbearing and its most significant needs. This concerns the whole lifecycle:

- communicating appropriately with politicians, professionals, and public;
- health education through each stage of our lifecycle, focusing on reproduction;
- establishing a scientifically sound culture.

The prenatal and perinatal societies—the International Society for Prenatal and Perinatal Psychology and Medicine (ISPPM), the APP-PAH, and, notably, *Congress 2002* in Nijmegen (Congress, 2002)—have taken us into many aspects of childbearing that have lasting effects on the child.

In January, 2006, my "Generating Healthy Brains" conference brought together ISPPM with the McCarrison Society for Nutrition and Health and the Institute for Brain Chemistry and Human Nutrition, with speakers of world standing on the various aspects. Together we are naturally trying to coordinate attention to the very beginnings of human life. Nutrition and toxins are the earliest factors in an individual's development that respond to care and need our fullest attention. This will be not just for the individual and the family, but for society as a whole and for the peace of the world.

PART D

PSYCHOLOGICAL HEALING AND PROTECTION

CHAPTER ELEVEN

Ways that a mother affects her child

"Following 2000 women through pregnancy and birth, Dr Monika Lukesch, a psychologist at Constantine University, in Frankfurt, West Germany, concluded in her study that the mother's attitude had the single greatest effect on how an infant turned out."

Thomas Verny, *The Secret Life of the Unborn Child* (1982b)

a.   *Pregnancy: attitudes*

In all societies there have always been those who believe that the outcome of pregnancy depends largely on the mother's own feelings and experiences, which are imprinted on the child in the same way as a film projector throws an image onto a blank screen. For thousands of years the Chinese have believed in creating a pleasant, relaxing atmosphere for the pregnant woman. The unborn child has been regaled with song and poetry. He is treated as a human being from the moment of conception. When the child is born, he is regarded as being one year old—presumably allowing three months for preconceptual preparation! This much, at least, modern research endorses.

Many Vaishnav Hindus believe that reading aloud religious literature—not fiction—throughout pregnancy influences the intelligence

169

and moral character of the newborn child and makes it easier, later in childhood, for him to learn the verses (or *slokas*) he had heard *in utero*.

In Victorian times women "in a certain condition" were advised by their doctors to avoid unpleasant experiences and expose themselves to pleasant stimulations; and educated women might visit art galleries—if they dared go out at all when they were "big with child"—or go to concerts and listen to the "good" sounds of classical music in the belief that this would produce offspring who were not only healthy, but also cultured.

Between the wars we went to the other extreme, and pregnant women were given *carte blanche* to behave more or less as they wanted, so long as they did not hit the bottle. They were told not to cosset themselves or worry about the outcome, but to carry on as far as possible living a normal active life. The trouble was that women tended to neglect what they frivolously called "the bun in the oven" because they believed that whatever they did, he was quite tough and could look after himself. They not only lived a normal, active life—which in the 1920s and 1930s was not always a healthy one—but made very little attempt to understand what was happening to them and how the child would change their lives.

Attitudes, however, began to change after the Second World War, when studies that I have described came to the conclusion that not only physical illness but also maternal stress could have a harmful effect on the fetus, producing behaviour disturbances in the child. But although much more attention is paid to antenatal care nowadays, and the physical needs of the mother and her unborn baby are well understood and usually taken care of, there is still a great deal of ignorance regarding psychological factors.

In recent years there has been an avalanche of information about psychological influences on the prenatal development of the child of which not even the average gynaecologist or paediatrician is aware in any great detail, let alone prospective parents.

Many of us in the West pride ourselves on knowing what is best for our children, but as a matter of fact Western children are retarded in the way they develop, both physically and emotionally, compared with the traditionally reared African baby—though the sad state of many African countries is clearly a hindrance to this today. But even when Simon House was in Uganda for two months, as General

Table 11.1.   Relative ages by which children reach motor-development stages in Africa and in the West

	Western baby	African baby
Holds up head	3 months	1 to 1.5 months
Picks up toy outside vision*	6 to 7 months	15 months
Sits up without support	7 to 8 months	4 months
Stands up and walks	12 to 14 months	8 months
Learns to run	24 months	12 to 14 months

Source: M. Geber in Uganda (Odent, 1986)

Museveni—President-to-be—was clearing out the gangster armies, he was deeply impressed by the closeness of community life, by the people's warmth and resilience from bereavement and shattering times. The traditional African mother is far closer to her child and much more aware of what is going on before birth; after birth, she will carry the baby everywhere with her on her back, which meets the neonate's need for continuous close contact. Table 11.1 shows the progress, in good times, of an infant in an African family compared with the Western baby.

In 1979 the US Department of Health, Education and Welfare, in reporting this, pointed out some of the things that I have emphasized in previous chapters—namely, that research shows that a child is affected by the emotional state of the mother before birth: a relaxed, well-nourished, well-prepared mother is necessary for a good pregnancy; and that newborn babies can see, hear, taste, smell, feel, and so they are learning from the beginning.

In her book *The Continuum Concept,* Jean Liedloff (1975) tells the story of how she and her Italian colleagues, who were searching for diamonds in the South American jungle, came across a tribe of Indians called the Yequana. She was fascinated with the way they lived their lives, working hard, sometimes doing the most arduous tasks, but always with good humour and always knowing "the right thing to do". They were, said Jean Liedloff, part of the jungle's ecosystem, as much as the plants and animals.

In the jungle Jean Liedloff had to help haul a large canoe, made from a tree trunk, inch by painful inch over rough and difficult terrain. She was tired and hot and sore, her knees and ankles cut and bleeding through rubbing against granite rocks, and she hated every moment spent working like this in the blistering heat. But the Indians just laughed and joked and did not complain once as they helped to haul the canoe. For them "each forward move was a little victory, enjoyed to the full". In their language there is no word for "work". They don't divide their lives into work and play—things they enjoy and those they don't.

So, of course, pregnancy and childbirth are natural and enjoyable; and the baby is always lovable. It is this "lovableness", so evident in Indian children, that—Jean Liedloff decided—is the natural condition of a baby or young animal not too far removed from our own species (you might not call young snakes or spiders lovable!). Lovableness in the baby is his way of getting attention. Even animals—wolves in particular—have been known to pick up a human baby, take it away to their den or lair, and take care of it there.

So what has gone wrong in many present-day Western homes, where mothers find pregnancy and childbirth so difficult and sometimes depressing and where babies are not always regarded as particularly lovable?

To so many of us the reason seems clear. It is the way we live, the way we think, the way we are searching for solutions outside ourselves to problems that arise within ourselves. It is our general attitude to all kinds of problems: we approach them mostly from our heads, not our hearts. It is our attitude towards ourselves and all our relationships, including our relationship to things, to our house, our car, our deep-freeze, and so on—the possessions we spend our lives protecting because we have invested so much of ourselves in them. All this has created tensions in society which affect everyone, including the pregnant woman and her unborn child.

What can we do about it? We are hooked to our way of life, and it is going to be as difficult and painful to cure ourselves of our addictions as it is for a junkie to give up heroin. But there is hope—there is hope because there are so many people now who are aware of what's wrong.

To see the problem only in terms of what is happening outside is to deny what is going on inside. Fundamentally, there is very little difference between the conflicts in the world and the conflicts within ourselves. Once we stop putting all the blame on others, we can take responsibility ourselves.

Individually, conflicts go back a long way—at least to childhood, but more probably to parents and grandparents and great-grandparents. We remain the victims of victims, until we somehow break through our internalized oppression. We need to wake up from what James Joyce described as "the nightmare of history".

Without blaming anyone, it is possible to start making some small changes in ourselves. The insights of people like Freud, Jung, Adler, and, today, Carl Rogers, Abraham Maslow, and Fritz Perls have shown us the way. Fritz Perls talked about "gaps" in our lives—the "unfinished business" of the past, the things we left undone in childhood. These are the things we need to do to fulfil ourselves—Maslow would say, to become "fully human" or "fully functioning".

Jean Liedloff (1975) puts it this way : "Missing experiences continue as a need as the deprived infant grows up and throughout his adult life. We go on seeking fulfilment of our infantile requirements. But as we have not been clear about what we are seeking, we have met with limited success."

The first step is to try to get to know ourselves a little better (although this may require some guidance in the first place); that does not mean listening to what others tell us, but actually listening to ourselves. It means paying attention to the things we have been writing about in this book: to the creative productions of the unconscious—to dreams, for instance. For a woman, childbearing tends to spark off early memories, dreams, and pictures.

b.   *Pregnancy: four dreams*

Dreams, as a route to the unconscious, can be interpreted in different ways, but the important thing is that they are *your* dreams: every image in a dream is a part of *you*, representing a subjective feeling. You need to own each image in turn. Some dreams are straightforward, dealing with some emotional problem and providing an obvious solution, which you could have worked out for yourself in your waking life; some are sexual, others seem to be archetypal. Their interpretation is a creative act, best carried out in the early morning between sleeping and waking, before the ego defences come into full play; later you may refuse to believe what your dreams are telling you if it is some unpleasant truth about yourself. Many dreams express, as Freud believed, unconscious wishes or fears, as demonstrated in the dreams of pregnant women. Pregnancy can produce a flood of conflicting emotions—perhaps a sense of triumph followed by feelings of apprehension and doubt and then worries about the birth. All these emotions can influence the dreams of a pregnant woman. The following material from four dreams of Ann C—who could be almost any pregnant woman today—is reported, with interpretations, by Dr Mildred Bressler-Feiner:

Ann C's four dreams in pregnancy

A—Conception:
In the first three months of my pregnancy I had several dreams of having a baby but not telling anyone. In these dreams I deliver a baby after going through a full-term pregnancy and don't tell anyone for a couple of days. Then I think that maybe I should tell everyone. Consciously I think that I am not really pregnant because I am not sick, just tired. (This dream is a clear message from the unconscious indicating Ann's ambivalence and denial of the reality of being pregnant—M.B.)

B—Growing:
In this dream the baby is big. He's not a monster, but there are funny things physically. The baby is big, like a two- or three-year-old child. (The manifest content of the dream reflects Ann's fear that her child may be born deformed. Ann's anxiety is a universal one—M.B.)

C—About breastfeeding:
I actually have not told anyone this dream because I felt embarrassed. This dream is about cats. I am nursing my cat, Meagan. I have had this cat for ten years and the cat is at my breast and I am cradling her in my arms. (According to folklore, cats are symbols of femininity. It may be that for Ann the cat is a representation of her childlike self and her wish for nurturing. The implication here is that Ann might have difficulty in assuming a mature role towards her own child. Apparently Ann's perception of breastfeeding is that it is bizarre and embarrassing instead of a normal pleasurable process. Ann's comment that she felt embarrassed about telling her dream is revealing. It is typical of people's reactions to dreams that deviate from cultural norms—M.B.)

D—Six weeks before birth:
I walked down a corridor holding a baby. Then a man came to-wards me with a long skinny knife. (In this dream Ann seems to be expressing two thoughts. The corridor seems to represent the birth canal through which the baby will be born. The knife is obvi-ously a phallic symbol and her reference to it seems to suggest re-sentment towards her husband's role in her impregnation—M.B.) [Bressler-Feiner, 1981]

Ann's dreams are typical of the dreams of many pregnant women whose fears never surface in their waking life. Her dreams were in-terpreted for her by a Freudian psychoanalyst, but there is another way Ann herself could have dealt with the dreams. In Gestalt therapy she would have been advised, if she wanted to work on her own, to write the dream down and make a list of all the details. Just writing it down, in a notebook by the side of the bed, can have an amazing effect. Sometimes you discover that you have been dreaming in puns, and sometimes Freudian slips are made. For instance Roy Ridgway tells us:

I once had a dream of a fox who had lost his tail; and when I was writing it down I wrote "tale" instead of "tail" and the meaning of the whole dream came to me in a flash. "Tale": my lifescript; "fox": the cunning child who had grown up with a script, as I had, "to please". As Sartre said, you can either live your life or tell a story; I was telling a story: it was all false. That, basically, is what the dream was about; and a slip helped me to understand it. [Ridgway, 1987]

The Gestalt therapist's client, however, is advised not to interpret, not to think too much—"lose your mind and come to your senses". After making a list of all the details in her dream, Ann would then have to transform herself into each of the different items—the mother, the baby, the cat, the skinny knife. "Ham it up and really become each item. Really become that thing, whatever it is", said Fritz Perls at a dreamwork seminar. In playing the part of each thing, Ann would then transform the thing, the symbol, into a feeling. This is the effect of turning it into I: for instance, "I am a tree" gives you a feeling, maybe, of standing erect in a storm, which is a symbol, a projection of some aspect of your personality (it is felt that way), spreading out its branches (your open arms), welcoming the storm (the tribulations, troubles, difficulties of life). "Every bit of the dream, every person in the dream, every mood is a part of our fractionalized life" (Perls, 1973a).

The next step is to write a script and get the different parts to have a dialogue with one another—the mother with the baby, the baby with the cat, the cat with the mother. It could go something like this:

Mother: What am I doing cradling you? You're not my baby—you're just Meagan, my silly old cat. What are you doing at my breast? It's obscene. Go away! I don't like you.

Cat: I'm not a cat. I'm just a figment of your imagination. You've just turned me into a cat because you don't like me at your breast. It embarrasses you. I'm your baby. Why are you so afraid of me?

As you go on writing down your dream, memories and feelings often come flooding back, and you may be surprised at some of the things you say, which can sound like a child speaking: it is the child you have suppressed in yourself. In the group situation, at a dream workshop, Ann would have been told to give a live performance of the dream. In this psychodrama, as it is called, all the dispersed and disowned parts of the self are gathered together and reintegrated in the conscious, waking life of the dreamer. They are the rejected, despised parts that have been reclaimed. As Fritz Perls says:

> The dream, is an excellent opportunity to find the holes in the personality. . . . Understanding the dream means realizing what you are avoiding, the obvious . . . And if you understand the meaning of each time you identify with some bit of a dream, each time you translate an *it* into an *I*, you increase in vitality and in your potential. Like a debt collector you have your money invested all over the place, so take it back. [Perls, 1973b]

c.   *Preventing the wounds*

The wounds can be prevented, but first of all one must have confidence in the treatment: pregnant women have recently been justifiably suspicious of the so-called obstetrics experts who have usually been men. There is also a cynicism in this country about prenatal psychology—a healthy cynicism, some would say. Research in this area is usually described by journalists in a mocking sort of way—for example, the report about research showing that the fetus could hear a mother reading a story was headlined in *The Guardian*: "Why a fetus likes to curl up with a good book", and in the *Sunday Times*: "Born with a sound education". Cracking jokes of this kind is irresistible, and, of course, I am not saying that one should approach the subject without a sense of humour. It is the English way. But humour can also be dismissive.

Perhaps it is because the Germans have a different sense of humour that they are more interested in, and less amused by, prenatal psychology. Or, to put it another way, perhaps it is because they take prenatal psychology more seriously that they are not able to crack jokes about it. Certainly in Germany and Austria and on the Continent generally, more interest is shown in prenatal psychology than seems to be the case in the United Kingdom.

As long ago as 1970, what has become the International Society for Prenatal and Perinatal Psychology and Medicine was founded in Salzburg. Its members include paediatricians, gynaecologists, obstetricians, sociologists, anthropologists, psychiatrists, and psychotherapists, who as a group believe that "not only the physical but also the psychic development of the human being should be viewed and understood as an inseparable whole, from conception, through intrauterine existence, birth, development after birth, to death itself".

Dr Dietmar Richter, of the University of Freiburg, is one of those who believe that much more attention should be given to psychological factors in pregnancy (Hau & Schindler, 1982): "It is important to know", he says, "how the expectant mother feels about the changes that are taking place in her body, and how in the course of pregnancy she, as well as her husband and parents, will experience the physical and psychological changes."

Richter is firmly convinced, as many others are today, that prenatal influences can have a profound effect on the shaping of the personality of the adult. "The disturbances in the behaviour of a child and later (if untreated) in the adult", says Richter, "are not confined to the home; they may erupt in social disturbances later on."

It is strange how people tend to grasp just one part of the truth but do not see how it is related to the whole. I think people generally agree that it is important to look after the pregnant woman's diet and to see that she is relaxed and gets enough rest and exercise. But even in this area there is a certain amount of ignorance. For instance, it has taken a long time for people generally to appreciate that alcohol and tobacco can have very damaging effects on the unborn child. And this does not only apply to the woman. The man also must look after himself, especially in the months before starting a family. An excess of alcohol or cigarettes can adversely affect the genesis and sustenance of the sperm months before conception. There is much research showing that the effects of alcohol, smoking, and drugs depend greatly on precise timing in relation particularly to spermatogenesis, ovulation, fertilization and implantation, and throughout pregnancy (S. House, 2000). What often happens when a woman becomes pregnant for the first time is that she and her husband are suddenly faced with emotional problems and conflicts that are completely unexpected. They have very little idea, apart from vague, unrealistic expectations, about how the birth of a child will affect them and how they are going to cope afterwards.

It is important, if a couple have problems of this kind, that they should talk about them, either with other couples at group meetings organized by antenatal clinics or at classes with understanding on the lines of the prenatal and perinatal societies, appreciating that bonding develops from conception and can be consciously sustained through pregnancy, birth, and so on.

Women respond to pregnancy in many different ways. It is helpful if a pregnant woman's whole life situation can be taken into account in assessing what kind of help she needs: her health, her own mother's experience of pregnancy and giving birth, her own experience with any previous child, her main relationships, her career prospects and financial situation.

Pregnancy has been described as one of those crises in human growth that, like puberty and the menopause, are points of no return, involving profound endocrinal and somatic changes that are irreversible. Once an adult, you can never be a child again; once menopausal, you can never bear children again; once pregnant, you can never be a single unit again—except, of course, through an abortion or the death of the child.

Pregnancy is a crisis that can be very disturbing, although for most women it is negotiated successfully and without too much anxiety. But we tend to put up with things if we think they are unchangeable, and that is what women have been told: it is a very difficult time, you will be anxious, the birth will be painful, and so on. And that has been true in the past and continues to be true for most women today. But things could be different, and more women today are beginning to realize this. They can and should be different.

From a psychological point of view, Grete Bibring sums up the pregnant woman's two main tasks of adjustment:

> Incorporating the image of the child within her self-image—the love object becoming part of the self,
>
> Perceiving the child as existing outside her self, as a separate person—this (used to) happen at what is called the quickening, when the mother becomes aware of the movements of the child. She suddenly realizes that the child moves of his own volition. (With scans this perception now tends to happen earlier). [Bibring, Dwyer, Huntington & Valenstein, 1961]

Bibring sums up the feelings of a woman who is pregnant for the first time by telling the story of a girl who arrived at an antenatal clinic in an agitated state and started to talk as she stood in the doorway: "I was terribly excited and anxious last night. I suddenly realized that I won't be Jenie much longer, but Mother for ever and ever after." She went on to talk, more calmly, about her own mother. She said that she was pleased when she had left home and become independent. After that she rarely visited her mother. But she said that "last night" she had realized that whenever she had some terrible problem, her first thought had always been, what would her mother say? And this, she felt, would be her role in the life of her own child. She would become her child's guide and confidante. Her relationship with her own mother would then change: she would become more of an equal.

Bibring says that, when a woman becomes pregnant, running like a thread through all her relationships is her relationship with her own mother. It is usually the mother who provided the prototype of a parental figure. This can be reassuring to the pregnant woman, but it can also create tensions between her and her husband and her husband's family. A survey has now shown prenatal depression to be even more common than postnatal, not necessarily to do with the maternal relationship, as Jenie's. Yet, like Jenie, a woman realizes, however much she wants the baby, that she is becoming "Mother for ever". She is no longer one. Her independence is gone. Her career is threatened.

The father's role in pregnancy has become better acknowledged. There was a time when the father was regarded almost as if he were an outsider. At the birth of his child, in the days when this usually took place in the home, he was sent into the kitchen to boil endless pans of water. They were not all needed, of course, but it kept him out of the bedroom. The midwife felt that it was best for him to be well out of the way. And this is still the case in the Soviet Union, where the father is not even allowed into the hospital after the baby is born, for fear that he will bring in some infection from outside. He must wait until mother and child go home before seeing the baby.

Now in the United Kingdom and the United States many fathers see their babies being born. Brian Jackson describes in his book, *Fatherhood* (1984), how he felt when he saw his own child born. It was, he said, "a personal Everest". Many fathers now share in a very intimate way the miracle of birth. And they also have powerful feelings—or, rather, they don't mind acknowledging powerful feelings any more, during the nine months of pregnancy. The couvade, which is a ritual in some primitive societies, in which the father pretends to experience the birth himself in a special ceremony, has become a reality in the West. The father may even suffer sympathetic labour-like pains. A father, of course, has feelings that are closely linked with the mother's. For him, too, pregnancy may bring back memories of his own childhood. As one father said, "It strikes me how regularly during the pregnancy I found the source of my feelings in the memories of my boyhood. . . . I drifted between thoughts of childhood and parenthood" (Bittman & Zalk, 1978).

The father's expectations will also have an influence on his wife's attitude to the unborn child. All relationships are extremely complex at this time. A father's expectations may conflict with his wife's, which may, in turn, be strongly influenced by her own mother's expectations and her memories of childhood. For the sake of the child, adjustments must be made all round before the child is born. Usually, however, parents do rally round, and usually their offers of help are not turned down.

d. *Fears and feelings of mother and child*

The essential difference between mother and father at this time is that there comes a point in most families when the woman will have to devote all her energies to the child while the man is able to continue with his normal occupation: at the beginning he is more a part-time parent than is the mother.

(This is not true of all fathers. According to his widow Sonia, Brian Jackson gave to fatherhood the same primacy in his life that most women accord to motherhood. He put his children before his work.)

And, as I have already said, one of the main problems nowadays is the conflict between a woman's role as mother and housewife and her wish to succeed in a career outside the home. Richter points out that a woman could be very positive about wanting a child, but unconsciously she may be anxious about her career and about being forced into a situation in which she is entirely dependent on her partner. The conscious wish to have a child does not in any way exclude an unconscious anxiety about the consequences.

Other anxieties include: the pregnant woman's fear of losing her sense of identity; regression to a child-like state of mind, which may in fact be necessary in forming a symbiotic relationship with the child; fear for the welfare of the child; fear of the aggression she sometimes feels towards the child—resentment, rejection, even a death wish, wanting an abortion—which cannot, very often, be expressed; and the fear of losing her sexual attractiveness.

Some of these fears were experienced by Nancy. All her unconscious fears were expressed symbolically in her drawings, but she was not fully aware of them herself. Richter tries to get the pregnant woman to discuss her conflicts quite openly; and, he says, the healthy woman always does. Healthy conflict that is brought into the open can resolve ambivalent feelings towards the child and result in an acceptance of the fact that the pregnant woman must give much of her attention to her child. A mentally unstable person such as Nancy will not be able to handle these fears because they remain submerged. She is not aware of what is troubling her. It is important to sort out the conscious and unconscious elements in her feelings towards the child. Yes, she says, she does want the child—a mother must want her child: not to want it would be unthinkable—but underneath she hates the child; she wants to get rid of it.

Problems, says Richter, do not remain static. Pregnancy is a dynamic event that is constantly changing, and adjustments have to be made all the time to the changes that take place. In general, pregnant women lose their initial fears with feelings of increased physical well-being. The initial fear—"Won't I lose out if the child demands more and more of me?"—fades. The conflict is resolved with feelings of "Now I must take special care of myself", "Now I must create the right kind of atmosphere around me to bring the child into the world."

As her confidence increases, so do her sexual feelings towards her husband, reaching a peak in the second trimester. With the approach of the birth, her sexual feelings may die down again as she turns her attention almost exclusively towards the coming event. Her emotional relations with the child will increase, and she will have less time for her husband except as a partner who is participating in the event.

e.   *Sex and the unborn child*

Dr Sepp Schindler, once president of the ISPPM, believes that the parents' sexual relationship can affect how the child becomes, his future behaviour and physical responses:

> To state that every child is the offspring of two different-sexed parents and is the outcome of the sexual act would be a platitude of almost unrivalled dimensions—if we take it purely as a biological statement. On the other hand, it must be said that there is a tendency to ignore this fact when speaking of the psychical development of a child. In the majority of accounts the newborn child appears psychically unstructured, a blank sheet of paper, as it were, who only acquires experience in post-natal life. [Schindler, 1981]

Schindler points out that newborn children perceive through different sensory channels from those of adults. Most of the child's information comes, not through vision, but through the sense of touch. It is worth comparing his belief with Francis Mott's, that "that every psychological feeling derives from an older physical feeling" (see ch. 4[c]). At 2–3 months the fetus is touch-sensitive, with constant opportunity, yet not visually sensitive to image till 5–8 months, with little opportunity in the womb. Schindler believes that the way the child perceives his world is similar, in the sense of physical closeness, to the way the adult feels during the sexual act. Sexual fulfilment is therefore important if the parents are going to meet the child's need for contact. If there is any rejection of sex in either or both parents, or any difficulty over physical contact between them, this will show in the way the child is handled. The word "handle" is significant here: it can be used both in its physical and in its psychological sense because the one is related to the other. "Handling" is what the child knows about in its physical sense; and the way he is handled will influence the way he handles others later in life, including sexual advances and responses.

f.   Predicting ease of birth

Many doctors know intuitively who among their patients is going to have a difficult pregnancy. There have been cases of doctors sending pregnant women to hospital on non-objective grounds and the patients then developing complications during labour that no clinical test could have predicted. A group of American psychologists and psychotherapists—Dr Lewis E. Mehl and associates—carried out a study of a number of doctors who used semi-objective guidelines in predicting who was at risk among a group of pregnant women. These women were not considered to be at risk from a purely medical point of view, so what the researchers were doing, in an indirect way, was to try to decide what were the psychosocial factors that were important in predicting the outcome of a pregnancy. They presented their findings in a paper at a meeting of the Association of Birth Psychology in New York in June 1980 (Mehl, 1981; Mehl et al., 1980).

Most researchers had found that significant predictors were past obstetric history, medical-obstetric disorders, pelvic or generative tract disorders. Maternal age, race, and nutrition were also regarded as important, but they considered emotional and psychological factors to be of little importance.

Mehl and colleagues set out to prove that in the past researchers had been wrong about psychosocial factors. Their approach was quite different from previous researchers'. They did not regard the pregnant woman merely as an "obstetric patient" similar to others in the same class, but as a "total human being, who must be understood as such and within the context of other human beings with whom she has developed and maintains intimate relationships".

They started off by interviewing the doctors mentioned above who seemed to make successful guesses not based on clinical evidence. They questioned them closely as to what had caught their eye about a particular patient: physical appearance, signs of stress, marital relations, living conditions—or what?

They also reviewed 200 childbirths, details of which they had collected over a period of time. They were able to produce a detailed list of possibly significant psychosocial factors for predicting high-risk pregnancies: whether an individual woman was passive or active, frail or robust, and so on.

After making what they called assessments of "psychophysiological status" in cooperation with the women concerned and the staff of the Berkeley Family Health Center, the researchers compiled a predictive scale. This was used to test certain basic assumptions, notably that as a woman lives her life, so will she give birth (and that problems and complications are not totally bad but have some learning potential). Would predictions based on these assumptions prove accurate?

One aim of the research was to help staff at the BFHC predict which women could safely have their babies at home and which should go into hospital. Such a decision was made easier by the fact that there was, if needed, an alternative birth centre at Mt Zion Hospital where women could enjoy the same comforts and caring environment as at home. Before this centre was established, the only choice, as so often, was between a home birth (usually a good emotional experience) and a safer but sometimes emotionally disturbing hospital birth.

Expectancy in obstetrics plays a significant role in determining the outcome. Many obstetricians are constantly looking for what can go wrong and in this way produce negative feelings in the mother. Modern medicine, in fact, may sometimes produce a biology of hopelessness: "A negative expectation will prevent the possibility of disappointment, but it may also contribute to a negative outcome that was not inevitable . . ." (Simonton, Matthews-Simonton, Creighton, 1978). The researchers in the study I have been describing had a high success rate in predicting the outcome of 200 pregnancies.

Women were placed into the following prediction groups:

5 Entirely normal delivery expected without the need for any medical or psychological intervention.

4 Probably normal delivery, but with possible/probable need for psychological intervention which would most likely be effective and/or minor medical intervention (episiotomy, etc).

3 Unpredictable or expected complication which could probably be handled at home, but we would prefer not to. Would much prefer hospital and will do what we can to accomplish that.

2 Expect complicated delivery with need for hospital intervention. Would not do at home.

1 Expect major complication in which every second is of the essence.

The predictions then allotted the 200 women into the five groups as shown in Table 11.2.

There was 100% success in predicting normal birth (Group 5). Of the 54 women predicted to be in Group 4, 65% did need minor interventions (Group 4), and 31% had entirely normal deliveries (Group 5). Taking these two groups together, 96% of the women predicted to have reasonably normal deliveries (who could theoretically deliver at home) did have normal deliveries.

At the other end of the scale, there was an 85% success rate for predictions in Group 2. Results in Group 3 were very variable, but this is not surprising as all women who were "enigmas to the prediction system" were placed in this group. Nonetheless, 61% of the women

Table 11.2. **Prediction groups for childbirth**

Group	Number of women	% of sample
5	32	16
4	54	27
3	48	24
2	66	33
1	0	0

did have the kind of complicated births (in Groups 1–3) that make a hospital delivery advisable. Taking Groups 1–3 as a whole, 76% of the women—all of whom, remember, would have been cleared for home births on medical grounds—were correctly judged to be at risk on psychophysiological grounds. Of the medically low-risk women, 57% became high-risk during labour.

This impressive study leaves little room for doubt that, contrary to what other researchers have said in the past, psychological and emotional factors are very important in predicting the outcome of a pregnancy.

CHAPTER TWELVE

Healing the original wound

"'People become so proficient at avoiding these things that they cease to realize they are doing it. . . . It becomes habitual', maintained Dr David Bohm.

'The wound remains', agreed Krishnamurti.

'We remember to forget, you see', added Bohm.

'We remember to forget', affirmed a psychiatrist from New York City, Dr David Shainberg, 'and then the process of therapy is to help the remembering and the recall—to remember you have forgotten, and then to understand the connections or why you forgot; then the thing can move in a more holistic way, rather than being fragmented.'"

Krishnamurti, *The Wholeness of Life* (1976)

"You are nothing but a set
Of obsolete responses."

T. S. Eliot, *The Cocktail Party*

a.   *Loving touch for primal pain*

A common thread runs through ways of healing. It is the immediate sense of being loved. Simon House writes:

> I was starting my first course teaching Re-evaluation Counselling. We were a group of sixteen people. I was just going to explain how it worked when one of our children ran in from the garden with (a grazed knee and) a pained look on his face. He quickly spotted his mother's face. As their eyes met he burst into tears. I said, "That's strange. The sight of his mother made him cry." We soon agreed that once there was the safety and loving support of the mother, the tears of relief could come, the pain of hurt and shock could be felt and released as the hurt heals. [House, 1999]

There are many people who have been hurt in the past and are still, like that boy, holding their pains in because they have never found a safe place to scream. The hurt that is held in is a bit of unfinished business; and it will go on being troublesome, in one way or another, until the person who has suffered the hurt is able to cry or to express his feelings in some other way—in art, for instance, or in creative play.

This analogy of the pain held in can be applied to all sorts of situations in life. We are unfulfilled in so many different ways. There is so much unfinished business. Fritz Perls called these unfulfilled needs "holes" in the personality. Any experience that has been cut off or not completed will remain in the system, interfering with our healthy development.

A person who has blocked off an early painful experience will very often organize much of his life around it, so that whenever he comes up against a pain that has some resemblance to the original pain, he will deal with it by some obvious or cunningly contrived avoidance technique.

According to prenatal psychologists, the original wound often occurred at birth or before birth. The object of therapy is to identify the pain and bring it into the open so that it can be given expression in the present and turned into something positive. When fully understood, the pain is usually a blocked need.

William Emerson works with children with behavioural problems that are believed to be related to birth trauma. Because regression to early experiences could be frightening for a child, Emerson uses indirect methods, such as dreamwork, artwork, and, quite often, play, which, he says, allows the child to be in control of what he does and able to change his approach to an intense feeling—such as anger or fear over a feeling of suffocation—from playful denial to playful confrontation. By keeping it all at the level of play, the child is never overwhelmed or incapable of managing intense feelings. It all becomes good fun, like any other game where fear might well be a component.

Emerson talks of recurring patterns of behaviour that have their origin in birth: "schemas", he calls them. Rank and others mentioned these recurring patterns, but in a broad sense: the trauma of birth creates a feeling of anxiety that is reactivated later in life at times of crisis. Emerson is more specific. He gives as an example the "schema" of a child who had cord complications at birth. His umbilicus was pinched between his shoulder and the maternal pelvis and was wrapped around his neck:

> During regression therapy, he "played with" intense feelings of suffocation, anoxia and fear. In his therapeutic process, he would push intensely forward and "go limp". It was as if he had learned that effort was futile: it would lead nowhere. His infant feeding, toilet training, walking and talking were all affected by this, resulting in a developmental lag. His general behaviour was characteristic of a younger age group. [Emerson, 1984]

Emerson has a videotape showing him in the classroom. "In slow motion, the 'schema' (his head turns clockwise and then back again to the normal position) could be seen to occur spontaneously and subliminally just before he gave up some task." This looked like the way he had to turn his head to free himself from the umbilical cord.

Emerson said he "reworked" the schema in a series of games: turning the head and then giving up; allowing the head turning to persist without the feeling of hopelessness; using the head turning in a number of other activities that are enjoyable and require very little effort; and finally being permitted to do any amount of head turning on social occasions; then the "schema" goes because it loses its meaning.

Fighting a habit often has the effect of strengthening it. Emerson's method is a bit like "paradoxical intention" (Frankl, 1970). If you suffer from insomnia and can't get to sleep, try staying awake. If you want to stop stammering, try playing the part of a stammerer on the stage.

In working with children, Emerson has three sorts of games, which he calls (1) *done-to games*; (2) *doing-to games*; and (3) *healing games*.

Examples of "done-to games" are:

Crushing earth mother.   Child topples mother, who crumbles onto child and makes crushing sounds.

Earthquakes.   Both parents surround child, making earthquake rumbles and movements, and encourage child to escape.

Tunnel crawl.   All adults form tunnel by arching back while on hands and knees. Children crawl through. Adults contract tunnel by dropping abdomens—often accompanied by darkness and heartbeat music.

Cave-in.   Children surround child and cave in; child attempts to escape through the tunnels provided by children's arms and legs.

The "doing-to games" are the same as the above only in reverse—giving parents a dose of their own medicine. Children surround the parents or surround other children. The games can be played with parents or with other children.

The "healing games" are created specifically to help children with special difficulties. For instance, children who feel socially isolated are given a game of breaking into and out of play groups, those with feelings of abandonment are sent alone on bus rides to new places, followed by a reunion with the family and pets and a celebration.

One boy who was being treated by Emerson had a fantasy while undergoing birth regression:

> "I'm in the woods, there's wild rhinos around and hanging leaves and this trail's going nowhere. It's getting narrower and smaller. I can't get further on this trail. I know, I'm getting down on my knees now and I'm pushing hard, I'm pushing through real hard, I'm crawling and ooh! it's, I don't like it. It's getting scary. Now there's snakes and there's viperous serpents. I don't like this. I'm getting out of here."

The reason why the boy had been referred to Emerson was because, although he was quite bright, he was making little headway at school. As Emerson put it, he was "stuck"—his head was stuck—where he was, and he could not move forward. Many of his drawings were of animals in cages or of animals tied down with spears stuck through their feet, pinning them to the ground. Sometimes, he said, he had the feeling of being in a cage; just as he was about to get out, he was suddenly pinioned in some way to the cage so that he could not move.

In the birth games the boy played, says Emerson, he did not experience any anxiety in the womb. The anxiety came when he was trying to get out. On these occasions, as he was struggling to get out, he felt angry and frustrated, and most of his anger was directed at his mother for not helping him very much.

Some of the games the boy played with Emerson and some at home with his mother. One game was called the attic crawl, where he and his mother would, once a week, go into their attic and crawl from the back to the front of the house. In this small, constricted place, where movement was difficult, he would complain, moan, and whine. His mother would offer helping hands, talk to him, tell funny stories. Bizarre though this may seem, it worked. Gradually the boy improved; he was less anxious, less agitated, and his mother wrote to Emerson: "He's really a different person, not so stuck in his head, and he's actively trying at school and getting on much better."

Another case, a girl of 8, re-experienced a stage of her birth in which she was entrapped in the contracting womb and unable to move forward. She had three sessions of 90 minutes with Emerson's group, in which she cried, experienced fear, and received the general loving support and understanding of her parents as well as other children in the group. Following this experience, her mother wrote to say how she never realized how much her daughter had been afraid of being touched: "I didn't realize how much she was withdrawn until after our sessions together." The child improved after the sessions, and this mother, too, was able to say that she "seems like a different person".

Another case, a boy with agoraphobia, was treated by Emerson because his fear of going out was making a misery of his life: he was even afraid of the playground. Emerson attributed his condition to a premature birth: moving him out too soon. Birth re-facilitation resulted in a remission of his symptoms.

A young girl who was brought to him with learning disability was found to have had a birth experience corresponding with Grof's third stage of birth (see ch. 5[b]). The success of her efforts was thwarted by a partial transverse position and broken waters. This, says Emerson, resulted in severe anxiety about "getting through" anything and a mental block (Emerson, 1984).

A young boy was referred to Emerson for periodic bronchitis: "His bronchitis, emotional fearfulness, and social withdrawal would periodically reappear and seemed to be stabilizing into a characterological pattern at the age of 5." The parents agreed to birth re-facilitation. The boy's problems were found to be connected with his continuing attempts to regurgitate fluids "inhaled" during the birth process. Rudimentary lung breathing, Emerson explains, occurs even before birth. The treatment successfully eradicated the emotional fearfulness and the bronchitis (Emerson, 1984).

Healing the breath

Leonard Orr describes his discovery for himself of "rebirthing breathwork" in 1962, though it was not until 1974 that he offered it to other people.

> I told them to get into their bathtubs and sit there until they felt it was time to get out. Then, to stay in the tub 30 minutes to an hour longer. The feeling that we must get out is an urgency barrier. Every time we sit through an urgency barrier we get a fantastic realization about ourselves and we learn about another program that is controlling us.

He found that something about the safety of his presence caused them to have spontaneous regressions and powerful spiritual experiences. Later he had the idea of using a snorkel and nose clips in a hot tub. In this womb-like environment, with him there, they instantly regressed to birth and prenatal states of consciousness. They did not just have memories, they regressed to a psychophysical state. "It wasn't just reliving the past, it was also a very high exploration into the spiritual dimensions of life. It was a complete spiritual, mental and physical experience." He stayed with each person until they felt peace. It usually took two hours. They breathed themselves out of pain and tension into relaxation and peace. "Most Rebirthing Breathwork sessions are physical, emotional, and spiritual. People experience breathing out pain, tension, drama, and trauma into relaxation and peace. Relaxed, gentle, connected breathing was the key."

In 1975, after giving hundreds of hot-tub rebirths, he noticed people having a "healing of the breath" experience.

I realized their breathing mechanism was totally transformed and their mind-body-spirit relationship was forever transformed. This healing took place after several sessions—when they felt safe enough to relive the moment of their first breath. Most people feel fear during this moment, so they have to feel safe to reach it. This is the experience of learning to breathe from the Breath Itself —directly from God. When we have enough completed Energy cycles and consciously learn to contact the Breath of Life, we have mastered breathing and have one of the greatest and most practical skills that humans are capable of having.

Orr next experimented with this connected breathing rhythm without the water and found that it was much better to do 10 one-to-two-hour Connected Breathing sessions out of the water before giving people a session in a hot tub with nose clips and a snorkel. He calls this Dry Rebirthing.

I found that most people can learn the connected breathing rhythm and how to breathe Energy as well as air in ten two hour sessions with a good Rebirther. I gave sessions to infants, to people in their nineties, and all ages in between. . . .It is important that people learn how our mind works and how to process our mind and feelings. . . We can breathe into and release our feelings. We can relax out of any kind of intense emotion or physical pain when we have this simple powerful skill of Conscious Breathing.

Orr practises conscious Divine Energy breathing every day, maintaining that Conscious Breathing is as important as good nutrition, exercise, working, or sunshine, and so on (Orr, 2002—http://www.rebirthingbreathwork.com/modules.php?name=DocTree&dtIsBlk=y&dtId=5&dtPath=3,5).

b.   Self and society

Breath release sounds fine and no doubt it works, as Orr and his patients say it does, but before anyone is carried away by the enthusiasm of those who practise the technique, I think it would be as well to sound a note of caution. Even though we may feel good after exercises of this sort and there may be "pleasurable possibilities", we still have to live in a world that is full of violence; not to be worried, not to be anxious, would be very strange indeed. We are all affected. It is not possible to separate the individual from society; his problem is to a large extent society's problem.

It would be unrealistic to say to anyone, "Look, I can cure you of your depression, your anxiety. All you have to do is to realize that you are mostly living in the past. Your responses to problems are quite inappropriate. They are the responses of memory. They belong to a different time and place." That is perfectly true of a great many people. But merely seeing the difference between our early distresses and the reality of our present situation does not make us less miserable or less anxious. It does give us the chance to work on it and find some release. Perhaps we need to ask ourselves seriously, what is it we are trying to cure? Do we imagine that life can be anything but a struggle, and do we think that there is something wrong about feeling depressed or anxious or afraid at times? Is it not human to have these feelings? Suppressing them is what throws us off balance.

Whatever it is that is wrong, it is not just the individual who is sick. Most of us suffer from the sickness of our times. So diagnosis, as Erik Erikson said, is a problem of relativities—a systematic going round in circles, in which you can clarify the relevances and relativities of all known data. There is so much we have to consider: food, chemistry, bacteria, viruses, allergies, attitudes, social and economic pressures, the family, the workplace, and so on. Roy Ridgway comments:

> In a world such as ours is it surprising that mothers sometimes say they don't want to be mothers? Is it surprising that they are less than perfect? And what is perfection? As someone once said of a state of perfect sanity, it would drive anyone mad the moment he reached it! Perfectionism is like that. It's like a disease, especially when the idea of perfection is imposed on mothers and children as if it is something that can be achieved. I remember when I was a teenager and tried to do what Marcus Aurelius advised—"Aim at perfect soundness in every word and every act"—I became a nervous wreck! In the end I gave up any such notion that it was possible to be perfect: it was just the fantasy of a mad Roman Emperor. [Ridgway, 1987]

Professor C. Henry Kempe, Chairman of the Department of Paediatrics at Colorado Medical Center, found from his research among 1,000 families that 20% of women felt unable to "turn on their mothering instinct": they just did not feel all-giving and protective towards their children (Kempe, Silverman, Steele, Droegmuller, & Silver, 1962).

"All right", a mother may say, "something went wrong at birth, or before birth. What do you expect? Something's bound to go wrong if, as you say, anxiety can damage a child. You tell me how I can stop feeling anxious when the world's in such a terrible mess and my husband is out of work. You tell an African mother whose child is dying of starvation to stop worrying."

It is a good argument. But one thing is certain. All research shows that battered children tend to become battering mothers. That is the past repeating itself and we must surely be able to do something about that. What's happened is that the child of a brutal, indifferent mother has "missed out on mothering". Something can be done about the "holes" in the personality. "The parent who lacks mothering herself is incapable of mothering", says Professor Kempe, "but expects her child to be capable of loving her; she expects far more than a baby is capable of and she sees its crying as rejection." He quoted a mother who had had a good education and was not unintelligent as saying, "When he cried it meant he didn't love me, so I hit him."

How does one deal with this? One way is to try to persuade the injured child who has grown up to become an indifferent and brutal mother to join a group where she will get all the love and support she missed out on herself when she was a child. This is what primal integration groups are for, whether adult groups such as Lake's, or children's groups such as Emerson's. In this case the mother must become a child again and find this time round the love she never got first time round. That will work, though it may take time; the main problem will probably be getting the mother to join such a group.

c.   *Working in groups*

It is in groups of one sort or another that we often fulfil ourselves. We all belong to groups, of course, but there are some that just add to our miseries. As Frank Lake pointed out, all groups can be perceived as wombs. They are sometimes seen as places of refuge where there is a "good-womb" feeling of warmth and security. For the teenager it may be the disco, where the beat of the music recalls the beat of the heart, where there is movement and a physical as well as an emotional closeness between people. On the other hand, there are groups that give us an oppressive feeling: constricted and confused places where there is a lot of tension and conflict and there does not seem to be a way out. One's place of work—a factory or office—may be like that. There are rules, regulations, rigid boundaries. It has the "bad-womb" feeling. One is dependent on this group for one's livelihood, just as a child is dependent on his mother for nourishment; and there is no escape. One is forced to accept the values and beliefs of the group.

"Prenatal and perinatal events", says Lake, "are so deeply imprinted upon the human organism that the uterine lifestyle imposes itself on all subsequent groups of which the person is a member." He goes on:

> Prenatal and perinatal events are so deeply imprinted upon the human organism that the uterine lifestyle imposes itself on all subsequent groups of which the person is a member. The boundaries of his place of work or worship, of his community or nation, or even the earth itself, (now more aware of its boundaries than ever before) can be experienced precisely as he or she experienced the boundaries of the womb. If the internal state of the group or institution becomes confused . . he or she will then add to the actual lack of clarity, the whole compendium of his or her intra-uterine confusion and its associated violent emotions. [Lake 1981]

How does one prevent this from happening? How can the mother who is herself the victim of the maternal–fetal distress syndrome help to change all this? She may not be so disturbed as the mother who batters her child. In fact, she might even imagine that she has done everything she possibly could do for her child: "I don't know what's wrong with her. She's had everything—a good home, good wholesome food, holidays, a good school. And yet look what she's like. She's so screwed up." Maybe it is in the mother's interest to keep the child in that state. Maybe the child is the "wooden leg" in the family, the one who makes all the others feel good about themselves.

The mother's attitude to her child has been determined by her own prenatal and perinatal experiences. Her very thoughts are the outcome of those experiences, so that the way she thinks about her problems or the way she tries to find solutions "in the head" is part of the problem. Inbuilt into the problem is an attitude to life that seeks to solve problems in a predetermined way. So what does she do?

Frank Lake says that the discovery that our basic, original injuries take place during embryonic and fetal life means that healing, if it is to be radical and not just patched up, should take place at the same deep level. To re-experience the original distress is not as difficult as it may seem, because, as he says, "the original wound is, or may feel to be, as real and raw now as in the hour it happened" (Lake, 1981). Though split off from consciousness, dissociated and repressed, no detail of the incident has been obliterated. Nothing is forgotten: only our ability to retrieve the memory has been blocked—but can be reopened. The way Lake sees it, the original "taped" input was so threatening, in view of the need to go on living in the same bad world, that it was often further split into at least four "tapes", each kept in separate "lead-lined cans". Sensations, emotions, images, and concepts that later found verbal utterance were all "gated off" from each other.

According to Lake, it is possible to play them back on a "mixer" with four inputs. "The adult", he says, "who is bent on achieving this integration can bring the hurt child of the past into the present, and give it a voice." Primal integration therapy works by the patient's consciously connecting their immediate sensations and movements with the original primal experience, so integrating their separate memory systems:

> Each person picks up the sensations and movements which be-
> long to their primal experience. As deep breathing provides the
> oxygen that facilitates both connecting and discriminating, and
> as a sober confidence in the group-assisted process grows, these
> are contextualised in their original time and place. The associated
> images of the self are connected to the "scripts" or summaries of
> experience and reaction, and these again to the associated emo-
> tions. In this way the four main tape recorders of past experience,
> . . . which had been gated off from each other in the primal dis-
> sociation, are brought together again. [Lake, 1981]

These four main tape-recorders are associated with:

- brainstem (sensations and movements)
- limbic system (emotions)
- right hemisphere (intuiting and symbolizing)
- left hemisphere (thinking and reasoning).

To connect these systems, the patient needs to recognize the original primal experience, with its pain or other feeling, and not just to leave the recalled memory in symbolized, dreamlike form. And it seems to have been Lake's insistence on this that led to more and more precise identification of memories (House, 1999; Lake, 1981).

The adult, still detached from his wants and fears, can, with the help of an experienced facilitator, permit the memory of primal hurts to break the surface of lifelong repression and emerge into consciousness. Lake stresses:

> Accurate recall may shatter some precious and long-cherished illusions. It is "nice to think" that the earliest relationships with one's mother, whether in the womb, or at birth, or after it, were idyllic. Parents often have a vested interest in retrospective falsification of incidents they are ashamed of, and "didn't mean" or "didn't want" to happen. It is as if obliterating from the record everything that didn't "go according to plan", and was far from their own "ideal" of parenting, could obliterate it from the intrauterine and peri-natal record of their offspring. Far from it. Such denials only add to the confusion. They generate the very distrust it was hoped to avoid.
>
> By contrast, a diligent search, behind the "cover up" of strenuous denial that is now natural to all of us, as "fallen" people, when inwardly accused of a guilty sense of responsibility for what we have (however inadvertently) done, clears the air. It promotes an exciting and growing trust in the parent-child relationships, twenty or fifty years after the offending occasion. [Lake, 1980b]

And change at such a level in people inevitably brings a change in society. Simon House finds through experience and reading that this common thread runs through those involved in primal work:

> Therapy can bring a change of values. Since the root of the human problem is neurosis, says Janov, we need a revolutionary consciousness, primal consciousness—a mind, integrated with and then liberated from internal realities, that is, pain. He adds, "Well people will logically produce a well society" (Janov, 1975). After therapy, he says, the patients' major difference is in their value system. They value their time, the preciousness of life, beauty, the environment and sanctity of living things. What a relief to be able to love and be loved (Janov, 1991). Grof says that deep inner exploration tends to foster reverence for life, empathy for other species, and ecological sensitivity (Grof, 1998). Horia Crisan puts it that the split of self into body and mind has rendered human

beings biologically superior yet matchlessly aggressive and cruel. The integrated self, healed of the split, could become the true jewel of creation, freely and creatively responsible for the world (Crisan, 1996). [House, 1999]

Finding the true self, one's true sense of values, may be for few adults. But if society can have a clearer understanding of the health needed to conceive children and nurture them successfully, this could affect many more people for life. A deeper feeling and sense of values, among more and more people, is a powerful source of healing for society as a whole.

d.   Generating peaceful people

We said that the neocortex has not become well integrated with the limbic system and brainstem (ch. 2[d]). When there has been poor nutrition or trauma in development, the connection may be even more tenuous and slow (ch. 8[b], "Second window"). The importance of improving such a connection in every way possible is strongly expressed by James Prescott (1996). In this way it is more than intellectual capacity we achieve; we gain spiritually. He sees his "basic thesis of *neurointegration* as the key to human transformation, sexual spirituality and states of Transcendental Consciousness", and as the antithesis of that ancient dualism that has proven so destructive to humanity, that subordinates body to spirit, woman to man. The ancient Greek philosophers "defined the nature of our humanity as 'schizoid' and woman was declared forever as unequal to man" (James Prescott is a developmental neuropsychologist and cross-cultural psychologist of distinction, referred to early in the Introduction under *Bonding*).

Prescott agrees with Teilhard de Chardin's comments in *The Evolution of Chastity* (1934): "At the (end) of the spiritual power of matter, lies the spiritual power of the flesh and of the feminine. . . . The feminine is the most formidable of the forces of matter."

Teilhard de Chardin (1976) also speaks of the individual, and one-to-one and cosmic relationships "as bonded by a unifying cement, by the Universal Feminine".

Prescott maintains that in his perspective, this evolution of Spirit only becomes possible with the evolution of the "neurointegrative brain", which makes possible the integration of "Passion" with "Spirit". This means integration of brain structures where "Love" is born—namely, the olfactory–limbic–cerebellar–frontal cortex. He adds that preliminary scientific data suggests that this neurointegration "is more fully developed in the human female brain than in the male human brain" (Kohl & Francoeur, 1995; Prescott, 1983, 1990, 1992).

He points out that "Physically affectional cultures do not inflict pain upon their infants; are highly nurturant to children with prolonged breastfeeding (2.5 years or longer); adult violence is low; and religious activity is low." And that:

> "movement therapies" and "movement sports", e.g. gymnastics, skiing, ice-skating, roller skating, roller blading, swimming-diving, snorkeling, water flotation, hang gliding, skydiving, bungee jumping, dancing, etc. produces such dramatic emotional-behavioral therapeutic effects. These "vestibular-cerebellar sports" are the "therapies of choice" for treating depression, impulse control disorders and addictive disorders. [Prescott, 1996]

Prescott endorses Ashley Montagu (1952). Woman must stand firm and be true to her own inner nature; to yield to the prevailing false conception of love, of unloving love, is to abdicate her great evolutionary mission to keep human beings true to themselves, to keep them from doing violence to their inner nature, to help them to realize their potentialities for being loving and cooperative.

Epilogue I

Roy Ridgway

Truth to build trust

Finally—if I may end on a more optimistic note than perhaps much that has gone before would seem to justify—it remains a fact, whatever hurts we have suffered, that there is part of the mind of all of us that is uncontaminated by the past. Strictly speaking, it is not a "part": it is everywhere, behind and in everything, and can be reached in meditation. David Bohm calls it "intelligence", which is not, he says, what people think it is: the mere capacity for design, remembrance, or communication. Knowledge, the accumulation of facts and experience, however wide, does not necessarily indicate intelligence. Intelligence, David Bohm would say, is sensitive aware-ness of the totality of life—life with all its problems, vexations, contra-dictions, miseries, joys. To be aware of all this, to accept it completely without rejecting anything, and to flow with the whole of life is intelligence.

This means scrubbing the ego off the slate, emptying the mind of all the chatter that goes on all the time: which is meditation. Medita-tion does not, of course, by itself solve your problems: in fact, it is just an escape for some: better than alcohol or drugs, but an escape all the same—an escape back to the "nothingness" of the womb. The important thing is to bring the meditative mind into the everyday world where there are so many problems, so many conflicts, irritations, frustrations. The meditative mind sees what is there and does not invent anything that is not there. It sees through the fog of self-deceit.

Krishnamurti talks about the thought process being a chemical or substance (Vedaparayana, 2006). Body chemistry is affected by alcohol, drugs, and all sorts of different agents. So, too, there are poisons in food that can affect the mind, and the thought process is affected by outside influences—that is, the thoughts of others. Probably some people's thoughts are literally poisonous. They affect not only the mind, but the body, and the pregnant woman may be poisoning her unborn child with her thoughts.

If thoughts are poisonous, my own thinking will not solve my problems. The poison in the mind cannot get rid of itself. So what is the purifying agent? Krishnamurti believes it is an energy outside the self—but is also inside, though not a part of the self, that is, the self-image—and this energy is truth. The ego twists the truth: so the truth is outside ego consciousness.

You will find the truth in dreams, in myths, in poetry, in the sudden insight—which David Bohm talks of as being "remedial"—in many artistic productions. Of course, science has an important part to play. But it is not enough. Or perhaps we are not scientific enough. As René Dubos (1965) said, as regards the attitudes and approach of the medical profession to problems of illness and their rejection of many alternative techniques: "Indeed, it is commonly stated that biology has lost contact with the humanities because it has become too "scientific" . . ., but the explanation of the difficulty, in my judgment, is that biology is not scientific enough." Modern medicine will become really scientific only when physicians and their patients have learned to manage the forces of the body and mind that operate in *vis medicatrix naturae*—that is to say, the body cures itself without medical intervention. We have some very powerful weapons to fight illness that you do not always find in hospitals, and they are: hope, love, faith, courage, tenacity, and a sense of humour.

Unearthing the truth about ourselves

In Gurdjieff's extraordinary book, *All and Everything: Beelze-bub's Tales to his Grandson* (1950), which is written in such a discursive way that it is difficult to extract any sense from it—a deliberate stratagem, like a Zen koan, to arouse thought in the reader—the all-wise Beelzebub tells his grandson, Hassein, about the strange customs and problems of the "three-brained beings of planet Earth". One of the strange traits he found in these beings when he visited the planet was the fact that "they didn't discover anything by their active deliberation alone". They only believed what the Smiths and Browns—that is, other people—told them. The beliefs of the Smiths and Browns had been "rooted" in them long ago, so that no one was saying anything any more.

And, of course, that is perfectly true: if people could see the truth of that, the world would be a better place. Who the Smiths and Browns are, nobody knows exactly: they are "something I saw in a book", "in black and white", "something the man on telly said", "something they say". The Smiths and Browns, though we call them by those names, don't in fact have names: the Smiths and Browns are they: the anonymous experts.

Now I am not saying that I am not as guilty as anyone in this matter. Of course I am! As a medical journalist I am mainly an interpreter or explainer of other people's ideas. I am not expected to have ideas of my own. It would not be possible to get along, of course, without the experts: the people who know how to build houses and fly planes and do all sorts of practical things, including the surgeon who sets bones or removes a rotten appendix or a physician who gives you an injection to ease your pain or provides you with much-needed vitamins if you are old or weak or pregnant. But as regards what I feel and who I am, I am the only expert. Nobody knows better than I do about the reality of being me.

But sometimes I hear people say things that I know, deep down, are true: true for me, I should say. It is just that I have forgotten certain things or I have blocked them off because they are so unpleasant: they do not fit the picture I have of myself. The people who uncover these truths, who speak to me as much as to anyone else, are the artists, the poets, and wise men like Gurdjieff.

Another extraordinary trait Beelzebub missed—though perhaps I should say it was something I missed in his rambling tale, which is supposed to deal with "all and everything"—was that the peculiar creatures on planet Earth with their reptilian instinctive Paleo-mammalian emotional and neo-mammalian thinking brains had a tendency soon after birth to start inventing fictions about themselves. At first the fiction is just a game children play to get their own way. But all too soon they begin to believe it and start defending it as if it were true, and then roles are invented for them in the working-class family, bourgeois family, religious family, disturbed family, and so on, onwards and upwards to the fiction of "my country, right or wrong", "Land of hope and glory", "Deutschland über alles", and they find themselves wearing a uniform—then whoomph! somebody drops a bomb; they dive for shelter, their self-image shattered; sometimes it is only then, in the hell of war, that people rediscover themselves.

Threads of remembrance in a diary

Turning back just to one page in my diary, I find that, if I think about it and remember what happened before and after, the past, present, and future were all there in that single journal entry. As Eliot said in *East Coker*, there is a whole lifetime burning in every moment.

When re-reading my diary, the fiction becomes obvious. I remember many people from the past who never fully lived their lives because they were always play-acting, and others who never really died because they still keep talking to me in my head and reminding me who I am. I remember passing moments that have never really gone away—some good moments, some awful moments keep coming back. I have memories of doors unopened that I keep on opening in my memory—"door[s] into the rose garden" (to borrow another memorable line from T. S. Eliot [*Burnt Norton*]).

Then there is the story-telling, the road one constructs for oneself as one goes along it—personal mythology. And there is what Cardinal Newman called the "poetry of the soul"—the style that is not superimposed but is an intrinsic quality of the self—how we are, the very essence or ground of our being on which those who are "in touch" try to build and re-build their world.

But even though I can see the connectedness of everything, a page in my diary can trigger an abreaction in which, for instance, I can find myself re-experiencing an isolated moment with no before and after. I can go back and re-experience some of the horrors of war or feel the emptiness and desolation of bereavement, as if the world had come to an end. This in fact is the characteristic of a traumatic or breathtaking (peak) experience: in either case the world stands still.

While reading my diary, I have occasionally experienced, as if for the first time, emotions I must have repressed long ago, even traumas of the past that go back to prenatal experiences, birth, and infancy. My diary shows me how the same person has been doing the same things again and again; and the emotions stirred up sometimes feel like the re-living of the ordeal or separation of birth. Or they feel like a "good-womb" memory. What comes up are memory traces of a process that has been well established objectively in developmental biology—namely, the process whereby stimuli or insults in sensitive periods in early life have an indelible effect on our behaviour and have lifetime consequences.

Unfinished business

There are gaps in everyone's story—the unfinished business that can be resolved later in life. A diary helps. For instance, my diary describes the part I played in the Battle of Cassino when I worked as a medical orderly in a field hospital. I was too busy at the time to take in the horror of it all, but there was a part of me that registered it and was damaged by the experience.

I never trembled with fear when the shells were exploding and shrapnel was ripping tents and human flesh apart, but I feel the tension now, all these years later, when I read about what happened, and I remember once finding my hands shaking when I talked about it in a co-counselling session in the 1970s. We are waiting on the side of a hill while heavy artillery is pounding the enemy lines opposite. The shells come over the hospital tents. The memory comes back as a feeling of trepidation about the bloody battle to come, when we expect the Germans to respond to our barrage. I realize now that there is a thread taking me from that moment of terror much further back to the implantation of the blastocyst (embryo), which was also quite a bloody affair.

Also, when reading my diary, I have found myself moved to tears at the loss of someone who was once very close to me. It is as if it has only just happened, and maybe it has just happened in its completeness because some part of me was not there at the death; tears were held back. Though the loss I remember is of a particular person, the emotion that tears me apart does just that because I believe it is linked to a memory of birth when the unborn child's sense of oneness with a mother is suddenly shattered—torn apart!

Prototype of bereavement

The primal integration therapist David Wasdell (1998) describes the trauma of birth as one of the most profound transitions in the experience of a human being, laying down patterns of change and loss that are formative for the whole of life. "In that sense birth", he says "is the prototype of bereavement. It is hardly surprising that the Kubler-Ross (1970) dynamics of bereavement reactions emerge also in perinatal abreaction."

Wasdell goes on to say that bereavement, as a break in bonding in later life, restimulates the imprinting of the perinatal impingement, so that reaction to death is overloaded by triggered emotion from the repressed unconscious field, underlying the current loss. The hell of the birth canal is seen in retrospect as "paradise lost"!—title for Milton's epic poem, written after he became blind. "There is no depth of grief", says Wasdell, "able to express such a cataclysm." The amazing thing is that the child survives it all unless something more traumatic happens—not only survives it but understands it emotionally and is able to treat loss as something final, not to be re-played in the imagination as something that never happened or need never have happened—the "if only" feeling—which is what adults do. That is the positive effect of the first break in bonding: the realization that we die to every moment. The joy, the "being-with" and "being-for" someone, is over—finished with! The child is plunged into utter despondency, then realizes something has gone for good and moves happily on to the next thing.

To the adult, the screaming of childhood seems out of all proportion to the cause of the distress. A broken toy, a mother walking out the front door—gone forever! as the child thinks—a sand castle washed away by the incoming tide, being left alone in a bedroom with the light switched off or a candle snuffed out. To a child it is the end—the prototype of bereavement. When someone we love dies, it is not so much a person as a relationship that is missing, and you are torn apart with grief because it feels like a big chunk of yourself has gone—the other part of the I–Thou relationship that Martin Buber wrote about:

> I see in the other not a stranger, not an "it" but a quality that is in me. When I see the other as Thou and not it, I see all that matters in life. All real living is meeting. [Buber, 1958]

Sometimes the sorrow is tempered by a feeling of freedom from what had become an unsatisfactory relationship that should have ended—say, when childhood ended—but dragged on beyond its natural duration. I am "diminished" by another's death, as John Donne said, but when I accept the fact that "the bell tolls for me" I become more aware of myself, more aware of life and death as one movement, more alive, and, in the case of the death of someone close to me, I become less dependent on the other, though I am usually grateful for what he/she taught me. We are still together in spirit, but love is no longer a bond, a place where I am trapped. As Khalil Gibran wrote:

> Love one another, but make not a bond of love
> Let it be rather a moving sea between the shores of your souls.
>   [Khalil Gibran, 1926]

In terms of birth, what we remember is a sense of relief following the "no-exit" sensation of the first clinical stage of delivery (Grof, 1990)—a feeling of being trapped—then suddenly, at this worst moment of your life, you are propelled into another world. It may be paradise lost, but it is also the end of a kind of paralysis that prevents you moving out of an uncomfortable environment that is gripping you tight: a crushing feeling with no relief.

At first a separation is felt as an intense pain, like any other pain in childhood; but as one grows older, the pain becomes more and more familiar and therefore not so intense. You know how you are going to survive the loss. You know how everything changes. In old age you become a child again. You experience total loss again and again as you lose your job, your health, your friends. And what you know is that each loss can also be a gain: it can be turned into a positive experience.

Peak experiences

When reading my diary, I can relive peak experiences as well as traumas, though the division is never clear-cut: "joy and woe are woven fine", as Blake wrote in *Auguries of Innocence*. I can, for instance, transport myself to a beach on the Costa Bella (the good-womb experience) or to a small cottage—Ty-Bach (small house) in Cwmyoy (happy valley) near Capel-y-ffin (the chapel at the end of the valley) on the road that leads to nowhere, losing its way in the mountains. There is the bliss of being wrapped around by mountains in this beautiful, peaceful place. There is no way out and no desire to move out: a wonderful amalgam of images connected with prenatal bliss, birth, and death—peace at the beginning and end.

For me 1941, when I stayed in Ty Bach, was the prelude to war. The calm before the storm. However, it was not all bliss. Sometimes at night German bombers would pass over the valley on their way to pour death from the sky on Birmingham and Coventry—the impingements, the anxiety, the noises of the world outside the womb. I knew the peace of the valley would not last, so it was all the more precious to me. As my days there came to an end, I felt a mixture of excitement and fear—but also something else: a feeling of sadness that I would be leaving people I loved behind when I joined the Friends Ambulance Unit training camp in Northfield, Birmingham.

I remember trudging along a snow-covered mountain path, in the early light of a freezing morning in January, on my way from Cwmyoy to Llanvihangel Station to catch a train to Birmingham—to new friendships (as I recall with pleasure now), a sense of purpose, but also to danger and possibly death. This memory brings back yet another feeling—one of resentment, of being put upon, of having to do something I did not really want to do—a sense of affliction or tribulation [a word derived from the Greek *thlipsis*, meaning "strong crushing pressure"]. This memory of a pressure being put on me can also be stretched back to the crushing pressure before birth.

The life you never lived

I can go on living my life again and again, and every time I look in my diary I understand a bit more about myself: the parts begin to connect to form a whole as I go back and back. I fill in the gaps—the unfinished business—and allow myself to live those parts of my life that I had failed to live in the past. Then it is a bit like living the fullness of a life postponed, and I am reminded of Oscar Wilde's words: "Your real life is the one you never lived."

You could perhaps describe my life as a true story about false situations—with all their fears, hopes, pains, pleasures, and so on at different times. The emotions are real, though sparked off by unreal situations. Krishnamurti (1934) describes those times of crisis when you felt threatened by a loss of some sort—loss of job, loss of property, loss of a spouse, and so on—as "living in a room with a poisonous snake". That is how it has sometimes been for me. The image of the snake explains it all. The original fear of separation—the loss of a holding environment—is about feelings of vulnerability: the fear of a predator. Gradually I abandoned the struggle, as many do in middle age, and learnt to accept the fiction. Finally, in old age, the past comes back with all its distortions: you see what might have happened and see the people you loved as they wanted to be and not as they were.

Epilogue II

Simon H. House

"After our industrial civilization has broken and the civilization of touch has begun, war will cease, there will be no more wars."

D. H. Lawrence, *Future War*

"The greatest single factor in the acquisition and maintenance of good health is perfectly constituted food."

Robert McCarrison, *Nutrition and Health* (1953)

In his Epilogue, Roy has shown us how he has reviewed his life, re-evaluated it, recognizing the impact on himself of life's events, all the way back through his times in his mother's arms, at birth, and in the womb, even to conception itself—almost as if this is an invitation to each of us.

All our work in this field has given me a new view of medicine. Not so long ago doctors regarded the child medically as a small adult, a paediatrician friend told me. The differences that have emerged are, of course, great. Doctors now will more likely learn much about the adult from childhood development. I am sure this trend will continue to trace back earlier and earlier in life, effectively reorienting medicine.

The overview of medicine taught will begin by looking at the building of the cells of human nature from the environmental elements and molecules. Our focus will be on the spermatagonium and the primary oocyte, and their subsequent meeting as mature sperm and ovum, all in the context of parental and evolutionary background, with full regard for hormonal influences, particularly the spiritual qualities of loving, gentle, and playful nurture.

Throughout the book, we have seen how many people have wrestled with the questions:

How do we come to be as we are?

How can we free ourselves, nourish ourselves, and nurture our children so that we and they can come closer to our potential?

The core answers seem to lie in sensitive, healing touch and bonding, and our relationship with and respect for the delicate biochemistry of our biosphere, creation.

These insights, scientifically validated, are seriously overlooked in the excitement and profitability of new technologies, yet they are focal to a growing number who have at heart society's life and health. And seeking a better world for all is part of our own personal health and peace.

REFERENCES AND BIBLIOGRAPHY

Adler, A. (1930). *Individual Psychology.* In: C. Murchison (Ed.), *Psychologists of 1930.* Worcester, MA: Clark University Press.

Agostoni, C., Trojan, S., Bellu, R., Riva, E., & Giovanni, M. (1995). Neurodevelopmental quotient of healthy term infants at 4 months and feeding practice: The role of long-chain polyunsaturated fatty acids. *Pediatric Research, 38* (2): 262–266.

Andin-Sobocki, P., Jonsson, B., Wittchen, H.-U., & Olesen, L. (2005). Cost of disorders of the brain in Europe. *European Journal of Neurology, 12:* 1–27.

APPPAH (1997). *Birth, Love and Relationships.* Forrestville, CA: Association for Prenatal and Perinatal Psychology and Health of North America (http://birthpsychology.com/congress/congress97.html).

Assagioli, R. (1971). *Psychosynthesis: A Manual of Principles and Techniques.* Tonbridge: Viking.

Associate Parliamentary Food and Health Forum (2003). *Diet and Behaviour.* Joint meeting with the All Party Group on Complementary & Integrated Healthcare (January, February) (www.fhf.org.uk/meetings/2003–01–21_minutes.pdf) (www.fhf.org.uk/Documents/Diet%20Behaviour%20Minutes.htm).

Barker, D. J. P. (1998). *Mothers, Babies and Health in Later Life.* Edinburgh: Churchill Livingstone.

Baum, M. (2002). Teaching the humanities to medical students. *Clinical Medicine,3:* 246–249.

Begg, E. (1984). *Myth and Today's Consciousness.* London: Coventure.

Berne, E. (1971a). *Sex in Human Loving.* London: André Deutsch.

Berne, E. (1971b). *Transactional Analysis in Psychotherapy.* New York: Grove Press.

Bibring, G., Dwyer, T. F., Huntington, D. S., & Valenstein, A. F. (1961). A study of the psychological processes in pregnancy and of the earliest mother–child relationship. *Psychoanalytic Study of the Child, 16:* 9–73.

Bindschedler, A. D. (1978). Rebirthing: A non-cathartic therapeutic process. *Self & Society* (July).

Birch, E. E., Birch, D., Hoffman, D., Hale, L., Everett, M., & Uauy, R. (1993). Breast feeding and optimal visual development. *Pediatric Ophthalmology and Strabismology, 30*: 33–38.

Birch, E. E., Hoffman, D. R., Uauy, R., Birch, D. G., & Prestidge, C. (1998). Visual acuity and the essentiality of docosahexaenoic acid and arachidonic acid in the diet of term infants. *Pediatric Research, 44*: 201–209.

Bitman, J., Wood, L., Hamosh, M., Hamosh, P., & Mehta, N. R. (1983). Comparison of the lipid composition of breast milk from mothers of term and preterm infants. *American Journal of Clinical Nutrition, 38*: 300–312.

Bittman, S., & Zalk, S. (1978). *Expectant Fathers*. New York: Hawthorne Publishers.

Bjerve, K. F., Thoresen, L., Bonaa, K., Vik, T., Johnsen, H., & Brubakk, A. M. (1992). Clinical studies with alpha-linolenic acid and long chain n-3 fatty acids. *Nutrition 8*: 130–132.

Blechschmidt, E. (1977). *The Beginnings of Human Life*. New York: Springer Verlag.

Blum, B. (1980). *Psychological Aspects of Pregnancy, Birthing and Bonding*. New York: Human Sciences Press.

Bohm, D. (1992). *Thought as a System*. London: Routledge.

Bonhoeffer, D. (1937). *The Cost of Discipleship*, trans. R. H. Fuller. London: SCM Press; New York: Macmillan, 1959.

Børresen, T. (2004). [Head Coordinator of *SeaFoodPlus*, Denmark.] Presentation to the Letten Symposium on Brain Function and Dysfunction, at the Royal Society (May).*The McCarrison Society Newsletter, 38* (2) (www.mccarrisonsociety.org.uk).

Bourne, G. (1973). *Pregnancy*. London: Pan Books.

Bower, T. (1984). The perceptual capacities of young children. *The Imaged World*. Television series, 16 July.

Bradley, S. G., & Bennett, N. (1995). *Preparation for Pregnancy*. Glendaruel: Argyll Publishing.

Brazelton, T. B. (1973). Effect of maternal expectation on early infant behaviour. *Early Child Development Care, 2*.

Breen, D. (1980). *The Birth of a First Child*. London: Souvenir Press.

Bressler-Feiner, M. (1981). Dreams of pregnant women. *Birth Psychology Bulletin*.

Brody, S., & Axelrod, S. (1970). *Anxiety and Ego Formation in Infancy*. New York: International Universities Press.

Brown, D., & Pedder, J. (1979). *Introduction to Psychotherapy*. London: Tavistock.

Brown, J. A. C. (1961). *Freud and the Post-Freudians*. Gretna, LA: Pelican.

Buber, M. (1958). *I and Thou* [*Ich und Du*, 1923], trans. R. G. Smith. New York: Scribner.

Caspi, A., Moffitt, T. E., et al. (2002). Role of genotype in the cycle of violence in maltreated children. *Science, 297* (5582): 851–854.

Caws, C. (2005). *The News* (retrieved 28 July from www.portsmouth. co.uk).

Chamberlain, G. (1961). *The Safety of the Unborn Child*. Gretna, LA: Pelican.

Channel 4 TV, UK (2001). *Damage to Mauritania's Fishing Industry*. Unreported World, 16 November, 7.30 p.m.

Chomsky, N. (1966). *Topics in the Theory of Generative Grammar*. The Hague: Mouton & Company.

Chomsky, N. (1968). *Language and Mind*. New York: Harcourt Brace & World.

Chomsky, N. (1971). *Selected Readings*, ed. J. P. B. Allen & P. van Buren. London: Oxford University Press

Chomsky, N. (1983). Things no amount of learning can teach. Interview by J. Gliedman. *Omni, 6* (11).

Clarkson, P. (1989). *Gestalt Counselling Verbatim*. London: Sage.

Cocteau, J. (1988). *Diary of an Unknown*, trans. J. Browner. New York: Paragon House.

Congress (2002). International Congress on Embryology, Therapy and Society (www.congress2002.com).

Connor, W. E. (2000). Importance of n-3 fatty acids in health and disease. *American Journal of Clinical Nutrition, 71* (No. 1, Suppl): 171S–175S.

Crawford, M. A. (1993). The role of essential fatty acids in neural development, implications for perinatal nutrition. *American Journal of Clinical Nutrition, 57* (Suppl.): 703S–710S.

Crawford, M. A., Costeloe, K., Ghebremeskel, K., Phylactos, A., Skirvin, L., & Stacey, F. (1997). Are deficits of arachidonic and docosahexaenoic acids responsible for the neural and vascular complications of preterm babies? *American Journal of Clinical Nutrition, 66*: 1032S-1041S.

Crawford, M. A., & Crawford, S. M. (1972). *What We Eat Today*. London: Neville Spearman.

Crawford, M. A., Ghebremeskel, K., et al. (2003). The potential role for arachidonic and docosahexaenoic acids in protection against some central nervous system injuries in preterm infants. *Lipids, 38* (4):303–315 (www.londonmet.ac.uk/ibchn_home).

Crawford, M., & Marsh, D. (1995). *Nutrition and Evolution*. New Canaan, CT: Keats.

Crisan, H. (1996). Das Ich und seine zwei Welten [The I and its two worlds]. In: *Jahrbuch für Ethnomedizin 1996* [Yearbook for Ethnomedicine] (pp. 159–212). Berlin: VWB.

Czeizel, A. (1995). Folic acid: Vitamins in pregnancy and infancy. *Annales Nestle, 53*: 61–68.

Darwin, C. (1842). *The Foundations of the Origin of the Species*, ed. Francis Darwin. Cambridge: Cambridge University Press, 1909.

Darwin, C. (1859). *On the Origin of the Species*. London: John Murray, 1868.

DeCasper, A., & Fifer, W. P. (1980). Of human bonding: Newborns prefer their mothers' voices. *Science, 208*: 1174.

DeCasper, A., & Spence, M. (1986). Prenatal maternal speech influences newborns' perception of speech sounds. *Infant Behaviour and Development, 9*: 113–150.

Dryden, R. (1978). *Before Birth*. Oxford: Heinemann.

Dubacq, J.-P., & Pham-Quoc (1993). Biotechnology of Spirulina lipids: A source of gamma-linolenic acid, K. *Bulletin de l'Institut Oceanographique (Monaco), 12* (Special issue): 103–107.

Dubos, R. (1965). Humanistic biology: Man's nature and man's history. *American Scientist, 53*: 4–19.

Emerson, W. (1978). Life, birth and rebirth: The hazy mirrors. *Self & Society* (July).

Emerson, W. (1984). *Infant and Child Birth Re-facilitation*. Petaluma, CA: Human Potential Resources.

Emerson, W. (2002). *Journal of Heart Centered Therapies* (Autumn) (www.findarticles.com/p/articles/mi_m0FGV/is_2_5/ai_99019062).

Farquharson, J., Cockburn, F., Patrick, A. W., et al. (1992). Infant cerebral cortex phospholipid fatty acid composition and diet. *Lancet, 340*: 810–813.

Feher, L. (1980). *The Psychology of Birth: The Foundation of Human Personality*. London: Souvenir Press.

Feldman, R., & Eidelman, A. I. (2003). Direct and indirect effects of breast milk on the neurobehavioral and cognitive development of premature infants. *Developmental Psychobiology, 43* (2): 109–119.

Ferreira, A. J. (1962). Emotional factors in the pre-natal environment. *Journal of Nervous and Mental Disease, 141* (1965).

Flanagan, G. L. (1962). *The First Nine Months of Life*. New York: Simon & Schuster.

Fodor, N. (1949). *The Search for the Beloved*. New Hyde Park, NJ: University Books.

Fordham, M. (1977). A possible root of imagination. *Journal of Analytical Psychology, 22* (4): 317–330.

Foresight (1990). *Preparation for Pregnancy Program*. Leaflet. London: Larkhall Green Farm.

Frankl, V. E. (1970). *Psychotherapy and Existentialism*. London: Souvenir Press.

Freedman, D. G. (1979). *Human Sociobiology*. New York: Free Press.

Freud, S. (1910). "Wild" psycho-analysis. *S.E.*, 11.

Freud, S. (1922). *Group Psychology and the Analysis of the Ego.* New York: Liveright, 1959.

Freud, W. E. (1980). Notes on some aspects of neonatal care. *The Course of Life, 1.*

Furst, A. (2002). Can nutrition affect chemical toxicity? *International Journal of Toxicology, 21* (5): 419–424. [University of San Francisco, International, Fremont, CA (artfurst@aol.com).]

Garnder, R. A., & Garnder, B. T. (1969). Teaching sign language to chimpanzees. *Science, 197* (1977): 664–672.

Gesch, C. B. (2002a). Foodstuff: Living in an age of feast and famine. *Demos* (December).

Gesch, C. B. (2002b). *Healthy Eating "Can Cut Crime".* London: BBC TV, June 25 (news.bbc.co.uk/1/hi/health/2063117.stm).

Gesch, C. B. (2003). Crime diet. In: *The Osgood File.* CBS Radio Network, November 3 (www.acfnewsource.org/science/crime_diet.html).

Gesch, C. B., Hammond, S. M., Hampson, S. E., Eves, A., & Crowder, M. J., (2002). Influence of supplementary vitamins, minerals and essential fatty acids on the antisocial behaviour of young adult prisoners. Randomised, placebo-controlled trial. *British Journal of Psychiatry, 181*: 22–28 (www.physiol.ox.ac.uk/natural.justice/Resources/PressPack.pdf).

Ghebremeskel, K., Bitsanis, D., Koukkou, E., Lowy, C., Poston, L., & Crawford, M. A. (1999). Maternal diet high in fat reduces docosahexaenoic acid in liver lipids of the newborn and suckling pups. *British Journal of Nutrition, 81*: 395–404.

Gibran, K. (1926). *The Prophet.* Oxford: Heinemann.

Global Forum for Health (1998). WHO forecast, March (www.globalforumhealth.org).

Glynn, M. L., Sandman, C. A., & Wadhwa, M. (2000). The influence of corticotropin-releasing hormone on human fetal development and parturition. *Journal of Prenatal and Perinatal Psychology and Health, 14* (3–4).

Goleman D. (1996). *Emotional Intelligence.* London: Bloomsbury Press.

Goodwin, J., & Jaramillo, J. (1976). Post-partum psychosis in an artist. *Birth Psychology Bulletin.*

Graber, G. H. (1974). *Pranatale Psychologie.* Munich: Kindler Taschenbucher.

Greenacre, P. T. (1978). *Trauma, Growth and Personality.* New York: International Universities Press.

Grof, S. (1972). Varieties of transpersonal experiences: Observations from LSD psychotherapy. *Journal of Transpersonal Psychology, 4* (1): 45–80

Grof, S. (1975). *Realms of the Human Unconscious: Observations from LSD Research.* New York: Viking Press.

Grof, S. (Ed.) (1984). *Ancient Wisdom and Modern Science*. Albany, NY: State University of New York Press.

Grof, S. (1990). *The Holotropic Mind*. New York: Harper Collins.

Grof, S. (1998). *The Cosmic Game*. New York: Albany, NY: State University of New York Press.

Grof, S., & Grof, C. (1980). *Beyond Death: The Gates of Consciousness*. London: Thames & Hudson.

Grof, S., & Halifax, J. (1978). *The Human Encounter with Death*. New York: Dutton.

Gross, W. (1982). *Was erlebt ein Kind im Mutterleib?* Freiburg: Herder-Taschenbuch.

Gruber, H. E., & Voneche, J. J. (Eds.) (1977). *The Essential Piaget*. London: Routledge & Kegan Paul.

Gurdjieff, G. I. (1950). *All and Everything: Beelzebub's Tales to His Grandson*. London: Routledge & Kegan Paul.

Guvenc, H., Karatas, F., et al. (1995). Low levels of selenium in mothers and their newborns in pregnancies with a neural tube defect. *Pediatrics, 95* (6): 879–882.

Haeckel, E. (1899). *Riddle of the Universe at the Close of the Nineteenth Century* (www.ucmp.berkeley.edu/history/haeckel.html).

Haire, D. (1978). *The Cultural Warping of Childbirth*. ICEA Special Report. New York: American Foundation for Maternal and Child Health.

Hamazaki, T., Itomura, M., Sawazaki, S., & Nagao, Y. (2000). Anti-stress effects of DHA. *Biofactors, 13* (1–4).

Hart, S., Boylan, L. M., Carroll, S., Musick, Y. A., & Lampe, R. M. (2003). Brief report: Breast-fed one-week-olds demonstrate superior neurobehavioral organization. *Journal of Pediatric Psychology, 28* (8): 529–534.

Hau, T. F., & Schindler, S. (1982). *Pranatale und Perinatale Psychosomatik*. Stuttgart: Hippokrates-Verlag.

Heidegger, M. (1953). *Being and Time* [*Sein und Zeit*, 1927], trans. J. Stambaugh. Albany, NY: State University of New York Press.

Helfer, R. (1978). The relationship between lack of bonding and child abuse and neglect. In: *Round Table on Maternal Attachment and Nurturing Disorder*. New Brunswick, NJ.

Helland, I. B., & Smith, L. (2003). Maternal supplementation with very-long-chain n-3 fatty acids during pregnancy and lactation augments children's IQ at 4 years of age. *Pediatrics, 111* (1): 39–44.

Heron, J. (1995). "Original Theory of Co-Counselling and the Paradigm Shift." Paper presented at Co-counselling International Teachers meeting, Harlech, Wales (July) (www.shef.ac.uk/personal/c/cci/cciuk/practice/paradigmshift.html).

Hibbeln, J. R. (1998). Fish consumption and major depression. *Lancet, 351*: 1213.

Hibbeln, J. R. (2001a). "Neurodevelopmental, Evolutionary and Epidemi-ological Perspectives: Dietary Deficiencies of Omega-3 Fatty Acids in Mental Health." Paper presented at McCarrison Society Conference, Post-Genome: Health Implications for Research and Food Policy, at the Medical Society of London (19 September).

Hibbeln, J. R. (2001b). Seafood consumption and homicide mortality: A cross-national ecological analysis. *World Review of Nutrition and Diet, 88*: 41–46.

Hibbeln, J. R. (2002). Seafood consumption, the DHA content of mothers' milk and prevalence rates of postpartum depression: A cross-national, ecological analysis. *Journal of Affective Disorders, 69* (1–3): 15–29.

Hill, M. (1999). *Carnegie Stages.* Kyoto Collection (http://embryology.med.unsw.edu.au/wwwhuman/Stages/Stages.htm).

Himmelberger, D. U., Brown, B. W., & Cohen, E. N. (1978). Cigarette smoking during pregnancy and the occurrence of spontaneous abor-tion and congenital. Sixth Congress of Social Psychiatry and Abnor-mality. *American Journal of Epidemiology, 108.*

H.M. Government (2004). Written reply to a Parliamentary Question asked by Lord Morris (July).

Hofmann, A. (1980). *LSD—My Problem Child* (trans. J. Ott). New York: McGraw-Hill.

Holmes, M. (2001). *The Blue Planet.* BBC2, October.

Holmes, M. (2002). *The Blue Planet.* BBC2, July.

Hooker, D. (1952a). Early human fetal activity. *Anat Rec, 113* (4): 503–504.

Hooker, D. (1952b). *The Prenatal Origin of Behaviour.* Lawrence, KS: Uni-versity of Kansas Press.

House, A. R. (2000). *Francis of Assisi.* London: Chatto & Windus.

House, S. (1999). Primal Integration Therapy—School of Frank Lake MB MRCPsych DPM. *Journal of Prenatal and Perinatal Psychology and Medicine, 11*: 437–457. Also in: *Journal of Prenatal and Perinatal Psychol-ogy and Health 14* (2000): 213–235 (www.healthierbabies.org/simon/simon.htm).

House, S. (2000). Generating healthy people: Stages in reproduction par-ticularly vulnerable to xenobiotic hazards and nutritional deficits. *Nutrition and Health 14* (3) (www.healthierbabies.org/simon/simon.htm).

Howe, E. G. (1965). *Cure or Heal?* London: Allen & Unwin.

Hudson, B. J. F., & Karis, I. G. (1974). The lipids of the alga Spirulina. *Jour-nal of the Science of Food & Agriculture, 25*: 759–763.

Human Genome Project (1990–2003) (www.ornl.gov/sci/techresources/Human_Genome/home.shtml).

Huxley, A. (1920). The Fifth Philosopher's Song. In: *Brave New World* (chap. 3). London: Penguin, 1975.

Ingalls, P. (1997). Neurosciences: Environment and violence [update of Birth traumas, violence begets violence]. *International Journal of Prenatal & Perinatal Psychology & Medicine, 9* (2).

International Justice Project (2002). *The Impact and Implications of Trauma and Abuse* (www.internationaljusticeproject.org/pdfs/trauma.pdf).

Irish Scientist (1999). Marine microalgae as a source of ω3 fatty acids (www.irishscientist.ie/GITIF114.htm).

Jackson, B. (1984). *Fatherhood*. London: Allen & Unwin.

Jahoda, G. (1969). *The Psychology of Superstition*. London: Allen Lane.

Janov, A. (1973). *The Primal Scream*. London: Abacus.

Janov, A. (1975). *The Primal Revolution*. London: Abacus.

Janov, A. (1977). *The Feeling Child*. London: Sphere Books.

Janov, A. (1991). *The New Primal Scream*. London: Abacus.

Janus, L. (1997). *The Enduring Effects of Prenatal Experience*. Northvale, NJ: Aronson; reprinted Heidelberg: Mattes, 2001..

Janus, L., & Kurth, W. (Eds.) (2000). *Psychohistorie, Gruppenphantasien und Krieg* (Psycho-history, Group-Fantasies, and War). Heidelberg: Mattes.

Johnston, W. (1974). *Silent Music*. Glasgow: Collins.

Kay, D. L. (1984). Foetal psychology and the analytic process. *Journal of Analytical Psychology, 29*: 317–336.

Kempe, C. H., Silverman, F. N., Steele, B. F., Droegmuller, W., & Silver, H. K. (1962). The battered child syndrome. *Journal of the American Medical Association, 181*: 17–24.

Kernberg, P., & Chazan, S. E. (1991). *Children with Conduct Disorders*. New York: Harper Collins.

Kitzinger, S. (1991). *Home Birth & Other Alternatives to Hospital*. London: Dorling Kindersley.

Klaus, M. H., & Kennell, J. H. (1976). *Maternal Infant Bonding*. St Louis, MO: C. V. Mosby.

Kohl, J. V., & Francoeur, R. T. (1995). *The Scent of Eros: Mysteries of Odor in Human Sexuality*. New York: Continuum.

Kotulak, R. M. (1996). *Inside the Brain*. Kansas City, KS: Andrew & McMeel.

Koukkou, E., Bitsanis, D., Ghebremeskel, K., Lowy, C., Poston, L., & Crawford, M. A. (1997). Both diabetes and maternal diets rich in saturated fatty acids alter fetal liver lipid composition and vascular-reactivity. Proceedings of the IVth International Congress on Essential Fatty Acids and Their Eicosanoids. *Journal of Prostaglandins, Leukotrienes and EFAs, 57*: 268.

Krishnamurti, J. (1934). Ojai 11th Public Talk 30th June, 1934 (http://66.249.93.104/search?q=cache:890BQuZZ7kUJ:www.krishnamurti.oddech.com/krishnajiworks_423.html+krishnamurti+poisonous+snake&hl=en&gl=uk&ct=clnk&cd=2).

Krishnamurti, J. (1970). *The Urgency of Change*. Madras: Krishnamurti Foundation.

Krishnamurti, J. (1972). *The Impossible Question*. London: Gollancz.

Krishnamurti, J. (1976). *The Wholeness of Life*. Abridged from videotape recordings at Brockwood Park, Hampshire, May.

Krishnamurti, J. (1981). *The Wholeness of Life*. London: Harpercollins.

Krishnamurti, J. (1992). *Choiceless Awareness*. Ojai, CA: Krishnamurti Publications of America.

Kubler-Ross, E. (1970). *On Death and Dying*. London: Tavistock; Carmichael, CA: Touchstone, 1997.

Laing, R. D. (1976). *The Facts of Life*. London: Allen Lane.

Laing, R. D. (1978). Existential topography. *Self & Society* (July).

Laing, R. D. (1982). *The Voice of Experience*. London: Allen Lane.

Lake, F. (1966). *Clinical Theology*. London: Darton, Longman & Todd.

Lake, F. (1980a). *Constricted Confusion: Exploration of a Pre- and Perinatal Paradigm*. Private publication by Bridge Pastoral Foundation (www.bridgepastoral.org.uk).

Lake, F. (1980b). Interview with Roy Ridgway.

Lake, F. (1981). *Tight Corners in Pastoral Counselling*. London: Darton, Longman & Todd.

Lancet (2004). *The Catastrophic Failure of Health Policy*. Editorial (6 March).

Leaf, A. A., Leighfield, M. J., Costeloe, K. L., & Crawford, M. A. (1992). Factors affecting long-chain polyunsaturated fatty acid composition of plasma choline phosphor-glycerides in preterm infants. *Journal of Gastroenterology and Nutrition, 14*: 300–338.

Leboyer, F. (1975). *Birth Without Violence*. Aldershot: Wildwood House.

Liedloff, J. (1975). *The Continuum Concept*. London: Duckworth; London: Arkana, 1989.

Liley, A. M. (1972). The foetus as a personality. *Australian and New Zealand Journal of Psychiatry, 6* (1972): 103.

Liley, A. M. (1977). The foetus as a personality. *Self & Society* (June).

Lipton, B. (1998). Nurture, nature and the power of love. *Journal of Prenatal & Perinatal Psychology & Health, 13* (1): 3–10.

Lipton, B. H. (2001). Nature, nurture and human development. *Journal of Prenatal and Perinatal Psychology and Health, 16* (2): 167–180.

Liu, J., Raine, A., Venables, P. H., Dalais, C., & Mednick S.A. (2003). Malnutrition at age 3 years and lower cognitive ability at age 11 years: Independence from psychosocial adversity. *Archives of Pediatric & Adolescent Medicine, 157* (6): 593–600.

Liu, J., Raine, A., Venables, P. H., & Mednick, S. A (2004). Malnutrition at age 3 years and externalizing behavior problems at ages 8, 11, and 17 years. *American Journal of Psychiatry, 161* (11): 2005–2013.

Livingston, S. (1972). *Comprehensive Management of Epilepsy in Infancy, Childhood and Adolescence*. Springfield, IL: C. C. Thomas.

Lucas, A., Morley, R., Cole, T. J., Lister, G., Leeson-Payne, C., (1992). Breast milk and subsequent intelligence quotient in children born preterm. *Lancet, 339*: 261–264.

MacFarlane, A. (1977). *The Psychology of Childbirth*. Cambridge, MA: Harvard University Press.

Mahler, M. (1975). *The Psychology of the Human Infant*. New York: International Universities Press.

Makrides, M., Simmer, K., Goggin, M., & Gibson, R. A. (1993). Erythrocyte docosahexaenoic acid correlates with visual response of healthy term infants. *Pediatric Research, 34*: 425–427.

Mandela, N. (2002). In: World report on violence and health. Geneva World Health Organization (www.who.int/violence_injury_prevention/violence/world_report/en/chap1.pdf).

Marsh, D. E. (2001). The role of the essential fatty acids in the evolution of the modern human brain. *Positive Health* (May) (www.positivehealth.com).

Marsh, D. E. (2002). The importance of minerals to health. *Positive Health* (www.positivehealth.com).

Maslow, A. (1968). *Towards a Psychology of Being*. New York: Van Nostrand.

Maslow, A. (1971). *The Further Reaches of Human Nature*. Tonbridge: Viking.

Maternity Services Advisory Committee (1981). *Maternity Care in Action. Part 1, Antenatal Care*. Victoria, Australia.

May, R. (1983). *The Discovery of Being: Writings in Existential Psychology*. New York: Norton.

McCarrison, R. (1953). *Nutrition and Health*. London: Faber & Faber. [Republished London: The McCarrison Society, 1982.]

McFerran, A. (Ed.) (1988). *Motherland: Interviews with Mothers and Daughters*. London: Virago.

Mehl, L. (1981). Psychophysiological risk screening for childbirth. *Birth Psychology Bulletin* (January).

Mehl, L. E., et al. (1980). "An Existential Approach to Childbirth Preparation." Association of Birth Psychology Conference (June 7–8).

Mental Health Foundation (1998). *Facts Not Fairy Tales: Mental Health and Illness in Children and Young People*. Briefing No. 15. London (www.mentalhealth.org.uk/page.cfm?pagecode=PBBZ0215#effects).

Mental Health Foundation (2005). *Lifetime Impacts. Childhood and Adolescent Mental Health: Understanding the lifetime impacts*. London (www.mentalhealth.org.uk/page.cfm?pagecode=PBNP#lifetime).

Miller, A. (1991). *Breaking Down the Wall of Silence*. London: Virago.

Moir, A., & Jessel, D. (1995). *A Mind to Crime*. London: Michael Joseph.

Montagu, A. (1952). *The Natural Superiority of Women* (revised edition). London: Collier, 1974

Montagu, A. (1961). *Life Before Birth*. New York: New American Library.

Montagu, A. (1978). *Touching: The Human Significance of the Skin*. New York/London: Harper & Row.

Morgan, E. (1982). *The Aquatic Ape*, London: Stein & Day (www.lamma .net/aquatic.htm).

Morris, J. N. (1951). Recent history of coronary disease. *Lancet, i*: 1–7; (January 13): 69–73.

Mott, F. J. (1964). *The Universal Design of Creation*. Edenbridge: Mark Beech.

Mowrer, O. H. (1961). *The Crisis in Psychiatry and Religion*. Princeton, NJ: Van Nostrand Insight.

Nemets, B., Stahl, Z., & Belmaker, R. H. (2002). Addition of omega-3 fatty acid to maintenance medication treatment for recurrent unipolar depressive disorder. *American Journal of Psychiatry, 159* (3): 477–479.

Neumann, E. (1955). *The Great Mother*. Princeton, NJ: Princeton University Press.

Neumann, E. (1973). *The Child*. New York: Harper & Row.

Neuringer, M., Anderson, G. J., & Connor, W. E. (1988). The essentiality of n-3 fatty acids for the development & function of the retina & brain. *Annual Review of Nutrition, 8*: 517–541.

Neuringer, M., & Connor, W. E. (1986). n-3 Fatty acids in the brain and retina, evidence for their essentiality. *Nutrition Reviews, 44* (9): 285–294.

NIH (1998). *Omega 3 Essential Fatty Acids and Psychiatric Disorders*. NIH Workshop, Washington, DC, National Institutes of Health (September) (efaeducation.nih.gov/sig/nihwork.html)

NIH (2005). *What Foods Provide Folate?* National Institutes of Health, Office of Dietary Supplements (ods.od.nih.gov/factsheets/folate.asp).

Odent, M. (1984). *Birth Reborn*. London: Random House.

Odent, M. (1986). *Primal Health*. London: Century.

Odent, M. (1999). *Scientification of Love*. London/New York: Free Association Books,

Older, J. (1982). *Touching Is Healing*. New York: Stein & Day.

Ouspensky, P. D. (1949). *In Search of the Miraculous*. London: Routledge & Kegan Paul.

Panksepp, J. (1998). *Affective Neuroscience: The Foundations of Human and Animal Emotions*. Oxford: Oxford University Press.

Patterson, T. (2002a). Excerpt from his last statement. [Executed, 28 May] (www.internationaljusticeproject.org/pdfs/trauma.pdf).

Patterson, T. (2002b). Latest news on Toronto Patterson (www.ccadp.org/ torontopatterson-latestnews2002.htm).

Pearce, J. C. (1979). *The Magical Child*. Boulder, CO: Paladin.

Pearce, J. C. (1997). "Effects of Technological Childbirth." Paper presented at the Eighth International Conference of the *APPPAH*, San Francisco (www.birthpsychology.com/birthscene/congress2.html).

Peerbolte, M. L. (1954). *Psychic Energy in Pre-Natal Dynamics*. Holland: Wassener.

Pelletier, K. R. (1978). *Towards a Science of Consciousness*. New York: Delta.

Penfield, W. (1952). Memory mechanisms. *Archives of Neurology & Psychiatry, 67*.

Perls, F. S. (1969). *Gestalt Therapy Verbatim*. Moab, UT: Real People Press.

Perls, F. (1973a). *The Gestalt Approach and Eye Witness to Therapy*. Palo Alto, CA: Science & Behaviour.

Perls, F. S. (1973b). *Gestalt Therapy: Excitement and Growth in the Human Personality*. London: Penguin.

Perry, J. (1974). *The Far Side of Madness*. Englewood Cliffs, NJ: Prentice-Hall.

Pert, C. (1998). *Molecules of Emotions*. London: Simon & Schuster.

Piontelli, A. (1992). *From Fetus to Child: An Observational and Psychoanalytic Study*. London: Routledge.

Popper, K. (1972). *Objective Knowledge*. Oxford: Oxford University Press.

Pregnancy & Birth (2005). Report (September). Also in: BBC News, 1 September (news.bbc.co.uk/1/hi/health/4202630.stm).

Prescott, J. W. (1983). "The Quadrune Brain: Cerebellar Regulation of Emotional Behaviors." Invited address, European Seminar on Developmental Neurology, Institut für Kindesentwicklung, GmbH, Hamburg, Germany (14–17 February).

Prescott, J. W. (1990). Affectional bonding for the prevention of violent behaviors: Neuro-biological, psychological and religious/spiritual determinants. In: L. J. Hertzberg et al. (Eds.), *Violent Behavior, Vol. 1: Assessment and Intervention* (pp. 110–142). New York: PMA.

Prescott, J. W. (1992). "Sexual Dimorphism in the Developing Human Brain: Evidence from Lateral Skull X-rays." Presented in Symposium on Genes, Hormones, and Sexual Behavior. The Society for the Scientific Study of Sex, 1992 Annual Meeting, San Diego, CA (12 November).

Prescott, J. W. (1996). The origins of human love & violence. *Journal of Prenatal & Perinatal Psychology & Health, 10* (3): 143–188 (www.violence. de/prescott/pppj/article.html).

Pribram, K. H. (1971). *Languages of the Brain*. Englewood Cliffs, NJ: Prentice-Hall.

Price, W. A. (1945). *Nutrition and Physical Degeneration*. La Mesa, CA: Price-Pottenger.

Prigogine, I., & Stengers, I. (1984). *Order Out of Chaos*. London: Flamingo.

Raine, A. (1995). *A Mind to Crime*. Channel 4 TV.

Raine, A. (2002). Annotation: The role of prefrontal deficits, low auto-nomic arousal, and early health factors in the development of anti-social and aggressive behavior in children. *Journal of Child Psychology & Psychiatry, 43* (4): 417–434.

Raine, A., Brennan, P., & Mednick, S. A. (1994). Birth complication com-bined with early maternal rejection at age 1 year predispose to violent crimes at age 18 years. *Archives of General Psychiatry, 51*: 984–988.

Raine, A., Mellingen, K., Liu, J., Venables, P., & Mednick, S. A. (2003). Ef-fects of environmental enrichment at ages 3–5 years on schizotypal personality and antisocial behavior at ages 17 and 23 years. *American Journal of Psychiatry. 160* (9): 1627–1635.

Rank, O. (1929). *The Trauma of Birth*. New York: Warner Torch Books, 1934.

Rank, O. (1932). *Myth of the Birth of the Hero*. New York: Alfred A Knopf.

Rayman, M. P. (2002). The argument for increasing selenium intake. *Proc Nutr Soc, 61* (2): 203–215.

Rayner, M. (2004). [Researcher, British Heart Foundation.] Presentation to the Letten Symposium on Brain Function and Dysfunction, the Royal Society (May). *The McCarrison Society Newsletter, 38* (2) (www.mccarrisonsociety.org.uk).

Reading, A. (1983). *The Psychological Aspects of Pregnancy*. New York: Longman.

Reich, W. (1933). *Character Analysis*. Vienna: Farrer, Strauss & Giroux, 1969.

Renggli, F. (2003). Tracing the roots of panic to prenatal trauma. *Journal of Prenatal & Perinatal Psychology & Health, 17* (4): 289–299.

Ridgway, R. (1987). *The Unborn Child: How to Recognize and Overcome Pre-natal Trauma*. Aldershot: Wildwood House.

Ring, K. (1974). A transpersonal consciousness. *Journal of Transpersonal Psychology, 7.*

Robertson, N. (2001). Scottish agriculture: Radical strategy for its survival. *Nutrition and Health, 15* (2).

Rodier, P. M. (2000). The early origins of autism. *Scientific American, 282* (No. 2, February), pp. 56–63 (www.unc.edu/~cory/autism-info/or-gautsa.html).

Rosenthal, P.-A., & Rosenthal, S. (1984). Suicidal behavior by preschool children. *American Journal of Psychiatry, 141*: 520–525.

Rugh, R., & Shettles, L. (1972). *From Conception to Birth*. London: Allen & Unwin.

Rutherford, M. (2004). "The Problem at Its Roots." Presented to the Letten Symposium on Brain Function and Dysfunction, at the Royal Society (May). *McCarrison Society Newsletter, 38* (2) (www.mccarrisonsociety.org.uk).

Sacks, O. (1970). *Migraine: Evolution of a Common Disorder*. London: Faber.

Sadger, I. I. (1941). Preliminary study of the psychic life of the foetus and primary germ. *Psychoanalytic Review, 28* (No. 3, July).

Sadger, I. I. (2005). *Recollecting Freud* (ed. A. Dundes, trans. J. M. Jaçobsen & A. Dundes). Madison, WI: University of Wisconsin Press.

Sahlberg, O. N. (1999) The prenatal self becoming conscious—Christ and Buddha, *International Journal of Prenatal & Perinatal Psychology & Medicine, 2* (1): 49–56.

Sansone, A. (2004). *Mothers, Babies and Their Body Language*. London: Karnac.

Sartre, J. P. (1964). *Les Mots* [The Words]. Amsterdam: Elsevier.

Sassone, R. S. (1977). *The Tiniest Humans* [Based on interviews with J. Lejeune & W. Liley]. Stafford, VA: American Life League.

Saugstad, L. F. (2001). Manic depressive psychosis and schizophrenia are neurological disorders at the extremes of CNS maturation and nutritional disorders associated with a deficit in marine fat. *Med Hypotheses, 57* (6): 679–692.

Saugstad, L. F. (2004). From superior adaptation and function to brain dysfunction—the neglect of epigenetic factors. *Nutrition and Health, 18* (1): 3–27.

Schindler, S. (1981). *Der Praktische Arzt, 35*.

Schindler, S., & Zimprich, H. (1983). *Okologie der Perinatalzeit*. Stuttgart: Hippokrates-Verlag.

Schultes, R. E., & Hofmann, A. (1979). *Plants of the Gods: Origins of Hallucinogenic Use*. New York: McGraw-Hill.

Schultes, R. E., Hofmann, A., & Rätsch, C. (1992). *Plants of the Gods: Their Sacred, Healing, and Hallucinogenic Powers*. Rochester, VT: Healing Arts Press

Seaborn-Jones, G. (1977). Interview with June Posey. *Self & Society* (June).

SF NEWS (1996). New international justice project to stress healing over punishment. *Simon Fraser News, 6* (No. 2, 23 May) (www.sfu.ca/mediapr/sfnews/1996/May23/justice.html).

Sherrington, C. (1951). *Man on His Nature* (2nd edition). London: Cambridge University Press.

Simonton, O. C., Matthews-Simonton, S., & Creighton, J. L. (1978). *Getting Well Again: The Bestselling Classic About the Simontons' Revolutionary Lifesaving Self- Awareness Techniques*. New York: Bantam.

Simpson, W. J. A. (1957). A preliminary report on cigarette smoking and the incidence of prematurity. *American Journal of Obstetrics & Gynaecology, 73*.

Skoyles, J. R. (2002). *Is Autism Due to Cerebral–Cerebellum Disconnection?* London: London School of Economics.

Sontag, L. W. (1941). The significance of fetal environmental differences. *American Journal of Obstetrics and Gynecology, 42*: 996–1003.

Sontag, L. W. (1944). War and the maternal fetal relationship. *Marriage and Family Living, 6*: 1–5.

Sontag, L. W. (1966). Implications of fetal behaviour and environment for adult personalities. *Annals of the New York Academy of Sciences, 134*: 782–786.

Spector, A. A. (2001). Plasma free fatty acid and lipoproteins as sources of polyunsaturated fatty acid for the brain. *Journal of Molecular Neuroscience. 16*: 159–165; 215–221 [discussion].

Spelt, D. K. (1948). The conditioning of the human fetus in utero. *Journal of Experimental Psychology, 38*: 454–461.

Spitz, R. (1965). *The First Year of Life*. New York: International Universities Press.

Stein, Z., Susser, M., Saenger, G., & Marolla, F. (1975). *Famine and Human Development: The Dutch Hunger Winter of 1944/45*. London: Oxford University Press.

Stettbacher, K. (1991). *Making Sense of Suffering*. New York: Dutton.

Stevens, L. J., Burgess, J. R., et al. (1995). Essential fatty acid metabolism in boys with ADHD. *American Journal of Nutrition, 62*: 761–768.

Stirnimann, F. (1940). *Psychologie des neugeborenen Kindes*. Munich: Kindler; reprinted Munich, Kindler, 1973.

Stirnimann, F. (1951). *Das Kind und seine früheste Umwelt*. Basel: Karger.

Stockdale, T. (1992). A speculative discussion of some of the problems arising from the use of ammonium nitrate fertiliser on acid soil. *Nutrition & Health, 8*: 207–222. [See also: Letter, *Nutrition & Health, 14* (2000): 141–142.]

Stoll, A. L., & Severus, W. E. (1999). Omega 3 fatty acids in bipolar disorder: A preliminary double-blind, placebo-controlled trial. *Arch Gen Psychiatry, 56* (5): 407–412.

Stott, D. H. (1978). Epidemiological indicators of the origins of behavior disturbance as measured by the Bristol social adjustment guides. *Genetic Psychology Monograph, 97* (February).

Stott, D. H., & Latchford, S. A. (1976). Prenatal antecedents of child health, development, and behavior: An epidemiological report of incidence and association. *Journal of the American Academy of Child Psychiatry, 15*: 161–191.

Stuart, K. (2004). "Indigenous Populations in Transition." Presented to the Letten Symposium on Brain Function and Dysfunction, at the Royal Society (May). *McCarrison Society Newsletter, 38* (2) (www.mccarrison-society.org.uk).

Swartley, W. (1977). *Self and Society* (June).

Swartley, W., & Maurice, J. (1978). The birth of primals in wartime Britain. *Self & Society*, 6 (7).

Tart, C. T. (1969). *Altered States of Consciousness*. New York: Wiley.

Tart, C. T. (1975). *Transpersonal Psychologies*, New York: Harper & Row.

Teilhard de Chardin, P. (1934). The evolution of chastity. In: *Toward The Future*, trans. R. Hague. New York: Harcourt Brace Javonovich, 1975. [Editions de Seuil, 1973.]

Teilhard de Chardin, P. (1976). *The Heart of the Matter*, trans. R. Hague. London: Collins, 1978.

Trimmer, E. J. (1965). *Before Birth: Fact and Fantasy*. London: MacGibbon & Kee.

Tuddenham, E. (2001). "Genome Evolution, Blood and Soil—A Message from Deep Time." Presented to the McCarrison Society Conference, Post-Genome: Health Implications for Research and Food Policy, at the Medical Society of London (19 September) (europium.csc.mrc. ac.uk).

Uauy, R., Hoffman, D. R., Peirano, P., Birch, D. G., & Birch, E. E. (2001). Essential fatty acids in visual and brain development. *Lipids*, 36 (9): 885–895.

UNCED (1992). *Nations of the Earth Report*. UNCED national reports summaries. New York: United Nations.

UNICEF (1998). *State of the World's Children* (www.eldis.org/static/DOC17004.htm).

UNICEF-WHO (2004). Low birthweight. In: *Country, Regional and Global Estimates*. New York: UNICEF (www.childinfo.org/areas/birthweight/LBW_WHO_UNICEF%202000.pdf).

US Senate (1936). *Farm Land Mineral Depletion*. Senate Document 264, 74th Congress, 2nd Session.

Valman, H. B., & Pearson, J. F. (1980). What the fetus feels. *British Medical Journal* (26 January).

Vedaparayana, G. (2006). The way of intelligence (pp. 210–211). In: *The Philosophy of Jiddu Krishnamurti* (http://www.here-now4u.de/eng/the_philosophy_of_jiddu_krishn.htm).

Verny, T. (1982a). Prenatal factors in character formation. In: T. F. Hau & S. Schindler (Eds.), *Pränatale und perinatale Psychosomatik*. Stuttgart: Hippokrates Verlag.

Verny, T. (1982b) (with J. Kelly). *The Secret Life of the Unborn Child*. Toronto: Collins.

von Varga, G. (1982). *Appropriate Care: A Bibliography of Recent Research Concerning the Biopsychological Needs of Infants and Mothers*. Private publication.

Wang, Y., Crawford, M. A., Chen, J., Li, J., Ghebremeskel, K., Campbell, T. C., Fan, W., Parker, R., & Leyton, J. (2003). Fish consumption, blood docosahexaenoic acid and chronic diseases in Chinese rural populations. *Comp Biochem Physiol A Mol Integr Physiol, 136* (1): 127–140.

Wasdell, D. (1998). Abstract. 12th Congress of the International Society for Prenatal & Perinatal Psychology & Medicine.

Whitman, W. (1891). *Song of Myself* (www.daypoems.net/poems/1900.html).

WHO (2002). *World Report on Violence and Health.* World Health Organization (http://www.who.int/violence_injury_prevention/violence/world_report/en/full_en.pdf).

Wilheim, J. (2002). Cellular memory: Clinical evidence. *International Journal of Prenatal and Perinatal Psychology and Medicine, 14* (1/2): 19–31.

Williams, C., Birch, E. E., et al. (2001). Stereoacuity at age 3.5 y in children born full-term is associated with prenatal and postnatal dietary factors: A report from a population-based cohort study. *American Journal of Clinical Nutrition, 73* (2): 316–322.

Winkler, J. (2004). [Director of Food and Health Research, London.] Presentation to the Letten Symposium on Brain Function and Dysfunction, at the Royal Society. *McCarrison Society Newsletter, 38* (2) (www.mccarrisonsociety.org.uk).

Winnicott, D. (1949). Mind its relation to the psych-soma. In: *Collected Papers: Through Paediatrics to Psycho-Analysis.* London: Tavistock.

Winnicott, D. (1954). Birth memories, birth trauma and anxiety. In: *Collected Papers: Through Paediatrics to Psycho-Analysis.* London: Tavistock.

Winnicott, D. (1958). *Collected Papers: Through Paediatrics to Psycho-Analysis.* London: Tavistock.

Winnicott, D. (1972). *The Maturational Processes and the Facilitating Environment.* London: Hogarth Press.

World Health Statistics Annual 1995. Geneva: WHO.

Wynn, M., & Wynn, A. (1981). *Prevention of Handicap of Early Pregnancy Origin.* London: Foundation for Education and Research in Child-Bearing.

Wynn, M., & Wynn, A. (2001). New evidence on the nutrition of British school children and conclusions drawn for school meals. *Nutrition and Health, 16* (2).

RELEVANT ORGANIZATIONS

American Association for Prenatal and Perinatal Psychology and Health (Maureen Wolfe), PO Box 1398, Forestville, CA, 95436-1398, USA (www.birthpsychology.com).

Amethyst (Sheila Ward), Ballybroghan, Killaloe, County Clare, Ireland (http://www.holistic.ie/amethyst).

Bridge Pastoral Foundation, Queen's College, Somerset Rd, Edgbaston, Birmingham, B15 2QH (www.bridgepastoral.org.uk).

Deep Release (Dr Chris Andrew), S Andrew's Centre/Road, Plaistow, London, E13 8QD (www.deeprelease.org.uk).

Emerson Training Seminars (William Emerson), 4940 Bodega Avenue, Petaluma, CA, 94952 (www.emersonbirthrx.com).

Foresight (Belinda Barnes), 28 The Paddock, Godalming, GU7 1XD, Surrey (www.foresight preconception.org.uk).

Institute of Brain Chemistry & Human Nutrition (Dr Michael Crawford), University of North London, 166–222 Hollywood Road, London, N7 8DB (www.north.londonmet.ac.uk/ibchn).

International Society for Prenatal and Perinatal Psychology and Medicine (Dr Ludwig Janus, Juliet Bischoff), Friedhofweg 8, Heidelberg, D-69118, Germany (www.isppm.de).

Marie Stopes International (Liz Tait), 153-157 Cleveland St, London, W1P 5PG (www.mariestopes.org.uk).

McCarrison Society (David Marsh), 37 Waterhouse Close, Hammersmith, London, W6 8BQ (www.mccarrisonsociety.org.uk).

Meridian Matrix (David Wasdell), Meridian House, 115 Poplar High St, London, E14 0AE (www.meridian.org.uk).

Mother & Child Foundation (Dr Michael Crawford), IBCHN, London Metropolitan University, 166–222 Holloway Road, London, N7 8DB (www.north.londonmet.ac.uk/ibchn).

National Birthday Trust (Elspeth Chowdary-Best), 27 Walpole St, London, SW3 4QS (www.wellbeingofwomen.org.uk).

National Childbirth Trust, Alexandra House, Oldham Terrace, Acton, London, W3 7NH (www.nctpregnancyandbabycare.com).

National Parenting Education & Support, c/o National Children's Bureau, 8 Wolsely St, London, EC1V 7QE (www.ncb.org.uk).

Parenting Education and Support Forum, The Director, 431 Highgate Studios, 53–79 Highgate Road, London, NW5 1TL (www.parenting-forum.org.uk).

Parent Network, 44–46 Caversham Rd, London, NW5 2DS (www.essex-mh.nhs.uk).

Parents in Partnership Parent Infant Network (Lena Snow), 9 Murray Ct, 80 Banbury Rd, Oxford, OX2 6LQ (www.pippin.org.uk).

Primal Health Care (Dr Michel Odent), 59 Roderick Rd, Hampstead, London, NW3 2NP (www.secure.serve.com/birthworks/primalhealth).

Primal Therapists, London Association, 18A Laurier Rd, London, NW5 1SH (www.lapp.org).

INDEX